CW01425970

UNFINISHED BUSINESS

The life and legacy of
Sir Tim Brighouse
– a tribute and a call to action

Edited by
David Cameron, Steve Munby and Mick Waters

Crown House Publishing Limited
www.crownhouse.co.uk

First published by

Crown House Publishing Limited

Crown Buildings, Bancyfelin, Carmarthen, Wales, SA33 5ND, UK

www.crownhouse.co.uk

and

Crown House Publishing Company LLC

PO Box 2223, Williston, VT 05495, USA

www.crownhousepublishing.com

British Library Cataloguing-in-Publication Data

A catalogue entry for this book is available from the British Library.

Print ISBN 978-178583729-6
Mobi ISBN 978-17583736-4
ePub ISBN 978-178583737-1
ePDF ISBN 978-178583738-8
LCCN 2024940064

Printed and bound in the UK by
CPi, Antony Rowe, Chippenham, Wiltshire

This book is dedicated to Tim's family, friends and colleagues and to teachers everywhere who will take Tim's legacy to future generations of children.

Acknowledgements

We would like to thank all those who contributed to the book so willingly, who met, or at least got close to meeting, some very tight deadlines and graciously accepted comments and edits. We also thank all of those who could have and would have contributed. We know that many of them will be making other contributions to keeping Tim's legacy alive and continuing his work. We would also like to thank the team at Crown House Publishing for making this book a reality.

Royalties and a share of profits from sales of this book will be donated to Tim's favourite charities and causes.

Contents

Contents

Contents

List of contributors

Professor Mel Ainscow, CBE FRSA

Mel Ainscow is emeritus professor, University of Manchester, professor of education, University of Glasgow and adjunct professor, Queensland University of Technology. He is internationally recognised as an authority on the promotion of inclusion and equity in education. Mel worked with Tim Brighouse on City Challenge in London and Greater Manchester.

Amjad Ali

Amjad Ali is a teacher, trainer, TEDx speaker, author and senior leader. He has a background in challenging, diverse schools and young offender prisons, and co-founded the BAMEed Network. Amjad has delivered continuing professional development at events alongside Sir Tim and was fortunate to have been informally mentored and supported by him.

Dr Fiona Aubrey-Smith

Fiona Aubrey-Smith is a consultant researcher and school system leader who is known for her infectious enthusiasm, pedagogy-first approach and championing of agency for young people. Fiona worked closely with Tim and Mick and an advisory team to curate the formation of Open School.

Kenneth Baker, Baron Baker of Dorking, CH PC

Kenneth Baker is a former MP and cabinet minister. As education secretary, he introduced the national curriculum, city technology colleges and grant-maintained schools. He is the chair of Baker Dearing Educational Trust which promotes university technical colleges. Over the course of the last 40 years, he had several healthy debates with Tim about vital educational matters.

Sir David Bell, KCB DL

David Bell is vice-chancellor and chief executive of the University of Sunderland. He has been a local authority director of education – paralleling Tim's time in Birmingham, Her Majesty's Chief Inspector of Schools and permanent secretary at the Department for Education where he engaged positively with Tim.

Melissa Benn

Melissa Benn is a writer and campaigner. Her books on education include *School Wars: The Battle for Britain's Education* (2012) and *Life Lessons: The Case for a National Education Service* (2018). A former chair of Comprehensive Future and co-founder of the Private Education Policy Forum, she was a great admirer of Tim's.

Louise Blackburn

First and foremost, Louise Blackburn is an advocate for disadvantaged learners. Having worked in education for over 20 years, she now supports schools to deliver equitable approaches through Challenging Education, which works with leaders to tackle inequalities through Raising the Attainment of Disadvantaged Youngsters (RADY). It is this passion for equity that brought Louise into contact with Tim.

David Blunkett, Baron Blunkett, PC

David Blunkett drew upon the experience, expertise and wisdom of Tim Brighouse when he was education and employment secretary between 1997 and 2001. Together putting ideas into practice and inspiring others led to a continuing friendship which David values to this day. What they started with Excellence in Cities led to Tim's success in leading the London Challenge.

Adam Boxer

Adam Boxer is a science teacher, teacher trainer and education director of Carousel Learning. Although he never met Tim, Adam corresponded with him on a number of occasions, often on points they disagreed upon!

Professor Harry Brighouse

Harry Brighouse is Mildred Fish Harnack Professor of Philosophy of Education and Carol Dickson Bascom Professor of Humanities at the University of Wisconsin-Madison. Tim Brighouse was his father.

Anna Bush

Anna Bush has worked in education for 20 years and currently works for United Learning. A role on the London Challenge meant working closely with Tim Brighouse and getting behind the efforts of the capital's most challenging schools. Anna is known for her passion and commitment – or, in Tim's words, 'Anna is easy to work with and gets things done.'

David Cameron

David Cameron has had a long and varied career in education. He met Tim at a conference years ago. Tim said he would tell people to book him instead of Tim. He did. They became colleagues and friends. David sees that as one of the greatest honours of his life and hopes this book repays that to some small extent.

Rosemary Campbell-Stephens, MBE

Rosemary Campbell-Stephens is an international speaker, author and consultant on leadership and decolonising system change. She first met Tim Brighouse when he was Birmingham's chief education officer. Over the years, they have shared various platforms on numerous occasions. Most notably, their paths crossed during the London Challenge work from 2003 to 2011.

Sir David Carter, KNZM

David Carter has been in education since 1983 as a teacher and leader of schools and trusts. David knew Tim for more than 20 years as a mentor and someone who inspired his own personal leadership journey, and believes he talked common sense in a world where at times this seemed to be lacking.

Lena Carter

Lena Carter started her career in Cambridgeshire in 1992. She is currently a shared head teacher of two rural Scottish primary schools. In 2017, she had the good fortune to spend a weekend with Tim and educators from across the UK, exploring how our four countries can learn from one another.

Dame Julia Cleverdon, DCVO CBE

In 1985, while Julia Cleverdon was working as director of education for the Industrial Society, she led a four-day leadership course with Tim for 50 deputy heads at St John's College, Oxford. Their 40-year collaboration continued through Business in the Community, his tremendous support for Teach First and the Fair Education Alliance Summit in 2023.

Sir Jon Coles

Jon Coles is the chief executive of United Learning. From 2002 to 2005, he was director of the London Challenge, where he worked closely with Tim.

Sir Kevan Collins

Tim's wisdom guided Kevan Collins' work as a school leader, local authority adviser and in his national work. He will always be grateful for the time Tim gave him and his unmatched ability to remind us that grace, humour and human connections are the lifeblood of our work.

Ellie Costello

Ellie Costello is executive director at Square Peg and a long-time fangirl of Sir Tim. Square Peg is a community interest company working to ensure that any young people who are marginalised or unable to attend, access or remain in education are at the heart of policy, development and improvement, giving us a brighter future for all.

Leora Cruddas, CBE

Leora Cruddas is the founding chief executive of the Confederation of School Trusts – the national organisation and sector body for school trusts in England. She had a feisty relationship with Tim founded on mutual respect. She is visiting professor at UCL Institute of Education. Leora was awarded a CBE in the New Year's Honours in 2022.

Ben Davis

Ben Davis is the head teacher at St Ambrose Barlow RC High School in Salford. Prior to this he worked as a head in Scotland, where he first encountered Tim through David Cameron, an association that continued after his move to England in 2015.

Professor Colin Diamond, CBE

Colin Diamond first met Tim in 2000 when visiting Birmingham. He recalls his abundant energy and chaotic office! Fast forward to 2015, and Colin took over as director of education in Birmingham, where everyone talked admiringly of the 'Tim years' and his legacy, and Colin felt that he was walking on the shoulders of a giant.

Professor Graham Donaldson, CB

Graham Donaldson and Tim have shared platforms on many occasions. Tim's unassuming manner and gift for connecting with an audience were unfailingly impressive, and Graham's admiration for him has continued to grow. They shared a passion for education and for supporting unfashionable football teams. Tim will be a huge loss as an inspiration and a friend. His wise counsel will endure.

Ed Dorrell

Ed Dorrell is a partner at Public First, where he leads on schools policy, strategic communications and qualitative research. He has authored several influential education policy papers. For 12 years before taking up this role, he was a senior journalist at the *TES*, and worked closely with Tim.

Maggie Farrar, CBE

Maggie Farrar first worked with Tim when she set up the University of the First Age in Birmingham. Since then he has provided support and inspiration as a mentor and friend through her time as a director at the National College for School Leadership and now as a leadership coach.

Evelyn Forde, MBE

Evelyn Forde was head teacher of Copthall School in Mill Hill, North London from 2016 to 2023, during which time she led the school to achieve significant improved outcomes and worked with staff to secure a range of accolades for the school. In 2022, Tim and Evelyn contributed to the Commission on Teacher Retention.

Sam Freedman

Sam Freedman has worked in education for 20 years, including as an adviser at the Department for Education. He is now a Senior Fellow at the Institute for Government. He never had a chance to work with Tim, but wishes he had.

Professor Michael Fullan, OC

Although they were very much the same age, Michael Fullan always thought of Tim Brighouse as a mysterious elder senior statesman. He was a practitioner, policymaker, professor. He never said much to Michael personally, but they had similar ideas. They borrowed ideas frequently from each other and Michael came to realise that they were quietly sympatico – a feeling that he deeply cherishes.

Professor Tony Gallagher

Tony Gallagher is professor emeritus at Queen's University Belfast and was honoured to read the citation for Tim's honorary doctorate. Tony and Tim were appointed as academic advisers to the Review Body on Post-Primary Education in Northern Ireland (1999–2000), and Tim chaired the governing body of a school collaboration project led by Tony (2010–2013).

Dame Christine Gilbert, DBE

As teacher, head teacher, director of education and Her Majesty's Chief Inspector at Ofsted, Christine was inspired by Tim for over 30 years and is proud to have worked with him. An Honorary Fellow at UCL, Christine is chair of the Education Endowment Foundation and of Camden Learning, a school company.

Ian Gilbert

Ian Gilbert is an educational author and speaker and the founder of Independent Thinking. Celebrating its 30th birthday in 2024, this organisation was in its infancy when Ian first saw Tim Brighouse speak at a head teacher conference in Oxford. It was an event that Ian still talks about to this day.

Ty Golding

Ty Golding was only able to hear Tim speak at a conference once, yet he was extremely grateful for a brief and memorable conversation at that event. It was from there that Ty began to read more about Tim's work, and his ideas began to influence Ty's thinking, leadership and, most recently, his role in the development of Curriculum for Wales.

Sir Mark Grundy

Mark Grundy has been associated with Shireland Collegiate Academy for over 25 years, initially as principal and more recently as CEO of the trust. Over the years, Tim was a frequent visitor, looking at the use of technology to support school improvement and the innovations in curriculum delivery across the trust's primary and secondary schools.

Professor Andy Hargreaves

Andy Hargreaves is an adviser to education ministers in Scotland and Canada. He co-founded and is president of the ARC Education Collaboratory. Andy worked at the University of Oxford when it partnered closely with Tim Brighouse's Oxfordshire local education authority in the 1980s, and has presented with Tim on many occasions.

Professor John Hattie, ONZM

John Hattie is emeritus laureate professor at the University of Melbourne and previously chair of the board of the Australian Institute for Teaching and School Leadership. Like Tim, he has worked within and outside government, been a critic and developer, and Tim and John have shared many conundrums about how to make a system work more effectively for educators and students.

Professor Louise Hayward

Louise Hayward has worked in practice, policy and research in Scotland and internationally to transform assessment experiences for all learners. Tim was a role model for her: a powerful educationalist who lived by the values he espoused and understood the potential for assessment to promote social justice.

Dr Javed Khan, OBE

Javed Khan is a former CEO of Barnardo's and a director of education. He first met Tim as a teacher in Birmingham, and was appointed to Tim's team in 2000 as assistant director where he saw Tim's magical impact at close quarters — and credits his success since then to what he learned.

Dr Debra Kidd

Debra Kidd is leader of learning and teaching at the British School of Brussels and an author and teacher trainer. As co-founder of Northern Rocks, she was grateful to benefit from the wise contributions of Tim Brighouse and proud to contribute to his and Mick Waters' book, *About Our Schools.*

Chris Kilkenny

Chris Kilkenny is a campaigner and activist striving to end the impact of poverty, when he is not busy sorting out his own life. He is currently working to get into university to become a teacher and make a difference for children from difficult circumstances, like his own. Tim Brighouse encouraged his ambitions.

Lucy Kirkham

Lucy Kirkham teaches geography at Bassaleg School, Newport, South Wales. Lucy met Tim when she hosted a discussion into young people's views on climate change. Lucy and her students went on to organise a climate education conference in June 2023 where Tim's speech was a highlight of the day.

Bridget Knight

Bridget Knight is a teaching head, CEO of Values-based Education and editor of *On the Subject of Values ... and the Value of Subjects* (2022). Tim Brighouse has been a standard bearer through her whole career. With him, we knew that teaching could be about educating the whole person.

Jim Knight, Baron Knight of Weymouth

Jim Knight chairs the boards of E-Act Multi-Academy Trust, the Council of British International Schools, Century-Tech and Educate Ventures Research. He worked with Tim as schools minister before serving as employment minister in the cabinet and joining the Lords in 2010. His continued work in education included regular discussions with Tim.

Emma Knights, OBE

Emma Knights was chief executive of the National Governance Association from 2010 to 2024, growing the organisation and the understanding of good governance. She had the privilege of representing the voices of school governors and academy trustees across England. It was through this national role that Emma knew Tim Brighouse.

Priya Lakhani, OBE

Priya Lakhani has deeply admired Tim's work for many years while building Century Tech. She was privileged to be on the National Teaching Awards board that honoured Tim with its inaugural Award for Lifetime Achievement, recognising his remarkable contribution to education.

Professor Bill Lucas

Bill Lucas is professor of learning at the University of Winchester, co-founder of Rethinking Assessment and an acclaimed education reformer. At the start of his career, Tim seconded Bill to develop the Oxford Certificate of Achievement, and Bill taught at Peers School where Tim's son, Harry, was a student.

Rachel Macfarlane

Rachel Macfarlane writes and leads training on various aspects of educational equity. As a programme leader for the London Leadership Strategy, Rachel heard Tim speak on many occasions. He kindly addressed leaders at various conferences that she organised from 2005 to 2023. On each occasion, he sprinkled gold dust and lifted and challenged colleagues.

Dr James Mannion

James Mannion is the director of Rethinking Education, a teacher training organisation specialising in self-regulated learning, implementation and improvement science. James is also the host of the Rethinking Education podcast, where he first met Tim, and the host of the Rethinking Education conference network, which hosted Tim as a keynote speaker in 2022.

Laura McInerney

Laura McInerney is the CEO of Teacher Tapp, a daily survey of over 10,000 teachers. As a former journalist for *Schools Week* and the *Guardian*, Laura had the pleasure of interviewing Tim Brighouse on several occasions and chaired a set of events alongside him at the Education Festival in 2023.

Niall McWilliams

Niall was formally the head teacher of the Oxford Academy, a school well known to Tim. Niall first met Tim when he arrived in Oxford to teach in the early 1990s. He continuously sought his advice throughout his numerous headships and leadership roles, including the managing director role that Niall held at Oxford United.

Fiona Millar

Fiona Millar is a writer and journalist specialising in education policy. She is also a school governor and campaigner for fairer school admissions. She first met Tim in 2003 and frequently spoke alongside him and interviewed him. They were also fellow members of the New Visions Group.

Professor Bob Moon, CBE FAcSS

Bob Moon began his teaching career in the Inner London Education Authority. He was head teacher of two secondary schools before becoming professor of education at the Open University in 1988. He has led many national and international teacher development programmes and was a member of Tim Brighouse's London Challenge advisory team.

Estelle Morris, Baroness Morris of Yardley, PC

Estelle Morris is a former secretary of state for education and was a Birmingham Labour MP during Tim's time in the city. Prior to being elected to Parliament she was a teacher in an inner-city secondary school. She is now a member of the House of Lords and chairs the Birmingham Education Partnership.

Professor Steve Munby, CBE

Steve Munby has held various educational leadership roles including chief executive of the National College for School Leadership in England. He regards Tim as having had a hugely positive impact on his leadership. Tim was his mentor for more than 20 years.

Mary Myatt

Mary Myatt is an education adviser, writer and speaker. She trained as an RE teacher and is a former local authority adviser and inspector. She engages with pupils, teachers and leaders about learning, leadership and the curriculum. Her work has been informed by the wisdom, insights and humanity of Sir Tim Brighouse.

James Nottingham

James Nottingham is a teacher, consultant and author of 12 books. He leads demonstration lessons and creates commissioned videos for schools. A highlight of his career has been the many pinch-me-now moments as a second keynote speaker to Sir Tim's headline presentations at education conferences across the UK.

Dame Alison Peacock, DBE DL FRSA

Dame Alison Peacock is chief executive of the Chartered College of Teaching. Her career spans secondary, primary and early years education. She is a lifelong teacher committed to the inclusive values of 'learning without limits'. Alison is grateful that Sir Tim Brighouse was a great supporter of the Chartered College and thoroughly embraced the philosophy of reducing practices that label children.

Hywel Roberts

Hywel Roberts is a teacher, writer, bassist and brewer. His books include *Oops! Helping Children Learn Accidentally* (2012), *Uncharted Territories* (with Debra Kidd) (2018) and *Botheredness* (2022). Hywel worked alongside Sir Tim at conferences where he would be found nodding his head a lot. He hasn't had enough of experts.

Liz Robinson

Liz Robinson is a school and system leader who has worked with underserved communities across London. Liz's work focuses on challenging leaders to 'think big' about the purpose of school and has worked to radically reshape practices, based on a human-centred belief in the capacity of every child. Tim was a mentor and friend.

Sir Anthony Seldon FRSA FRHistS FKC

Anthony Seldon was head of Brighton College and then Wellington College and first came across Tim in both institutions. They shared a fascination with education in its broadest sense, and what gives meaning and purpose to life. They also shared an interest in politics. Anthony has written the inside books on every prime minister from Margaret Thatcher to Liz Truss.

Rachel Sylvester

Rachel Sylvester is a journalist at *The Times* and chair of the Times Education Commission. Tim gave evidence to the Commission.

Dr Mick Walker

Mick Walker is a former executive director of education at the Qualifications and Curriculum Development Agency and Honorary Research Fellow at the University of Leeds. Mick first met Tim Brighouse in 2006 when he was an adviser to the Expert Group on Assessment of which Tim was a member.

Mick Waters

Mick Waters was a colleague and friend of Tim for 25 years. Mick worked as a head teacher and in initial teacher education before joining Tim as chief adviser in Birmingham He later became chief education officer in Manchester and director of curriculum at the Qualifications and Curriculum Development Agency. Mick and Tim collaborated on *About Our Schools* (2022), which looked at policy change in English schooling since 1976.

David Woods, CBE

After an early career in teaching, teacher training and as a local education authority adviser, David Woods worked with Tim as chief education adviser in Birmingham until moving to the Department for Education. The partnership resumed when Tim was appointed as the commissioner for London schools and David became the lead adviser for the London Challenge.

Introduction

David Cameron

David Cameron has had a long and varied career in education. He met Tim at a conference years ago. Tim said he would tell people to book him instead of Tim. He did. They became colleagues and friends. David sees that as one of the greatest honours of his life and hopes this book repays that to some small extent.

This is a book filled with admiration, gratitude, love, respect and a host of other emotions all evoked by, and dedicated to, Tim Brighouse. We suspect Tim might have hated the attention. At the very least, he would have been very uncomfortable with all the emotion. We think he would have been much happier with the fact that it is full of ideas, forward-looking and determined to finish the work to which he devoted his life.

We wanted a book that commemorated Tim, and those who have contributed to it have done that well. He is captured in the round, with all his eccentricity, passion, enthusiasm, kindness and remarkable range of qualities and skills. His achievements are celebrated by others, but Tim was never likely to celebrate them himself. Despite all that he did, he never lived in the past, nor used his laurels for siestas.

He was always more likely to start a conversation with a new idea, a fresh plan or what we came to think of as 'one of his ploys'. They often began with the relatively harmless, 'I've been thinking ...' He never stopped 'bloody thinking', as he might have said, but he was brilliant at turning thoughts into action and action into achievement.

He had only recently finished *About Our Schools* with Mick Waters (2022). It is an epic which makes Tolstoy look like a short story specialist and *Finnegan's Wake* resemble a graphic novel, without the graphics. He was already thinking about the next book.

That is why this book is not just a tribute; it is a call to action. He wanted to do more to make education more humane, more fair and more effective. He wanted us to be more creative, to think more widely and more deeply and, above all, to help young people create a better future.

He often quoted George Bernard Shaw:

> This is the true joy in life, the being used for a purpose recognized by yourself as a mighty one; the being thoroughly worn out before you are thrown on the scrap heap; the being a force of Nature instead of a feverish selfish little clod of ailments and grievances complaining that the world will not devote itself to making you happy. (Shaw, 1903: Epistle dedicatory)

> I am of the opinion that my life belongs to the whole community, and as long as I live it is my privilege to do for it whatsoever I can.

> I want to be thoroughly used up when I die, for the harder I work, the more I live. I rejoice in life for its own sake. Life is no 'brief candle' for me. It is a sort of splendid torch, which I have got hold of for the moment; and I want to make it burn as brightly as possible before handing it on to future generations. (Shaw quoted in Henderson, 1911: 512)

This book asks you to pick up the torch.

We are grateful to all who have contributed to the book and deeply apologetic to all those who could have and didn't get the opportunity. We are proud of the range of issues that are covered and of the diversity of the authors.

We hope that we have done him justice.

References

Brighouse, T. and Waters, M. (2022). *About Our Schools: Improving on Previous Best*. Carmarthen: Crown House Publishing.

Henderson, A. (1911). *George Bernard Shaw: His Life and Works. A Critical Biography*. Cincinnati, OH: Stewart & Kidd.

Shaw, G. B. (1903). *Man and Superman: A Comedy and a Philosophy*. Available at: https://www.gutenberg.org/files/3328/3328-h/3328-h.htm.

Part I
A tribute

Chapter 1
Finding the Holy Grail
Harry Brighouse

Harry Brighouse is Mildred Fish Harnack Professor of Philosophy of Education and Carol Dickson Bascom Professor of Humanities at the University of Wisconsin-Madison. Tim Brighouse was his father.

When Tim died, the obituaries – as well as the outpouring on social media – emphasised two things. He was idealistic, in the sense that he was driven by an infectious vision of a better world and better education. And he related well to people, especially to teachers but also to children, who wanted to tell their stories to him and were inspired by the ideas he shared.

Those *were* essential parts of him. But you cannot achieve what he did with mere ideas and good relationships. You need also to be canny: to keep a close eye on opportunities and be able to take them.

Tim attributed his entire career success to a single canny decision. He loved university and enjoyed studying history, but didn't devote himself entirely to the academic side, and so, when he finished his exams, he faced a viva which he knew would determine whether he would come out with a second-class or a third-class degree. He was confident that they would either viva him about the paper in which he had done best or the one in which he had done worst. His strategy was simple: focus entirely on preparing for a viva on the worst paper, and hope that if they ask about the best, his pre-existing expertise would suffice. They did indeed focus on the worst paper: he passed with flying colours and came out with a second. He confidently believed that a third would not have been good enough to get him his first job as a head of department at a girls' grammar school in Buxton, which, in turn, was the essential springboard for other opportunities.

After he started work in Oxfordshire, he became aware of a central government scheme supporting sabbaticals for teachers from his friend Barry Taylor (CEO in Somerset). A teacher could spend one year in professional development (take a university course, visit schools in another country, research pedagogy, write a novel), and the local education authority (LEA) would continue to pay their salary, while central government paid for the salary of a replacement teacher. LEAs had discretion over whom and what projects to approve. Suddenly, a lot of teachers in Oxfordshire (including novelist Philip Pullman) were taking sabbaticals, which was good both for morale and for enhancing the workforce: sabbatical-takers would return refreshed, loyal and often with new knowledge and skills. The same thing happened in Somerset and … nowhere else, because Tim and Barry kept their knowledge of the scheme to themselves. Of course, something like that cannot last; after a few years, other LEAs cottoned on and the government ended the scheme.

Tim was a fierce opponent of corporal punishment. Becoming the CEO in a Conservative-led local authority, he realised that it was pointless having an argument about whether it was okay to beat children, and that unilaterally ending it was beyond his remit. As he put it, 'In a time of cuts, if I'd gone to the politicians and asked them for money for canes they'd ask me how many I wanted, and did I want the luxury versions.' But when, in the mid-1980s, councillors began panicking that it might be impossible to comply with the then inevitable law against corporal punishment in schools, he assured them that they needed to do precisely nothing because he knew that none of the schools practised it.

He had initiated an annual survey on how often schools caned pupils. When the results were in, he gave each school the full list, showing the numbers of canings at each school, but with the names of all other schools redacted. The head at the top of the list was shocked to see that his school administered 25% of all the canings in the LEA, but Tim said something to the effect of, 'It's okay, that's the way you like to do things at your school; I often hear the swish as I drive by' [I realise he might have made that bit up, although many readers will know it is believable]. The following year canings were down substantially, even at that school, which was still at the top of the list, now accounting for 33% of all canings. Again, he was reassuring. Within two years, the league table was empty – there were no canings.

In political philosophy, we distinguish between *ideal theory* and *non-ideal theory*. Crudely, ideal theory is about what a just society would be like; non-ideal theory takes those values and asks how they tell us to act in our unjust society, which we might be able to improve but cannot expect to make just by our actions. You cannot do non-ideal theory without ideals; but you also cannot do it without a clear vision of where you are and without acknowledging the unwelcome constraints you face. Tim was principled, yes, but also pragmatic and, in the best sense of the word, opportunistic.

This explains why he was willing to work closely with academies and academy trusts. He thought the academy programme and its predecessors were a serious policy mistake, not because he saw them as a neoliberal plot (I never heard him utter the word 'neoliberal'), but because he believed that central government lacked the capacity to understand schools well enough to both support and regulate them. But once academies were a political reality, of course, there was no point in withholding resources from them: his view was that we should be doing everything we can to improve the quality of state schools, regardless of the form of governance.

I will finish with two non-professional stories: a success and a failure. The success: my godfather, John Walker, told this story at Tim's funeral. Both families purchased a small, almost derelict (and very cheap), holiday cottage in mid-Wales in the 1970s. Tim was brilliant at many things, none of which involved DIY. So, John took on the many tasks of fixing up the place. Tim, meanwhile, got to know the local people, reducing the risk that the cottage would be burned down by nationalists. And, of course, he was brilliant at that, not only because of his egalitarian manner and genuine interest in other people, but because he was happy to give useful advice on educational matters for their children. Even the fiercely nationalistic Welsh language speaker in the nearest house was cordial. The cottage survived.

The failure, and it is less than disastrous: Tim loved Monty Python and was often compared with John Cleese (of whom he did an excellent impression). In 1977, he took me (14) and my sister (10) to see *Monty Python and the Holy Grail* at the Maidenhead Odeon, asking for 'two adults and one child'. On being told that children weren't allowed to see the film (incredible, really), he instantly said, 'In that case, I'd like three *adults* please.' I didn't see *Holy Grail* until my own daughter turned 14, and I am not sure Tim ever did.

Chapter 2

A talisman for the teaching profession

Bob Moon

Bob Moon began his teaching career in the Inner London Education Authority. He was head teacher of two secondary schools before becoming professor of education at the Open University in 1988. He has led many national and international teacher development programmes and was a member of Tim Brighouse's London Challenge advisory team.

Tim and I first met in the early 1970s. He was the education officer in Buckinghamshire with responsibility for planning schools in the new city of Milton Keynes. I was one of a small group of teachers appointed to open the city's first new comprehensive secondary school, Stantonbury Campus.

We went on to become good friends with a shared interest in county cricket, lower league football and more egalitarian versions of golf. And, of course, we debated educational issues, going on to write and occasionally speak together. We also had overlapping membership of some of the progressive pressure groups that sought to influence government. When we met up, Tim always had a new idea to share. A few days before he died, he rang me from his hospital bed. 'Bloody boring in here,' he said. We talked about the operations he was about to undergo, the signing of a new Australian spinner by Lancashire and then he said, 'But, look, the reason I rang was to try out on you a devilishly fiendish plan I've thought up to finally deal with Ofsted!'

How did Tim come to be such a towering figure in the educational world? Why was he such a talisman for the teaching profession?

Early experiences were important. Tim was unhappy in the first grammar school he attended, but the family then moved and Tim, with his brothers, transferred to Lowestoft Grammar School (now Ormiston Denes Academy, still in the Grade 2-listed school building Tim knew). It was a transformative experience. 'The teachers were just more human,' he once said to me, 'and the atmosphere was different. I looked forward to going to school.'

Tim did well at school, went to Oxford and taught successfully for a few years, but he was then tempted by the offer of a post as an educational administrator in Monmouthshire. He had found his metier. 'An LEA officer might sound a bit boring, but I discovered, even in junior positions, that I could make things happen, do things for schools,' he told me. In that period, local education authorities (LEAs) were the equivalent of a local civil service, negotiating with the government as equals. Tim revered this world. He would frequently quote from the writings and work of chief officers like Alec Clegg and Henry Morris. During his time in Buckinghamshire, he became a protégé of Roy Harding, then one of the most influential chief education officers. Tim and Peter Newsam, the former Inner London Education Authority (ILEA) education officer, maintained a correspondence throughout their lives.

Tim was embracing the world of LEAs, and in his early jobs he was learning his trade. Later in his life, I heard people say that Tim was not a details person. Not true. His time in Monmouthshire, Buckinghamshire, the Association of County Councils and the ILEA allowed him to come to terms with the intricacies of financial planning, sites and buildings, school admissions and all the minutiae of running an education system. His abilities became well known, and he was soon the youngest education officer to serve on the influential expenditure steering group for education services, coordinating policy between government and the LEAs.

Tim's first major leadership role in education was as chief education officer in Oxfordshire, a county with a progressive approach to primary education and with a fully comprehensive secondary school system. He was young to the role, in his late 30s, but he soon began to establish a national reputation as an education reformer. I was a secondary head teacher in Oxford (Peers School) through most of Tim's time with the authority. Looking back, I think it was another period of apprenticeship for him, this time in leadership.

Tim had become a hugely inspiring person with whom to work. He was bubbling with ideas, and Oxfordshire was his first opportunity to put these into practice. I would point to three as of particular significance. First, he felt schools should be more accountable, but he believed this should come from internal school self-evaluation. Second, he thought the way young people were judged in school should go beyond marks and grades, so he developed a new portfolio model (this time working in cooperation with a group of other LEAs). Third, he believed the structure of the school day was too inflexible and needed to be adjusted to allow for the provision of activities that did not feature in the traditional curriculum. These were all initiatives with a strong basis in the sort of values that Tim sought to foster.

Tim had a unique leadership style, one that it would be difficult to copy but one that had attributes from which anyone could learn. He had a natural patience, courtesy and kindness, and he was a good listener. He was passionate about schools becoming fairer and more welcoming (friendly) places for all children, and I have seen him almost personally wounded if he came across examples to the contrary. Tim was wary of prescription. He would have aims, but he felt that the way these could be achieved required deliberation and debate. I had a second period of working directly with Tim as one of the small advisory team implementing the London Challenge. The aim was clear, a rapid improvement in the performance of all London secondary schools, but advisers were given discretion as to how they worked with schools to achieve this.

In Oxfordshire, Tim had the limited support systems of the time, given the size of the authority. He would tirelessly tour the county giving talks and speeches extolling the rationale behind reform proposals. Later, in Birmingham and then in London, he had much more extensive support systems. Tim loved working in the wider team context. In Birmingham, where he faced political challenges and an initially hostile Ofsted inspection, he needed the emotional support that a good team gives. In London, he worked with a high-flying civil service team led by Jon Coles as well as an advisory group drawn from across the country. This gave him the space to do what he was so good at, winning the hearts and minds of the more than five hundred London secondary head teachers and the leaders of the 33 London education authorities.

Tim never stopped working. Tens of thousands of teachers have heard him speak and many more have heard about him. He was a wonderful raconteur whether from a stage or amongst a group of family or friends. He had a superb memory for people, places and events. He had a restless, even incorrigible, intellectual energy that made him so revered in the world of education.

Debating with Tim was intellectually challenging, but it was also great fun. I recollect, just after the COVID-19 pandemic, discussing with him the idea of establishing an Open School. I had worked at the Open University for over 20 years, and it was an institution Tim greatly admired. We wrote an article for the *Guardian* (Brighouse and Moon, 2020), and I will always remember Tim's delight at the positive feedback we received. Tim then gave a major place to the Open School concept in the book he wrote with Mick Waters, *About Our Schools* (Brighouse and Waters, 2022). Discussions about the Open School are ongoing. I do hope something could come of this. It would provide yet another marker for Tim's extraordinary impact on the world of education.

References

Brighouse, T. and Moon, B. (2020). Like the Open University, We Now Need an Open School for the Whole Country. *The Guardian* (12 May). Available at: https://www.theguardian.com/education/2020/may/12/like-the-open-university-we-now-need-an-open-school-for-the-whole-country.

Brighouse, T. and Waters, M. (2022). *About Our Schools: Improving on Previous Best.* Carmarthen: Crown House Publishing.

Chapter 3

Inspirational, creative and innovative leadership: a tale of two cities

David Woods

After an early career in teaching, teacher training and as a local education authority adviser, David Woods worked with Tim as chief education adviser in Birmingham until moving to the Department for Education. The partnership resumed when Tim was appointed as the commissioner for London schools and David became the lead adviser for the London Challenge.

When Tim became chief education officer in Birmingham in 1993 and London's school commissioner in 2003, many schools and educational communities were underperforming with generally low morale and ambition. There was a significant need for radical reform to get these cities to achieve excellence. Tim readily embraced these challenges. His approach was to get to know the schools, build relationships and seek partnerships to establish shared vision, values and beliefs to underpin improved education achievement. He astutely built leadership teams and capacity from the outset in both cities. He wanted people who would be energy creators, enthusiastic and always positive, using critical thinking, creativity and imagination – matching his own – to stimulate and spark others.

He shared his clear educational principles with everyone, and from these came a set of core purposes to secure success. The most crucial was to achieve a substantial increase in aspiration, ambition, expectations and outcomes. In both cities, his style involved visiting many schools and education partnerships, debating and communicating core principles and practice. Remarkably quickly, he won the trust and respect of various education communities.

His values and ideas concerning moral purpose, social justice and school improvement took hold quickly. He strongly believed that moral purpose dictates that schools should be engines of social mobility, helping children to overcome the accidents of birth and background to achieve more than they ever imagined. His constant repetition of the importance of 'success for all', 'improving on previous best' and 'optimism and hope' with 'generosity of spirit' struck chords everywhere.

He also believed in the power of a positive common language as part of his 'climate-setting' agenda for these cities. He taught everyone that we could best support and improve education through our own personal example – what we do, think and say and through the practice we celebrate. His approach was always to encourage school staff to have confidence in themselves and be generous in sharing their expertise and practice. Tim knew instinctively that you get the most out of people by telling them what they can do, not what they can't do. His genius was to hold people to high standards and expectations to drive change, whilst convincing them that they could do it – that they had it within themselves to succeed. He changed the climate in both cities from negativity and cynicism to positivity and hope, building a momentum to do much better.

In both cities, Tim strove to break radically with the past and create a culture of achievement. He achieved this by securing agreement on principles and purpose, and led a strategic plan for school improvement to focus everyone's minds. He made school improvement a collaborative challenge through his special qualities of empathy, creative energy and charisma. Everyone wanted to meet the challenge together.

He fizzed with ideas (not always practical!), sufficient to fire up colleagues, education leaders and school communities. The bedrock of school improvement was a better understanding and use of data and evidence. Tim was keen on using comparative data to benchmark performance and tried this with inner-city primary schools in Birmingham. In London, with the help of Department for Education statisticians, he was able to create 'families' of schools with similar intakes – and published the data annually, first for secondary and then for primary schools. This proved to be a stimulus for all schools, and it soon became possible to identify those schools most in need of improvement and those already performing well.

This led in London to the creation of Keys to Success schools, as opposed to the term 'failing', often used by the media and some politicians – another great example of his positive language. These became 'high challenge' and 'high support' schools, and the great majority made remarkable progress – a key reason why London became the highest performing region in the country rather than the worst.

Of course, school improvement initiatives and interventions varied across the cities. Tim's inspiration led to an innovative collection of initiatives in Birmingham which inspired the city and gained national attention. There were the Birmingham 'Guarantees' in every phase of education covering inputs, processes and outputs; a climate calendar with yearly themes such as reading or the arts; a University of the First Age; a Children's University; quality development programmes and curriculum conferencing; and a number of 'butterfly' collections (small ideas for improvement with high leverage).

Tim introduced some of these ideas in London, but there were others for the capital, like the families of schools datasets already mentioned, a specific London Leadership Strategy, the Chartered London Teacher programme, university/school partnerships and the use of highly focused London Challenge advisers working in the field. There was an extensive programme of school-to-school support, and the development and use of consultant heads and leading teachers to promote the sharing of ideas and practice.

To transform education in Birmingham and London, Tim quickly realised, would take a huge, shared endeavour from education leaders and all school staff. Many meetings and conferences were organised alongside extensive school visits to secure buy-in. Instead of top-down approaches, he energised education systems to work both laterally and from the bottom up to an agreed agenda. In Birmingham, there were quality circles and local consortia to carry out the mission. In London, consultant heads and lead teachers were identified and trained as 'system leaders' to provide very effective school-to-school support and lead programmes of professional development. The ambition was to develop knowledge-sharing education systems and learning cities. Increasingly, education professionals were encouraged and incentivised to 'improve on their previous best' and take an increasing pride in their city's success.

At the heart of all his educational leadership, Tim kept an unremitting focus on the needs and aspirations of young people. There could be no compromise on implementing a broad and balanced curriculum where all could flourish and achieve. That is why he introduced the Birmingham and London student pledges across schools, which described the opportunities children should have by the ages of 11 and 16. For him 'it takes a whole city to educate a child'. To that end, he worked tirelessly with colleagues in both cities with business partnerships, arts and cultural organisations and sports bodies, as well as many agencies promoting the welfare of children. In London, he encouraged all the universities to partner with schools, share their expertise and learning, and provide greater opportunities to access higher education, particularly for disadvantaged groups. This was very successful.

Tim always recognised and celebrated the critical importance of teachers in making children's lives better. He was very aware that the quality of an education system cannot exceed the quality of its teachers. That is why he ensured that the London Challenge introduced the Teach First scheme and then the Chartered London Teacher programme. He wrote thousands of letters after his extensive school visits in both cities conveying his appreciation of the massive contribution of teachers to education transformation. He was one of those rare educationalists equally at home in schools talking to teachers and children as in strategic discussions about educational policy and practice. He was loved, admired and respected for his inspirational and creative leadership, and remains a legend in both, remembered for his personal example and his enormous impact.

Chapter 4

Tim in London
Jon Coles

Jon Coles is the chief executive of United Learning. From 2002 to 2005, he was director of the London Challenge, where he worked closely with Tim.

The first time I heard Tim Brighouse's name, I learned instantly of the loyalty he inspired. Charlie. my PGCE tutor at the time of John Patten's libellous comments, knew Tim and his work in Oxfordshire and told me with unusual intensity: 'He is a *wonderful* man.'

The first time I heard Tim speak, some years later, was at a Department for Education conference focused on a white paper I was responsible for. He quoted George Bernard Shaw's 'Life is no "brief candle" to me' – as he sometimes did, although he didn't quite like to quote the man responsible for 'those who can't ...' – and had the audience mesmerised. I promised myself never to speak after him.

But the first time I had a proper conversation with him was after we had both committed ourselves to London. By the time he was appointed as schools commissioner, I had been working for a while on strategy and plans and we had some pieces in place. His reputation from his work in Birmingham couldn't have been higher, but I had no idea what to expect.

When someone has had a lot of success, it may be forgivable if they try to repeat themselves. That was not Tim. He retained an unusual openness, alongside a strong instinct for which ideas might travel well if reworked. He was not interested in redoing or undoing anything already in place – nor did he ever act as if he knew best, even when he clearly did.

They say, 'culture eats strategy for breakfast'. It is a phrase which I suspect might have made Tim wince. But the sentiment – that how we habitually behave one to another is a more powerful force than any other – was at the centre of Tim's practice.

So we took great care about our use of language. We had committed to a direct focus on turning round some of the lowest attaining schools. Tim saw that if our aim was to break the link between deprivation and low educational attainment, then these schools were the 'Keys to Success' of the London Challenge. The language and attitudes of the Keys to Success programme were critical to schools seeing us as alongside them and on their side.

Tim proposed surprising approaches. We planned case conferences with local authority directors on the Keys to Success schools – what the issues and solutions were, and what we each should do. Tim suggested conferences with three local authorities together at a time. I feared that in London's competitive and sometimes uncollaborative climate, this might close down rather than open up solution-focused discussion. His assurances that it would work were proven triumphantly correct – one of many interventions that helped to build a problem-sharing and collaborative culture.

Tim was never in my experience ideological. His starting point was not that certain ideas, practices or policies were essential, or that all issues should be approached from a particular theoretical standpoint. As a result, he didn't suffer from the 'theory-induced blindness' of many who have strongly adopted one outlook or always think from one perspective. He could be open to new perspectives, wherever they came from, and could get behind the efforts of those he didn't wholly agree with if their goals and values were good.

He was pragmatic. He was willing to challenge ministers and the prime minister about issues – like admissions – that weren't being addressed. But he could work productively with them at the same time. He didn't love every programme the department was running, and in his ideal world some of them might not have existed. But they did exist, and Tim could see that getting them focused on London in the right way was one of our best ways of drawing resource and energy into the capital.

He could add huge value to a policy debate, but the civil service's desiccated approach to grinding theoretically towards an answer was a long way from Tim's. He was instead endlessly fascinated by schools, teachers and children and the possibility of growth and change. He didn't assume that there would be 'an answer' to a problem that might apply everywhere, and was more interested in finding, extending and sharing others' good ideas and practices than in promoting his own; more interested in triggering and energising improvement in the humanly messy real world than in analytically pure 'solutions'.

And if the task of educational improvement is the task of helping more teachers to succeed with more children, then Tim went at it very directly. He more than anyone rebuilt the identity of 'the London teacher' – a teacher who is part of a great enterprise of developing a city of learning and creativity, concerned about all the children of the city, breaking down gaps between rich and poor, and determined to learn, improve on previous best and operate at the peak of the profession.

He visited at speed a huge number of schools. He asked questions of head teachers, teachers and children that they might not have expected and that focused not on policy questions but on teaching and learning practices. Which teachers are the best markers? And, to heads, how do you use their expertise to help other teachers?

After visiting a school, as he always had, he wrote to everyone he had met, remembering details of what they had done and said, and thanking them. He wrote to people he didn't meet – for example, to the teachers mentioned by the children or by the head teacher as the best marker – thanking them for their work.

When he spoke to an audience, he followed no known rules of public speaking to quite extraordinary effect. He used overheard projector slides long after everyone else used PowerPoint. His slides sometimes appeared to have no particular order. He would put a quote on screen and extemporise on a theme – reminding teachers of their sense of purpose, what brought them to the most important job in the world, the difference they make and the values they hold.

He energised, inspired and even electrified audiences. Teachers felt seen, valued and uplifted. His apparently disordered presentation was in truth hugely skilful. His deep personal knowledge of the schools he was talking about and the lives, experiences, priorities and values of teachers created a deep connection. He had mastery of pace and pause in delivery, a great feel for an audience – making eye contact with many so that they felt he was speaking to them personally, humour, timing and the actor's ability to embody what he said, take risks and be vulnerable. He knew exactly what he was doing. It was a high-wire act with the real possibility of an embarrassing fall, but he did it anyway.

I have no idea how many hundreds of teachers he met or wrote or spoke to. But there can scarcely have been a London school whose staff did not have many touch points with Tim – moments of uplifting positivity and appreciation – which stayed with people. He was as close as could be to a one-person cultural change in London's teaching profession.

I never did speak to an audience after him.

And he *was* a *wonderful* man.

Chapter 5

Tim as a mentor

Steve Munby

Steve Munby has held various educational leadership roles including chief executive of the National College for School Leadership in England. He regards Tim as having had a hugely positive impact on his leadership. Tim was his mentor for more than 20 years.

'I have five heroes in my life: Kevin Keegan, Mark Knopfler, Bob Dylan, Leonard Cohen and Tim Brighouse. And Tim is in the top three.' This is how I introduced my education hero and mentor, Tim Brighouse, at a conference in Knowsley in 2002.

Many years earlier, I had invited Tim to speak at an event in Oldham. He was inspirational, as I knew he would be. I had an opportunity to talk with him privately beforehand, and he told me that he was about to take up the role of chief education officer in Birmingham. He said that he had been doing a lot of thinking since he had left Oxfordshire and had worked out the approach that was now needed to lead local education authorities (LEAs). Tim's approach was completely new. With Ofsted having just been established and funds drastically cut, most of us in LEAs were focusing more narrowly on the criteria to get a good Ofsted outcome and developing traded services for schools. The idea that a CEO could be a transformational leader focusing on school-to-school collaboration and improving on previous best was unprecedented.

It was while he was in Birmingham that Tim agreed to be one of my mentors, but not my coach. 'I could never be a coach because I am too keen to give advice and to give my opinion,' he said. Since his advice and opinion were exactly what I was looking for, the mentoring relationship worked very well indeed. We met in coffee shops, in bookshops, in his office and, in later years, at his house in Oxford. The advice was always pragmatic, emotionally intelligent and insightful. He helped me in so many ways to become a better leader.

I. Being honest about mistakes and being okay about being imperfect

During a session in Birmingham, Tim shared something that shocked me. He told me how many hours he worked each week. It was unremitting. He started with breakfast meetings and finished with meetings over dinner, and then went home and did his administrative work and wrote thank-you cards. He did this every working day! I told him that I thought this was unsustainable and he couldn't continue to put himself under such pressure. He replied that his senior team worked equally hard and that he didn't think anyone could transform a big LEA like Birmingham without putting in those hours. Fifteen years later, when he was well into his 70s and his health wasn't too good, he said to me during one of our mentoring sessions, 'On reflection, maybe I overdid it when I worked such extreme hours in Birmingham!' After his retirement from full-time work, he relished talking to me about some of the other mistakes he had made in his leadership and how he had learned from them. He helped me to feel positive about being an imperfect leader.

2. The importance of getting the right people on your side

When I was appointed as CEO of the National College for School Leadership, Tim was insightful in advising on big-picture strategy. He talked me through which influential people I needed to try to get 'onside'. His first recommendation was: 'Meet Ted Wragg and ask him for his advice – then he won't write negative things about the National College in the *Times Educational Supplement.*' I travelled to Exeter to meet with Ted, and he was both wise and supportive. Although he died a year later, he did not write a single critical thing about the National College in that time.

3. Personal relationships with school leaders are important, even when working in a national organisation

Tim helped me to think through how to stay connected with schools in my role as CEO of the National College. I had moved from an LEA where I was responsible for 80 schools to a national organisation where I needed to work with 22,000 schools. Tim's experience of leading in big cities like Birmingham and London was invaluable. He said, 'Find a way of writing personal cards to head teachers when you hear they have done something well, and to every new head teacher in the country. You can get a lot of powerful messages across through personal contact, and it will mean a great deal to them.' Tim gave me the confidence that this approach could work, even at a national level. He could not have been more right about this. Being a school principal can be such a lonely job, so being thanked or congratulated in a personal way really mattered.

4. Dealing with criticism without beating yourself up

Tim had immense resilience and had learned to cope with criticism from powerful people like Chris Woodhead (Her Majesty's Chief Inspector) and John Patten (education secretary). Years later when I was deeply upset about what I regarded as unfair articles in the *TES* and the *Guardian* about my time as director of education in Knowsley, he chided me. 'I have read the pieces, and they weren't that bad,' he said. 'Get over it and move on.' He gave me a better perspective and prevented me from dwelling too much on the negatives.

5. Using feedback to communicate high expectations and confidence at the same time

Tim had exceptional emotional intelligence. He understood the importance of acknowledgement and praise but also the need to have high expectations. When I started as CEO of the National College, he wrote a note to me saying: 'You are so important to the future of education, you know.' It made me both pleased and terrified in equal measure.

6. Looking for small opportunities to make a difference and to change things

He was insightful and analytical, always looking for a way forward or 'the gaps in the hedges' as he put it. He was such a creative and innovative thinker. Every time I met with him, I came away with an idea.

7. The importance of staying humble

What stood out above all was Tim's humility. The last thing he wrote to me on the inside cover of his excellent new book, *About Our Schools* (2022), written with his close friend Mick Waters was: 'Steve. Thanks for teaching me so much over the years. Tim'. It was *he* who had taught *me* so much, not the other way around.

8. The value of good mentors

Whatever kind of leadership role we are in, we need mentors to help us make better decisions and to give us another perspective. Tim gave me the precious gift of his time and his wisdom. He was my role model and my sage. Even when he wasn't around to talk to, I would say to myself, 'What would Tim do in this situation?'

I have never had a conversation with any of my other four heroes, but I did get the chance to spend many hours talking with Tim Brighouse. For me, he was not only Tim the hero but also, for 20 years, Tim the mentor. It has been one of the great privileges of my life to have known him.

References

Brighouse, T. and Waters, M. (2022). *About Our Schools: Improving on Previous Best.* Carmarthen: Crown House Publishing.

Chapter 6

Working with Tim –
a real joy

Estelle Morris

Estelle Morris is a former secretary of state for education and was a Birmingham Labour MP during Tim's time in the city. Prior to being elected to Parliament she was a teacher in an inner-city secondary school. She is now a member of the House of Lords and chairs the Birmingham Education Partnership.

At the start of the 1990s, Birmingham was changing. The National Exhibition Centre and the International Convention Centre were landmark developments, transforming the face of the city and refocusing the local economy. They were seen as trail-blazing both here and in Europe, and the city's leaders were right to herald their success as groundbreaking.

Yet, this spirit of investment and innovation wasn't a strand that ran through all the city's infrastructure. For a number of years, Birmingham's schools had been something of the poor relation: buildings in need of repair, low teacher morale and poor examination results. The subject of national comment for all the wrong reasons.

As a response to this, Ted Wragg had been asked to lead a commission into how to improve the city's schools. Following the publication of his report (Birmingham Education Commission, 1993), the key recommendations were accepted and the council committed itself to giving education the priority that it had so long needed.

Tim Brighouse was asked to take on the challenge of leading the implementation of these changes and was appointed as the city's director of education. It is not an exaggeration to say that things were never quite the same again.

The story of Tim's decade leading Birmingham's education system is well documented. The council kept its promise to invest more money and Tim led a transformation of the service, touching every school and every teacher, not only changing what happened in the classroom but how schools related to each other. The mood changed almost immediately: teacher morale improved, aspirations were raised and a year-on-year improvement in results followed. Birmingham was no longer shorthand for neglected and failing schools but a beacon of what was possible with good leadership.

It was during these years that many of the initiatives so closely associated with Tim were developed: improving on previous best, the pupil guarantee, family of schools' comparative data, the University of the First Age, learning from each other and so many more. These underpinned the progress in schools, and in the following years, a Labour government and countless local authorities looked to Birmingham and to Tim for best practice.

If there was any thought that Birmingham was merely a fluke, it was dispelled a decade later when Tim's leadership of the London Challenge moved the capital's schools from the bottom of the achievement table to the top.

Tim's reputation as a national and international educationist, academic and local government officer are beyond doubt, but if you speak to those who worked with him, that is rarely how he is described. They choose to recall a personal story, a note received, a good idea given, encouragement that made a difference – and that is what made Tim so special. It was as much who he was as what he did that marks him out as one of the best education leaders we have ever seen.

Even now, teachers recount their memories of working with Tim. They will tell you about a time he unexpectedly turned up to offer support when there was a problem, Balti restaurant tables booked so that issues could be explored and conversations that left them feeling anything was possible. All of this transformed the climate in which teachers worked and children learned.

Tim's time in Birmingham wasn't without challenge. He had some well-known critics whose battles with him also became part of the Birmingham story. They thought that Tim's approach meant he lacked rigour, was soft on standards and excused failure. How wrong they were. They failed to understand that Tim knew you didn't have to choose between treating someone kindly as a person and asking more of them as a professional. Where else in the 1990s did teachers willingly sign up to their school improving results year on year or openly sharing performance data with the school down the road?

Teachers gave more and did more because Tim made them feel part of a team. Their professionalism was valued and respected, and they knew that success would be built on what each one of them did and how they managed to work together. always thought that one of the reasons for Tim's success was that he was such a good teacher himself. He made people feel secure and confident enough to aim higher than they might otherwise have done, and he worked with them to develop the skills they needed to do the job.

Collegiality was writ large and teachers were proud to be part of the journey. Birmingham and London became good places to teach and good places to send your children to school.

The word 'charismatic' is often ascribed to Tim, but it wasn't the sort of charisma that said, 'look at me and follow', but a quieter charisma that made people look at themselves and realise how much more they could achieve. His speeches were inspirational not because they were barnstorming but because they gave people both hope and good ideas, and they were uncompromising in the message that education underpinned social justice.

I count myself immensely lucky to have worked with Tim. I became an MP in Birmingham the year before he began his work there, and his personal and professional friendship were cornerstones of my life for 30 years. I can't really remember a time when he said he disagreed with me, but I can remember lots of conversations where he would respond to an idea I had by asking, 'Have you thought about ...?', 'What if ...?' and 'Great, and you could also ...'

I came away with a much better idea – as well as thinking that it was all my own work! He really did bring out the best in so many of us.

References

Birmingham Education Commission (1993). *Aiming High: Report of the Birmingham Education Commission. Part 1: The Report. Part 2: The Oral and Written Evidence.* Birmingham: Birmingham Education Authority.

Chapter 7

Tim's national influence

David Blunkett

David Blunkett drew upon the experience, expertise and wisdom of Tim Brighouse when he was education and employment secretary between 1997 and 2001. Together putting ideas into practice and inspiring others led to a continuing friendship which David values to this day. What they started with Excellence in Cities led to Tim's success in leading the London Challenge.

If Tim Brighouse had not chosen to enter teaching and then become a nationally renowned educationalist, he might have become a psychologist. But it is clear from his whole career that an understanding of human nature and the importance of motivation was central to his thinking and to his success.

This was not an 'all-must-have-prizes' or 'children-should-simply-be-happy' caricature of inspiration and inclusion. Tim was a believer in data; in understanding what was happening, where and how it was happening, and what lessons could be learned. He believed in spreading best practice, in being rigorous and rooting out failure, but doing so in a way that carried others with him.

To achieve this, he needed to be – and was – a great communicator. In my contribution to the commemoration of Tim's life on BBC Radio 4's *Last Word*, I said, truthfully, that I was always reluctant to follow him onto a public platform. Not because I'm a shrinking violet, but because the empathy he created with an audience and his ability to take them with him was so effective that it was difficult to get across your own message.

I write all this because understanding Tim's contribution – not just to the past but to the future – requires an appreciation of what made him special. And, for the purposes of this publication, what we must learn and how we can take his legacy forward.

Not, I hope, unique.

We need more Tim Brighouses and, above all, we need to learn the lessons of Tim's success and inculcate it, in any way we can, into the future of excellent teaching and the routing out of failure.

What we are extremely bad at in this country as a whole – not least in the education service – is identifying excellent practice, appreciating the ingredients and then scaling it up. That is why I am personally disappointed that it hasn't been possible for Britain, over the last decade, to embrace the lessons from the success of the London Challenge and replicate it in a manner that would have avoided the massive educational divide that exists in the country, which – with the exception of extremely good schools, often with the benefit of a benign intake – reduces the life chances of too many youngsters, across the north of England in particular.

One of the reasons that Baroness Estelle Morris (who is paying her own tribute to Tim in these pages) and I embraced Tim Brighouse's wise counsel is precisely because he demonstrated what he believed in practical action and not just in theory. It is critical now, therefore, with Tim's passing, that the lessons of his success should be very rapidly infused into reform and modernisation, so we don't just wish for greater equality of opportunity but practise and deliver it.

We all pay lip service to the fact that excellent leadership and world-class teaching are at the root of giving every child the opportunity to flourish, develop and display their talent, and make a contribution to the world around them. Persuading potentially outstanding individuals to join the teaching profession and, above all, to be prepared to take on leadership roles is easier said than done. The lesson of Tim Brighouse's contribution was to ensure that people knew just how wonderful teaching could be, that they were valued in what they did in the most difficult circumstances, and that they would be supported and encouraged in developing their own talent and capability to communicate.

Nearly three decades have passed since we invited Tim to play his part in the development of a step change in delivering early years provision across the country. The establishment of the literacy and numeracy programmes drew on Tim's work in Oxfordshire and Birmingham. Although, all these years on, it is possible to be honest about the fact that we were in such a hurry that we didn't always take Tim's advice on bringing the education profession with us. Both Estelle Morris and I were qualified teachers; we knew about pedagogy and the importance of recognising that each student is an individual, and that what we deliver through the education system should be tailored to them rather than seeking to tailor the student to what, as a nation, we are prepared to offer.

The data can tell us what is working, but not always what is working for different cohorts of students from very different backgrounds, maturing at different rates and requiring an adaptation of approach. This is an approach that, if focused solely on an ever-narrowing qualification route, will deny success to tens of thousands of individuals, but also to meeting the challenge of a very different economic, social and cultural world of tomorrow.

If I had to sum up the lessons we must take forward into the future in a few words, it would be about cooperation, encouraging collaboration, and understanding that mutuality and reciprocity across the education sector is the prerequisite to learning the lessons of the past and applying the best of them in the future.

We must leave behind the atomisation described by a former chief inspector of schools, Sir Michael Wilshaw, and put back the glue that enables schools to work together and teachers to learn from each other. The success of our future adults and the leading of fulfilling and rewarding lives is for the many and not just the few.

Chapter 8

Tim Brighouse – a canny man of nuance

Michael Fullan

Although they were very much the same age, Michael Fullan always thought of Tim Brighouse as a mysterious elder senior statesman. He was a practitioner, policymaker, professor. He never said much to Michael personally, but they had similar ideas. They borrowed ideas frequently from each other and Michael came to realise that they were quietly sympatico – a feeling that he deeply cherishes.

When Tim Brighouse was appointed chief education officer of Birmingham in 1992, he wasn't what John Patten, secretary of state for education, expected. Upon hearing of the appointment, Patten muttered (a comment which was unfortunately (for Patten) recorded) that they had appointed this 'nutter'. Tim sued, and one libel suit later, he was awarded a good sum of money, which he promptly turned into the 'John Patten Innovation Fund'.

Have rumpled suit, will travel! And travel Tim did, usually in his car, often seemingly (or even actually) showing up in scores of schools early in the morning as he made the rounds in visiting his five hundred schools in Birmingham. As a young sociologist from Canada focusing on applied innovation, I would come across Tim fleetingly, mostly wondering what his modus operandi was. He was primarily a practical innovator, carving out ever more fundamental transformations – in Birmingham and later in the prestigious London Challenge. I stayed at his house once, feeling like a guest in a royal residence in an offshoot road in outer Oxford, which was beside a bridge and small creek. A road that, as far as I could tell, had no street numbers. A fitting circumstance for this man who was impossible for me to categorise.

Eventually, I thought of him as exemplifying what was becoming my main change theory preoccupation – nuance and deep change. He became my Leonardo da Vinci (the founder of innovative nuance as far as I was concerned). Tim became famous for leaving positive handwritten notes for people – everywhere. I am speculating that there must some 30,000 bits of Tim's notes strewn around England. It was his micro theory of change: praise people for small acts of change, which (in a nuanced way) did two things: made them feel valued, and reinforced, subtly, effective actions that were taking place. When I eventually asked him to provide a blurb for my book, *Nuance* (2019), he wrote: 'I love this book – enabling leaders to see what was under their nose with sharp action-oriented clarity.' I was proud because it is what Tim himself always did in subtle and informal ways, day in and day out, for decades.

He didn't write much, which is why I was thrilled to read and write about Tim and Mick Waters' magnum opus *About Our Schools* (2022). From 1990 to 2020, I was always scrounging to find anything that Tim had said or spoke about. In most of those days, media accounts were much less publicly available, so I had to chase Tim's stories and commentary. If I found out he was speaking somewhere, I searched to get copies of what he said. When I could be on a conference platform with him, I jumped at the chance, because what he said included gems of insights that weren't otherwise available. I was visibly excited when I found anything he had authored. It was always succinct, incisive like no other and oh so different. It was like a rare treasure when I found a piece he had written, like *How Successful Head Teachers Survive and Thrive* (Brighouse, 2007). He presented his practical wisdom in 'Four phases of headship, five uses of time, six essential tasks and seven ways to hold on to your sanity' – all in 31 pages!

I was like a groupie when Tim brought me into his confidence. In 2009, he was asked by the new director of the Toronto District School Board (TDSB) to serve on a small panel for 12 months to be 'a critical friend'. Tim noted that the board aspired to 'have the fastest rate of improvement and highest standards among all large cities in North America'. He knew a thing or two about transformation of large city boards, and wondered (somewhat doubtfully I would say) in writing to me: 'Is that the trustees' ambition? Is it stated, in what measures by when? There is an impressive and shared commitment to "equity" or "social justice". How far that translates into practices which support optimum practice is another matter.' He then proceeded to ask eight 'practical questions'. He very much wanted to see: 'How to set out the expectations and support for school leadership by the principal, but also the role of others in leadership.' (TDSB is still searching for the answers to these questions in 2024.)

Over most of the years I knew Tim (1980 onwards), I thought he liked what I was writing, but it wasn't until 2018 that he wrote to me:

> What you may not know is that I bought copies of your book *What's Worth Fighting for in the Principalship* for all the heads of Oxfordshire where I was CEO from 1978–1988; I repeated the giving of your book when I first went to Birmingham (1993–2002). And I gave them out at workshops (11 in all) I held with the heads of schools. I reckoned that the new heads would be keen, and therefore stories of the workshops would be positive, and that by the time I got to the 11th workshop and the 'old lags', I would have ironed out any glitches. (personal communication, 19 July 2018)

'Stories' are the best indicators (and strategies) of the transformation of cultures. Tim was the master storyteller in his actions. In commenting on his modus operandi of buying good books and having workshops upon workshops to cultivate a new culture, Tim reflected to me: 'Was that "nuance" or was it "canny"?' I never said that they were mutually exclusive, so let's call him canny.

On 15 February 2022, Tim wrote to me: 'I am writing with an unusual and bit cheeky request. Mick [Waters] and my book is going well, and we are organising a book launch for 30th March at 6pm with the hope that you could help launch the book.' Tim didn't mind being cheeky for a good cause. He taught me other precise English words: 'knackered', which he was the odd time; 'blag', which he advised leaders never to do; and 'chuffed', which today he has earned every right to be!

About Our Schools, the magnum opus by Tim Brighouse and Mick Waters, is a legacy opportunity for Tim Brighouse to *be more*! Lucky us, lucky learning for Tim's ideas to live on.

References

Brighouse, T. (2007). *How Successful Head Teachers Survive and Thrive.* Abingdon: RM.

Brighouse, T. and Waters, M. (2022). *About Our Schools: Improving on Previous Best.* Carmarthen: Crown House Publishing.

Fullan, M. (2019). *Nuance: Why Some Leaders Succeed and Others Fail.* Thousand Oaks, CA: Corwin.

Chapter 9

Tim Brighouse – sustainability maker

Andy Hargreaves

Andy Hargreaves is an adviser to education ministers in Scotland and Canada. He co-founded and is president of the ARC Education Collaboratory. Andy worked at the University of Oxford when it partnered closely with Tim Brighouse's Oxfordshire local education authority in the 1980s, and has presented with Tim on many occasions.

Nothing Tim Brighouse said to me had a transformational impact on my work.

It is a strange start to a tribute. But what Tim *did*, not what he said, transformed my career. It was not through modelling or example, but through the systems and cultures he created that he shaped my work and that of others like me.

Take just two examples. In the early 1980s, I was a lecturer at the University of Oxford while Tim was chief education officer for Oxfordshire Local Education Authority. He was committed to continuous professional learning for head teachers and middle leaders, and established a system of secondments to the university's Department of Educational Studies. Many of the teachers at that time did not even have university degrees – they had qualified through teacher training colleges. He was a believer in teaching as a profession and in the capacity of all educators to learn, grow and move further into leadership.

The secondments were intended to stimulate teachers' professional learning, refresh them professionally and personally, connect their dissertation studies to the needs of their schools and figure out how to improve their practice when they returned. One result of this ingenious programme was the arrival at my office door of five diploma students; neither they nor I had any idea what they would be doing. I was totally responsible for them. All were older than me. I was an academic, but I was barely 30 years old.

I designed the curriculum for the first term – a smattering of curriculum theory and studies of schools. Like characters in a 1950s novel, we sat in my office in moquette-covered chairs discussing readings around a gas fire. In the second term, I said that they would design the curriculum, based on common interests rooted in our readings and their roles in school. Our focus became personal and social education. We went to one of the group's schools to observe and discuss their social education course. We brought in trainers of a life skills programme, so we could engage in and reflect on their learning activities.

Their work in these classes and their dissertations were impressive. They matched many doctoral-level theses I have supervised since. They manifested Tim's belief that if you give teachers time and space to engage collaboratively in high-quality professional learning linked to practice, they will achieve far beyond the initial expectations that levels of certification might have suggested.

Halfway through the second semester, I suggested to the group that 'there might be a book in this!' So, throughout the rest of the course and for over a year beyond it, far beyond their period of secondment, we met to co-author what became *Personal and Social Education: Choices and Challenges*, published in 1988. They went back to their schools, implemented what they had learned and, in some cases, went on to become school leaders, national level directors and senior local authority advisers.

It was a transformative experience for us all. Tim had the vision. He believed in the power of his middle leaders and fledgling academics like me to create something magical and practical together. And he established the structure and culture that made it possible.

The experience lasted a lifetime for me too. I began to see schools, teachers and leaders as partners in creating new knowledge and practice together. It has stayed with me as I have done collaborative research with school systems, advised ministers and brought together system leaders from different countries to advance human rights. I have had opportunities to make a difference at levels and in ways I could never have imagined at

30. And this commitment, this respect for people in school systems as professional equals, began with Tim Brighouse.

He was also the mastermind of an extraordinary innovation called the Oxford Certificate of Educational Achievement (OCEA). Before the creation of the national curriculum in 1988, the secretary of state for education, Sir Keith Joseph, set out to transform secondary education to motivate young people in vocational studies who had become disaffected with a traditional curriculum. Joseph's energy and initiative brought together people from across the ideological spectrum to try and radically change secondary education.

Never one to miss an opportunity to improve learning, especially for the most marginalised, Tim formed a partnership with three large local authorities and the education department in my own university to create OCEA. It used a diverse assessment process to recognise the breadth of young people's accomplishments. It consisted of three components. The 'E' component collated conventional examination results, the 'G' component curated other out-of-school certificates, and the 'P' component might include part-time jobs, acting as a carer, taking on leadership positions in school and so on. This record was to be discussed periodically with a tutor who knew the young person well and could use the ongoing record to support their development. Together, these components made up a portfolio – a record of achievement – that could be presented to potential employers or people in further and higher education.

The initiative was quickly assassinated by the national curriculum in 1988, but, for many of us, the memory remained. I drew on it when I advised the Ministry of Education in Ontario on its transition years policy and on developing assessments to support young people's transition to high school. It was still in my head in 2023, when I reviewed the Irish examination system as part of an Organisation for Economic Co-operation and Development team. These learnings about alternative and inclusive assessments, picked up in people's formative years in their 30s, have had a lasting influence on the work, perspectives and policy impact of today's leading minds in UK educational assessment, as the ideas behind records of achievement are now being reinvented in the age of artificial intelligence.

Remembering Sir Tim Brighouse helps me, and may help others, to think differently about sustainability. We tend to consider policy impact as research evidence that academics produce, which then gets rolled out through implementation. But when I talk to senior leaders now, it is not what they have read recently that has influenced them. Most don't have time to read. It is what they did or read 20 or 30 years ago during these formative years that sticks with them as they use their power to make change on a large scale.

Many writers in this volume recall things that Tim said to them or modelled for them earlier in their careers. My treasured conversations with Tim came in my late 40s when we were both working with systemic change in different countries. But sometimes what matters in how people influence us is the frameworks they create that enable others to thrive in their own way. My collaborations with schools and school systems, the way I approach issues as a policy adviser, and what I keep trying to do in working with the profession to create more inclusive and equitable environments for all young people, owe a huge amount to the systems and cultures that Tim Brighouse constructed, and the memories he created for all of us.

References

Hargreaves, A., Baglin, E., Henderson, P., Leeson, P. and Tossell, T. (1988). *Personal and Social Education: Choices and Challenges*. Oxford: Basil Blackwell.

Part II

A call to action

About Our Schools by Tim Brighouse and Mick Waters was published in 2022. In it, the authors sought to chart the development of school policy and the influences upon it over the period since 1976. They describe the impact of policy on the teacher in the classroom, those in school leadership positions and, most importantly, the pupils in our schools.

The book is extensively referenced, taking interviews with 108 people as the basis for further research both in academic texts and in the autobiographies of the central characters. It tries to offer a fair analysis of the effect of change over time: the successes, failures, bright sparks and damp squibs (the policies rather than the politicians!).

The final part of *About Our Schools* summarises what has been learned and points the way to the next era of schooling – one based on hope, ambition and collaborative partnerships. Aware of the complexity of the agenda, Tim and Mick tried to avoid certainty in the book. Hence, they offer suggestions rather than proposals, and invite people to consider possibilities away from the trap of arguments over polarities that have bedevilled schooling for so long.

Similarly, in Part II of *Unfinished Business*, each chapter offers a perspective on the significant educational issues of our time. We have split these into four main sections:

1. Policy, politics, accountability and governance

2. Curriculum, pedagogy and assessment

3. School improvement, leadership and technology

4. Inclusion, equity and diversity

We invite the reader to dip into the thinking of our contributors and follow threads, spot possibilities, raise sights and grapple with the complexity of our schooling world. And, whatever our position, to ask what we can each do to take forward with clarity some unfinished business, as we work with others in a spirit of hope, ambition and collaborative partnership.

Chapter 10

From opinions to action ... improving on previous best

Mick Waters

Mick Waters was a colleague and friend of Tim for 25 years. Mick worked as a head teacher and in initial teacher education before joining Tim as chief adviser in Birmingham. He later became chief education officer in Manchester and director of curriculum at the Qualifications and Curriculum Development Agency. Mick and Tim collaborated on *About Our Schools* (2022), which looked at policy change in English schooling since 1976.

In *About Our Schools* (Brighouse and Waters, 2022), Tim and I wrote about the way government policy since 1976 had affected children's lives. That was the year when Prime Minister James Callaghan questioned school effectiveness and began the progress which led to the Education Reform Act 10 years later.

We built the book on interviews with all but two of the living secretaries of state, tracing their influence on the development of schooling policy and the impact in classrooms. Our experience had taught us that the teacher creates the weather for children, and the weather is part of the climate brought about by politicians, civil servants, special advisers, local authorities, multi-academy trusts, head teachers, inspectors, unions, employers and so on.

Our research showed us that much of the last 45 years had been beneficial, but there were many side effects that had inhibited progress. The final chapter of the book sets out 'foundation stone' suggestions for moving on from this extended period of centralisation, marketisation and managerialism in schooling.

Our first foundation stone was a Schooling Framework Commission. Many argue that policy power should be taken away from the secretary of state, but we thought that untenable. Instead, we suggested a commission comprised of the great and good and a modern civic conversation to establish a 10-year plan for schooling with scheduled reviews. The secretary of state would not be bound by the plan, but would need to explain any significant diversion from it. The first task of the commission would be to establish a set of purposes for schooling based on agreed principles about childhood and youth in our nation. Unbelievably, we have no statutory purposes for schooling.

We had been concerned about the impact of secretaries of state. The average tenure since 1976 is less than two years. Of the 25 since then, we judged that only four had made a significant strategic impact: Kenneth Baker, David Blunkett, Ed Balls and Michael Gove. Most cared and some had impressed because of commitment: Estelle Morris, Gillian Shepherd (both previously teachers), Charles Clarke (with a deep awareness of the power of e-technology while holding firm to developing the spirit of the learner) and Justine Greening (with an active pursuit of social justice). Yet almost all had brought their own 'policy adjustment' to address a crisis, make their mark, divert political attention or raise their own profile, with consequent reverberations in classrooms.

We believed that we need to incentivise the right things for learning to flourish. The accountability regime is stifling the work of the very system it seeks to monitor. It is constraining teachers who are being over-managed into a technical and operative outlook rather than being the drivers of the system. This led to our fifth foundation stone, the building of teacher expertise, seeing teachers as the lifeblood of the system and driving their own agenda through consultants based in schools engaging in deep research on the detail of pedagogy. We firmly believed in teachers forging new practices.

Many of the obituaries on Tim highlighted the time he spent in schools and classrooms, often unannounced. Portrayed as a delightful idiosyncrasy (alongside his dress sense), that same trait had often been used previously as a criticism. Throughout my career, I have been similarly affected by the veiled disapproval that too much time was spent in schools and classrooms (and laboratories, gyms, studios, workshops, fields and residential centres). From headship, through my leadership roles in local and national government, I have experienced the exasperation of people believing you should be with them and not with teachers.

Visiting schools was not some indulgent romantic escape from reality. It was, and remains, a calculated leadership approach. Being close to teachers, even fleetingly, was our way of gauging the weather that affects the pupils. Leadership within and beyond schools creates the climate which affects the weather. We wanted to feel the weather rather than be told about the climate.

Unlike most inspectors, we had seen classrooms and schools for real. We would see the brilliant and the appalling, the sunny and stormy days, the talented and troubled children. The kaleidoscope of images told us where we needed to help to develop policy to support a changing climate.

We both enjoyed the hard work of talking at conferences, structuring meetings to solve problems, writing papers or justifying our actions to elected representatives (although Tim enjoyed that more than me). In the two years since the publication of *About Our Schools*, Tim and I spoke to multiple gatherings ranging from large national conferences to literature festivals, such as the Hay Festival. In our many travelling hours, conversations would range widely: family, cricket, football, TV shows and books, DIY, royal accessions, prime ministerial accessions, politics, reminiscences of when we worked together ... and, of course, schools.

We would muse over the issue of the day, relate it to our book and wonder whether we had addressed it fully. We were never 'rear-view mirror' people who longed for a mystic yesteryear. But we did know when developments were likely to take us backwards and held firm to the notion of always seeking improvement on previous best.

As we assembled this book, we were said to be experiencing a school attendance crisis. It was described as the fading Conservative government's 'number one education priority' – well, along with teeth-cleaning, chess, mathematics, signing and mobile phones (and that is just one term's list). We reflected that Boris Johnson's rejection of Sir Kevan Collins' proposals for funding for post-pandemic programmes had been the portent of problems to come.

Would it not be better described as a 'school absence crisis'? Is attendance really the issue, or is it the symptom? Could it be that schooling as it is does not work for too many children? The euphemistic 'home schooling' numbers increase. The unmet needs of many children with special educational needs and disabilities (SEND) can make school a torment. We insist that a day of school missed is a day of learning lost, and at the same time lose half a million school days a year to pupil suspension.

Have children picked up the tension in their teachers about accountability? Many families have realised that their children are in a race that cannot be won in an assessment system that is designed to secure failure for a third. Is there any wonder that some children can't be bothered and their families don't see school as the answer? Adolescence begins earlier and lasts longer. Have schools been able to respond to that over the last generation?

We thought that the creation of an Open School would change the concept of schooling dramatically. With increasing numbers at best tolerating school and artificial intelligence advancing speedily, we wanted to reshape schooling to include access to a vast range of learning opportunities, with pupils guided towards expertise and wider interest groups, actual or virtual, that could nurture their talents and excite their interest.

We suggested two programmes that could be aimed at pupils, Extraordinary Learners with Exceptional Creative Talent (ELECT) and the Seeking Talent and Extending Participation Scheme (STEPS), and made sure they had acronyms in the hope they would catch on – and then we couldn't remember them ourselves.

So many issues from our book emerge in the discussion of school absence: welfare, teaching, leadership, SEND, disadvantage, behaviour, technology, curriculum, assessment and others, all intertwined or not through education policy-making.

It is these issues that are addressed in the second part of this book. Tim and I thoroughly enjoyed the extended hours we spent interviewing people for *About Our Schools*: always interesting, mostly fascinating and revealing. Occasionally, we were discomfited by the certainty we met in our witnesses. We were never 'certain' people, favouring conjecture, deliberation and ideas. We avoided standpoints that polarised issues and preferred discussion to debate, consensus to dogma. The chapters that follow encourage the reader to pick up the baton on a range of issues as we work together as an education community to improve outcomes for all pupils.

Writing this piece in the past tense has been very difficult. Tim's death and my own retirement from active involvement with schools, teachers and pupils have forced me to revisit the truths that Tim and I, and many others, knew throughout our careers, which began well before 1976. We always knew that good schools were human places: exploiting every moment for learning, warm in every crevice and celebrating learning for every person. Good schools are joyous and purposeful places too, where people enjoy being together, connect with a real world, and have memorable and funny events, happinesses and sadnesses. They help pupils to think for themselves and act for others.

We also knew that schooling is better nowadays than ever before, and so we should recognise and celebrate success. But we should also note that we can always do better, 'improving on previous best' as Tim urged. One way to do that is to secure a better future through hope, ambition and collaborative partnerships as, for children everywhere and for our world, we continue to address unfinished business.

References

Brighouse, T. and Waters, M. (2022). *About Our Schools: Improving on Previous Best.* Carmarthen: Crown House Publishing.

Policy, politics, accountability and governance

Chapter 11
Open School
Fiona Aubrey-Smith

Fiona Aubrey-Smith is a consultant researcher and school system leader who is known for her infectious enthusiasm, pedagogy-first approach and championing of agency for young people. Fiona worked closely with Tim and Mick and an advisory team to curate the formation of Open School.

Every conversation or interaction with Tim was a learning experience. He would listen carefully, pause reflectively (or chortle loudly!) and then offer a gem of an insight that both warmed the heart and inspired practical action. His pedagogy was personal, knowledgeable, ambitious and supportive – unsurprisingly, four outlooks that form the heart of Tim's aspirations for an Open School.

In 2020, mid-pandemic, Tim characteristically considered the landscape and, alongside Bob Moon, set out a compelling case in the *Guardian* to launch an Open School (Brighouse and Moon, 2020). His idea drew upon the foundations of the Open University – to provide access to high-quality and flexible teaching and learning resources and activities which could guide new models of educational provision. The idea was developed further in *About Our Schools* (Brighouse and Waters, 2022), where Tim and Mick set out a vision to bring teachers and learners closer together – with teachers acting as personal guides to curate personalised pathways for young people – leveraging both in-person experiences and the opportunities offered by global digital access. At its heart, the emphasis is on the equity such a model might offer – bringing human partnerships and high-quality experiences to young people who might not otherwise be able to access them due to disadvantages either at home or at school.

Post-pandemic, there have been two parallel trends affecting this space. First, a mainstreaming of large-scale initiatives offering online access to teaching and learning materials, with many teachers now using these as scaffolds for their own classroom practice. The staffroom has already become global. Second, a correlation between national school absence issues, increased home education and tutoring, and the global rise of new models of schooling. Young people and families are increasingly disengaged, with many considering alternatives to mainstream schooling.

In 2023, under Tim and Mick's guidance, the World Education Summit initiated a series of discussions with global thought leaders and existing success stories from open, blended and virtual schools.[1] These sessions unpacked implications on access and inclusivity, partnerships and relationships, curriculum and assessment, operations and teacher development.

Over the last year, a wide range of voices and perspectives have tabled discussion papers and contributed through roundtables and working groups to shape collective thinking. We have learned from those who are already bringing teacher subject expertise into their classrooms from other countries and from organisations that are already using data insights to provide students with dashboards signposting personalised academic and personal development. We have explored opportunities for supporting teacher recruitment and retention through new, professionally rewarding, flexible models of teaching. We have considered a range of financial and operating models which could enable the Open School to launch as a charitable, commercial or state-funded proposition. Perhaps most importantly, we have thought deeply about approaches to providing a scalable network of personal learning coaches, so that every young person has an appropriate and continuous champion to support their individual journey and aspirations. As Tim would say, someone who knows their favourite flavour of crisps!

The Open School is a huge ambition. It could make a life-changing impact on learners and teachers whose potential is currently capped by existing inflexible systems. In an increasingly consumer-led global landscape, it is illogical to structure schooling around the convenience of an organisation rather than the needs of the human being. Now, post-pandemic, and in a world of artificial intelligence and personalised everyday technologies, young people recognise this mismatch; even our quiet conformists see traditional schooling as increasingly irrelevant.

---

1   See https://www.worldedsummit.com.

Beyond school, young people are learning from personal networks that span schools and countries. They are collaborating through gaming projects with children from a diverse range of backgrounds. They are seeking out connections, ideas, inspiration and meaning through social channels. The problem is not that young people are disengaged from learning. The problem is that they are disengaged from schooling. Political insistence on attendance in school as a proxy for re-engaging young people with learning does not fix the problem. It simply increases frustration and anxiety where young people and teachers have to battle with a structure and system which both know is no longer fit for purpose.

We *must* do something about it. If we consider ourselves as teachers, leaders and educators, we must listen – really listen – to what our learners really want and need. What should learning, teaching and schooling look like beyond 2024? What is the purpose of schooling – for individuals as well as collectively? We must rethink the route map.

The Open School is in gestation but not yet born. To work at scale, it needs to demonstrate a scalable, high-quality provision that benefits learners, teachers, communities and the system. A series of prototypes are under development, combining personal data dashboards, teacher–student coaching, signposting of high-quality resource and provision and, importantly, a clear interplay between existing school structures and systems and gradual new ways of working. It needs funding but not politicising.

It is early days, but we are on this journey.

So, reader, here is the question for you. You have read this book, and this chapter, because you value the life and legacy of Sir Tim Brighouse. Think back to how and why he touched your life and shaped your thinking. How can you pay that forward? What might your contribution be?

Reach out. Opt in. Help us to shape this journey towards the Open School.

What greater homage could there be than to join this crusade and – as Tim might say – 'Get the bloody thing up and running.'

References

Brighouse, T. and Moon, B. (2020). Like the Open University, We Now Need An Open School for the Whole Country. *The Guardian* (12 May). Available at: https://www.theguardian.com/education/2020/may/12/like-the-open-university-we-now-need-an-open-school-for-the-whole-country.

Brighouse, T. and Waters, M. (2022). *About Our Schools: Improving on Previous Best*. Carmarthen: Crown House Publishing.

Chapter 12

Policy into practice – the Brighouse way

David Bell

David Bell is vice-chancellor and chief executive of the University of Sunderland. He has been a local authority director of education – paralleling Tim's time in Birmingham, Her Majesty's Chief Inspector of Schools and permanent secretary at the Department for Education where he engaged positively with Tim.

Tim Brighouse was a man of action. His indefatigable approach meant that he never stood still as he swept in and out of schools and classrooms, invariably leaving those he met feeling so much better about themselves and their work.

Running two large education authorities did not afford much time for review and reflection either. Yet, Tim was a man deeply interested in policy – he was a distinguished professor, after all – but always with an eye to classroom practice and how it could be improved.

It is hard to imagine Tim gliding effortlessly through the corridors of Whitehall with the smoothness and polish that characterised the mandarin class. He was too impatient for all of that. Yet, his approach can still teach us about how education policy can be better crafted and implemented.

First, evidence-based policy was central to Tim's approach whether it related to early learning, raising attainment or school improvement. He wanted teachers to know about the latest thinking and apply it to the classroom through research-informed teaching. He abhorred ideological certainty and was restless in his quest to find out new knowledge and how it might be utilised to help teachers.

The rhythms of politics and government and the search for the latest fix might seem antithetical to such an approach. However, the creation of national evidence centres in the early 2000s, to which Tim and others contributed, provided an opportunity for academics to bring their research to bear as policy was crafted at the same time as helping ministers to dig deep.

Tim was always curious about what was happening elsewhere in the world and what relevance it might have in the UK. This was no mere educational tourism which, at worst, seeks to implant methods in a way that takes no account of context or culture. For example, he wanted to know how today's best-performing education systems across the world were using assessment to drive quality rather than whether qualifications mirrored yesterday's incarnation.

Second, Tim wanted policy-makers, whether in local or central govern-ment, to 'touch and feel' the classroom or the science laboratory or the assembly hall. He would frequently encourage even the most senior people to spend a day in Birmingham's schools. Famously, he asked the then chief inspector of schools, Chris Woodhead, to do that after one of their well-publicised battles about the shape and direction of the educa-tion system.

Tim was too polite to castigate what he saw as 'armchair generals' whose ideas were generated far from the front line of learning and teaching. Rather, he preferred to trust the professionalism of those who worked in schools as they were closest to the action.

Yet, and third, Tim was no soft touch when it came to underperformance. Indeed, he could be at his most animated when talking about the children and young people who were failed by the education system. Tim's great insight was to create a high-trust, high-accountability environment.

In his mind, trusting the teachers, with no challenge implied, had allowed bad practice and poor educational outcomes to go unchallenged for too long. Equally, he abhorred a high-stakes inspection system that offered no support and could be punitively damaging to both pupils and teachers.

So, in both Oxfordshire and Birmingham, and through his writings as an academic, Tim promoted a model of school improvement where credible expertise was deployed to support teachers in the classroom.

Unsurprisingly, the brightest and best wanted to work for and with Tim, so he recruited fine people who had a profound impact on schools across the country.

Tim was not naive about the failings of some local authorities when it came supporting their schools. That is why, quietly and behind the scenes, he would mentor and support senior leaders who were struggling to make an impact. Yet, one of his abiding regrets was to see, in the latter part of his life, the hollowing out of local authorities and the increasing atomisation of the education system.

While it appeared increasingly unfashionable to support such a notion, Tim believed in a community of schools in which everyone supported everyone else, with high-performing local authorities acting as the glue that bound everyone together. But he did that in a way that respected school-based autonomy and leadership, ensuring that the choice was not a false one between the total control and dead hand of the local authority on the one hand, or the isolated and potentially selfish independence of the individual school on the other.

Finally, Tim believed in a rich, broad and balanced curriculum in which the arts and creative subjects had similar prominence to the sciences and technology. He promoted a range of initiatives to ensure that children could experience the excitement of live performance, corralling to the cause many great arts institutions in both Oxfordshire and Birmingham.

He gave the most talented children, across academic disciplines, the opportunity to work with others away from their own school. His own deep and wide intellectual hinterland gave him a credibility and authority to champion the cause of breadth in the curriculum, recognising early the suffocatingly narrow direction in which too many politicians were tempted to go when it came to subject choice.

Although Tim has gone, his approach to policy and his ideas seem more relevant than ever, as much of the orthodoxy of the past 15 years is reassessed with increased scepticism.

Tim's work is now being looked at with fresh and sympathetic eyes, whether it is in rebuilding a sense of community among schools in a locality where everyone takes their share of burdens, or in bringing back joy to the curriculum and revalidating the central role of the arts, or in ensuring that school accountability, while maintaining its rigour, is done in a proportionate, sympathetic and supportive manner.

When it comes to the legacy of Professor Sir Tim Brighouse, that – and much more – will do.

Chapter 13

The state/private divide: why old problems need new voices

Melissa Benn

Melissa Benn is a writer and campaigner. Her books on education include *School Wars: The Battle for Britain's Education* (2012) and *Life Lessons: The Case for a National Education Service* (2018). A former chair of Comprehensive Future and co-founder of the Private Education Policy Forum, she was a great admirer of Tim's.

At over six hundred pages, *About Our Schools* is exceptionally heavy on a reader's wrists, but it is worth its weight in rich thinking. Too much writing about education is replete with certainties and denunciations; it is refreshing to be drawn instead into an extended, almost ruminative, conversation that makes welcome room for differing perspectives. Through it all, however, runs a principled commitment to 'truly public' – that is, state – education and the values that should shape it: the same commitment and values that ran through the entirety of Tim's inspiring, imaginative and impressive professional life.

Nowhere do the tom-toms of argument beat more passionately than in the debate around the growing inequalities between private and state provision. In *About Our Schools*, Tim and Mick make clear that they do not want to see private schools abolished, but they admit to having felt 'unwonted envy and anger' on visits to those 'conveyor belts of privilege', such as Eton, Harrow and Winchester (Brighouse and Waters, 2022: 564).

The book includes some thoughtful proposals to rebalance the funding of private and state education, including a local 'equity tax' to be levied on the private sector at 'half the difference by which the average local independent schools' fees exceed the average per-capita unit cost of the age group in the local state system' (Brighouse and Waters, 2022: 595). The income from this tax would be pooled nationally and paid to the parents of children on free school meals aged 9–13 to buy them 'enhanced experiences': the kind of cultural education that is a middle-class child's by right. Tim and Mick also set out a 20-year plan to increase state-school funding from one-third to two-thirds of the average private school fee: this last, a scaled-down version of Gordon Brown's never-realised 2006 pledge to close the gap in funding between the two sectors.

The book's proposals for reform tap into the zeitgeist around private education in two important ways. First, they reflect the fact that after a long period of quietude the private school question is back on the agenda, partly due to the impact of deforming austerity imposed by a series of entitled Conservative politicians, but thanks also to a number of publications on the private school issue and the establishment of two organisations committed to serious discussion and reform. Admission of interest here: I was an early supporter of one of them – the cheekily named Abolish Eton – and a co-founder of the other – Private Education Policy Forum (PEPF). PEPF has undertaken valuable investigations into hitherto neglected areas, such as the global expansion of many well-known public school 'brands', and is exploring positive avenues for change, such as the conversion of private schools to state schools.

Second, Tim and Mick's proposals are designed to channel any additional taxation of private schools to the now chronically underfunded state sector. The Labour Party, having stopped short of abolishing charitable status (too tricky, legally), has made a similarly explicit connection. Its plan to charge 20% VAT on private school fees (with exemptions for special needs schools) will raise, roughly, £1.5 billion, which will be used to recruit 6,500 new teachers and expand mental health services.

On paper, such proposals seem both rational and just. However, recent reaction to the Labour plan gives us a different insight into the zeitgeist, illustrating just how hard it remains to tackle the inequalities between state and private education in a political sense.

Principally, there continues to be a deeply unhealthy connection between educational privilege and the power of civic voice. I have directly witnessed this over two decades in relation to the grammar school debate where, in those areas that still operate the 11+, those who lead or attend grammars have a virtual stranglehold on educational discussion and one barely hears from the contemporary, largely academised, secondary moderns and the families that are pushed into them.

This imbalance is even more noticeable in recent fevered debate over Labour's VAT plans, with opposition led by the formidably well-organised Independent Schools Council. Since it became clear that Labour would stick by the policy (one of its few bold moves on redistributive taxation), there has been a constant and unrelenting stream of newspaper and wider media coverage claiming that the plan threatens to push disadvantaged pupils out of grammar schools (where very few gain entry anyway), bring single-sex education to its knees, slash bursaries and force the closure of a number of small independent 'community schools' (a contested claim). This, despite private school fees having risen by a whopping 55% over the past 20 years with few of these catastrophic impacts.

Unsurprisingly, there has been little comment from the Etons and Winchesters whose annual fees now nudge £50,000, thus highlighting the irrationality – if not, the absurdity – of a charitable status that has enabled VAT exemption down the years. Instead, like so much educational debate from the Thatcher era onwards, it is increasingly parents who take the lead in public discussion and campaigning. However, to return to my earlier point about civic power: which parents? Whose voice? How many people realise that Labour's policy commands a consistent majority of public support, including among over 40% of private school alumni?

What are the lessons for reformers here? Certainly, the current furore over VAT points up the need for this and any future government to stay firm on plans for redistribution, of whatever kind. But it also illustrates how important it is that the public realm makes room for a different set of voices: the head teacher battling with a collapsing roof, the school in a deprived coastal area that has never been able to recruit a physics teacher, the parent who cannot afford a single 'enhanced experience' for their child. *About Our Schools* nobly champions such perspectives throughout, but if the argument about rebalancing resources is to cut through, we need to rebalance our culture as well as our economy and hear these voices more directly and frequently.

References

Brighouse, T. and Waters, M. (2022). *About Our Schools: Improving on Previous Best*. Carmarthen: Crown House Publishing.

Chapter 14

The champion of vulnerable children: who deserves this title and how do they achieve it?

David Carter

David Carter has been in education since 1983 as a teacher and leader of schools and trusts. David knew Tim for more than 20 years as a mentor and someone who inspired his own personal leadership journey, and believes he talked common sense in a world where at times this seemed to be lacking.

The relationship between academy trusts and local authorities has been a work in progress for nearly 20 years. The challenge of leading a system that sees roughly half of schools belonging to the maintained sector and the remainder being academies overseen by the Department for Education remains one of the structural challenges that governments could park in the 'too difficult to resolve' box. We are unlikely to see any legal mandate for all schools to become academies in the future, so this dual structure will be the norm for future generations of children and school leaders.

Whilst this is frustrating for some, there is a powerful advantage to be gained from purposeful collaboration. Many trusts have secured significant sustainable improvement in schools that previously had been failing for decades. Whilst all is not perfect in the trust sector, there are many outstanding leaders of school improvement working in academy trusts. The same can be said of many local authorities, where the support they provide is welcomed and often of high quality. The challenge is that an academy trust has a responsibility for all the children who attend one of its schools, whilst the local authority has a responsibility for every child, irrespective of the school they attend. The intelligent conclusion is that both sectors need each other more than at any time in the last decade. Arguably, there is no alternative other than to forge new partnerships that are focused on safety and standards and worry less about the 'tribe' you might belong to!

One of the key challenges facing the education system over the next decade is to resolve the issue hinted at in the title of this chapter. Who exactly is the champion of the vulnerable child? What we used to call inclusion is now neatly framed around four major crisis points for schools: (1) attendance levels, (2) behaviour concerns, (3) children with a special educational needs and disabilities (SEND) diagnosis but little or no support, and (4) mental health challenges that are fast becoming an epidemic for young people. The only alternative is to work sector-wide to innovate, pilot, implement and evaluate strategies that will make a difference. The role of central government is not to lead this but to fund it adequately, so that those closest to children in classrooms can execute their plans.

The four areas highlighted above need oversight beyond a single academy trust and beyond a single local authority. We will need porous borders across towns and cities so that a child living in one area and attending school in another can still access support. The framework for solving this challenge needs to be built around the five priorities outlined below. Local partnership groups should start from the premise that every child in a community is the responsibility of every adult working in the education sector, irrespective of the school they attend or the postcode in which they live. The partnership groups should be led by an independent chair and board members recruited because of the level of expertise they can bring to the agreed terms of reference. These members should be recruited from across the education sector, drawing on the full range of experiences from schools, further and higher education, and local and regional authorities. Only when we achieve this cultural shift will we start to build a less fragmented system.

Where would we start?

1. Ensuring there are enough good school places for every child close to where they live. Here, the responsibility is placed firmly on trust and school leadership teams, trustees and governors to build exceptional educational experiences for children.

2. Ensuring that every child who is disadvantaged can attend a good school, even if this means maintained schools and academies amending their criteria for the allocation of a school place and those responsible for school-place planning assuring the quality of the process. A child already falling behind at the age of 5 or 11 should have the right to attend a school that has been judged to be at least good if their parents and/or carers want them to. If transport is a concern, then local or national government should pay for it.

3. Ensuring that every school takes a fair allocation of children with SEND and that disadvantage is in line with the local authority averages. It cannot be socially or morally fair that this responsibility sits with the schools that take more than their fair share when it is clear that some schools admit considerably fewer children with complicated levels of social and educational need.

4. Ensuring that the system works better to build parent confidence in the support a child will receive to help them attend more frequently. This will entail collaborative partnerships across the sector that go beyond best practice sharing. More attendance hubs is not the answer. We need trained experts who understand the psychological reasons why children refuse to come to school, who can then build successful strategies that can be transmitted at scale.

5. Ensuring there are mental health experts and champions who are able to support schools and families where there is clear evidence that a child's education is on hold because of their well-being and confidence. Teams that might work in this area could be based in trusts, the local authority or charities that are new to the sector. What matters is the competence to provide sustained support, not who employs them.

Many of these suggestions are not new. For too long we have sought the perfect answer to an imperfect set of questions. Now is the time to think differently and put children even more at the centre of policy-making and delivery. The prize is a school system that delivers on the promise of equality and fairness. The winners will be families and communities in the future.

That would be a legacy to make Tim proud.

Chapter 15
A legacy for Tim
Julia Cleverdon

In 1985, while Julia Cleverdon was working as director of education for the Industrial Society, she led a four-day leadership course with Tim for 50 deputy heads at St John's College, Oxford. Their 40-year collaboration continued through Business in the Community, his tremendous support for Teach First and the Fair Education Alliance Summit in 2023.

My last words to Tim came when sharing a platform with him at the Fair Education Alliance Summit in 2023 where he spoke brilliantly on the importance of place and context. He had told the starfish story to great effect – telling of two people walking along a beach with one occasionally picking up starfish and throwing them back into the sea. What was the point of that the other asked? Well, it mattered a lot to the starfish that was saved! That was all we could do until we could build breakwaters to save them all. The breakwaters, however, would need to be subtly different depending on whether it was Blackpool or Doncaster. The context and the community mattered, as Tim had pointed out to David Blunkett when he had invited him to lead the London Challenge. 'Just do what you have done in Birmingham' David said. 'It wouldn't work,' Tim told him. 'Birmingham is different.'

I closed his brilliant session on place by saying that if, alas, he tried to die, he must be put on life support until we had managed to achieve all that he believed in. Reflecting on all I had learnt from him, starting with the leadership courses for deputy heads that we ran together in the early 1980s, I realised that I was most influenced by his passionate belief in the practice of teachers as leaders who could make the difference for every individual starfish in their class. It was that belief which drove Teach First, which I commissioned when chief executive at Business in the Community and later chaired to persuade many more talented graduates to come and teach in the poorest communities. Having learnt so much from him over more than 40 years, what must we do now that we are without him?

Think long term

Do everything we can to call for a Royal Commission, to shape a long-term, 10-year view on the UK's vision for education – as the Foundation for Education Development, which he so inspired, is trying to do. We have seen 10 secretaries of state for education between 2010 and 2024 and 10 ministers for universities and higher education in the same period, most of them relentlessly claiming the vital importance of setting up a new initiative or legacy-builder – generally just a lunch, a launch and a logo that disappears with their successor. If an incoming government could hand the setting of interest rates to an appointed independent board supervised by the Bank of England, surely the same could be achieved for an education system with widening inequity, faced with challenges with the workforce, the curriculum, the technology, the relevance and, in many places, a 20% absentee rate with consequent unsustainable costs.

Encourage educationalists to work across sectors to rebuild the wider moral purpose of education with communities, young people, businesses and public service

As Tim and Mick wrote in *About Our Schools*:

> Having criticised both the increase and exercise of powers at a national level, it may seem perverse that we should argue for much clearer exposition of values, aims and purpose by ministers at the centre – suitably advised, of course, by a Schooling Framework Commission. We do so, however, because we think that the professionals involved in schooling, especially teachers, will respond to being part of a great enterprise with a clearly articulated moral

belief and purpose. In heavily urbanised and rural areas, what unites teachers and school leaders is a passion to change the world for the better through unlocking the talents of their pupils, and the ability to convey this with a clarity which their pupils recognise and which brooks no denial. (Brighouse and Waters, 2022: 535)

Engage national stakeholders from business, communities and civil society but convened by educationalists like Sir Kevan Collins, Sir Michael Barber, Dame Alison Peacock, Alan Francis and Sir David Bell, with young people drawn from the #iwill movement. Hold a modern, civic, cross-sector conversation to establish a set of purposes for schools and colleges, laying to rest the unhelpful either/or of inspiring through knowledge or building skills and developing character. Use the Times Education Commission (2022) recommendations as the agenda-setter. Build on the purpose, reach and authority of two important structures shaped in the last 10 years – the Education Endowment Foundation and the Chartered College of Teaching.

Engage the business world in connecting schools with the future world of work

Build on the real progress and momentum made by the Gatsby Foundation and the Careers and Enterprise Company in benchmarking high-quality engagement by schools and employers. Take careers education from the margins to the mainstream and resource full-time careers leaders – and start in primary. Scale up the ambition of teacher encounters and co-create the curriculum with teachers and employers to prepare young people for the future, not the past, with Skills Builder and speaking skills woven in.[1] Reinvent work experience as work inspiration starting in Year 7. Reform Progress 8, and drive a relentless conversation on arts, music and performance in schools to build a resourced creativity curriculum to inspire the creativity we need. Establish Tim's timeline of the 10 things every child should do by the time they are 10 as his legacy.

---

1   See https://www.skillsbuilder.org.

Seize the metro mayor energy to drive the place agenda

Convene the last five children's commissioners, led by Dame Rachel de Souza, to develop their joint recommendations on how to put the child at the centre of the system, and ask the #iwill movement with the Fair Education Alliance and partners how to listen to and distil young people's experience. Examine the #BeeWell Survey in Greater Manchester, showing a 96% response rate on young people's experience of well-being and mental health.[2]

In cracking the public service silos, consider the relevant experience of the Cradle to Career team in North Birkenhead backed by the metro mayor, and the work of UK Youth in their Joined-Up Institute. In tackling the random academy challenge, examine the replicability of Blackpool's 10-year plan, where eight secondary schools with strings pulled by different academy chains took a more concerted and generous place-based approach to exclusion, primarily driven by new incentives to retain students.

References

Brighouse, T. and Waters, M. (2022). *About Our Schools: Improving on Previous Best*. Carmarthen: Crown House Publishing.

Times Education Commission (2022). *Bringing Out the Best: How to Transform Education and Unleash the Potential of Every Child*. London: The Times and The Sunday Times. Available at: https://nuk-tnl-editorial-prod-staticassets. s3.amazonaws.com/2022/education-commission/Times%20Education%20 Commission%20final%20report.pdf.

---

2   See https://beewellprogramme.org/research/survey.

Chapter 16

A man for all seasons – and eras

Ed Dorrell

Ed Dorrell is a partner at Public First, where he leads on schools policy, strategic communications and qualitative research. He has authored several influential education policy papers. For 12 years before taking up this role, he was a senior journalist at the *TES*, and worked closely with Tim.

Tim Brighouse was an extraordinary figure in the public life of this country. I consider myself incredibly lucky to have known him – and learnt from his wisdom – over the last 15 years.

A genuinely brilliant educationalist, he thought deeply about schools policy and yet was also beloved of the hundreds of thousands of teachers that his career touched. In this, Tim was unique.

He was also a connection to a bygone era. Born in 1940, he was too young to be a contemporary of the great generation of educational administrators – Sir Alec Clegg and Sir John Newson, for example – who had emerged after the Second World War with a mission to transform education for all children, but he learnt from them and probably knew them.

Indeed, Tim was working in Oxfordshire with my grandfather (John Dorrell) when the grammar school system was being dismantled and, like so many of his contemporaries, he held comprehensive education to be a wonderful example of democratic reform in public life. We need to renew this faith in authentic inclusivity.

Tim's understanding of the education system was profound, but it was his way of working that set him apart. It was predicated on something all too unusual among his caste of public servants: he loved, respected and cherished classroom teachers. The core of his philosophy was that if we could motivate teachers to have confidence in themselves and their professional knowledge, and then to share that insight with as many other teachers as possible in semi-formal and formal professional dialogue, we would lift the whole system.

I remember him telling me with a high degree of confidence that, in every single classroom in the country, something innovative was happening. If only, he pointed out, we could somehow surface and share each and every example of professional brilliance, from the smallest to the biggest, think of the power that would have.

This was the grounding for his way of working with schools too. On another occasion, I remember him reminiscing about his time in Birmingham, where he had been chief education officer during the early 1990s. At the time, Tim explained, there were a number of underperforming schools. He visited all of them. Ahead of each visit, he would ask his officers to iden-tify one brilliant thing the school was doing. 'I've come to see your school because I hear you're doing wonderful things with X,' was how he would start these potentially difficult meetings. The results would follow.

It is said, and I have no reason to doubt this, that during this time, Tim per-sonally wrote to every single teacher joining a school in the Birmingham local authority to welcome them.

Over the course of his career, Tim's reputation grew and grew, despite the best efforts of certain Conservative politicians to tarnish it. Under Tony Blair, he was appointed to lead the London Challenge, a singularly vast school improvement project that aimed to lift the results of schools throughout the capital. He set about this initiative with his usual zeal: his vision was to bring together schools in similar circumstances, wherever they were located, to learn from one another and to work out shared strat-egies for improvement. He was also determined to avoid any stigmatising language about failure.

There was, of course, a lot more to the London Challenge than that, but that was the core of the idea.

Today, London has one of the best state school systems in the world. There is a never-ending debate about why and how this has happened, and many are keen to point out that the advantages the capital enjoyed (demographics, funding, young and enthusiastic teachers) rendered the improvement we have witnessed as inevitable. But ask any head teacher who was around at the time to explain this step change in improvement, and Tim's name will be among the first words that come out of their mouths. School leaders and teachers simply loved working with him.

Tim was a deeply charismatic human being (in a peculiarly English way), and yet he somehow managed to combine that with being down to earth. His educational philosophy was at once both highly idealistic and grounded in common sense. Embodying these two apparent contradictions was his great achievement.

In Tim's personal mission, his life's work, his moral compass and his pragmatism, we can see a model for rebuilding the confidence of this country's education system as it recovers from the COVID-19 pandemic, austerity and the recent years of maladministration.

Tim was, discreetly, a Labour man to his core. The incoming Keir Starmer-led government could do a lot worse than learn from his approach to public service and public administration. Tim believed in a confident, high-performing state as a way to bring about long-term social change – and he believed in caring for, and respecting, those who choose to provide this service in the classroom.

This country – not just its teachers and its children – needs more people like Tim Brighouse.

An edited version of this article first appeared in the TES.

Chapter 17

Finding the Brighousian balance in school improvement

Sam Freedman

Sam Freedman has worked in education for 20 years, including as an adviser at the Department for Education. He is now a Senior Fellow at the Institute for Government. He never had a chance to work with Tim, but wishes he had.

It is a matter of deep personal regret that those of us working for the Coalition government after 2010 to reform education in England never asked Tim Brighouse to help us. The vision of school improvement set out in Secretary of State Michael Gove's white paper, published that year, was, after all, strongly rooted in the success of the London Challenge (Department for Education, 2010). It took many of the ideas developed by Tim and the rest of that team, including teaching schools and national leaders of education, and tried to apply it nationally.

Over time, though, the collaborative elements of the model got downplayed and punitive accountability became too great a focus. Schools within strong multi-academy trusts (MATs) have benefited from improvement approaches pioneered by Tim – the largest, United Learning Trust, is led by Jon Coles, one of his co-leads on the London Challenge. But too many schools are stuck in ineffective trusts or with seriously diminished local authority support due to heavy cuts in council funding.

There are reasons for this beyond the Department for Education, like the UK government's broader austerity policies which particularly targeted local government, but there was also a belief among some of the Gove team that collaboration was a fluffy, cuddly waste of time. And, of course, it can be. Poorly designed programmes can easily become schemes for justifying collective failure.

What made the London Challenge unique was that it found the right balance between collaboration and accountability; enough edge to create extrinsic incentives but enough focus on moral purpose and partnership to bolster intrinsic ones too. As many others have testified, Tim's personal warmth was critical to making this approach work, as it created the space for difficult conversations about poor exam results or a bad Ofsted inspection.

Whilst in opposition, Labour shadow ministers spoke about a more concerted national school improvement policy. This is an opportunity to rethink the approach, but it also comes with plenty of risks. A national programme designed by civil servants in a heavily centralised system would completely fail to take local context into account, even if it was professionally informed.

Moreover, it is not 2002 any more. We have some very successful MATs doing a great job, and a policy that tried to impose national directives on them would undermine the progress they have made in some of the most challenging schools in the country.

The key question is how to improve schools that are in weak, and often very small, trusts, or that have been left adrift as maintained schools with minimal local help. While this can't be done nationally, it also can't be done through local authorities, given they have been denuded of cash and expertise.

In any case, one of the most important elements of the London Challenge was the combination of localism and scale (something that Tim also utilised when running education for Birmingham City Council, which has more schools than any other local authority).

Had it been attempted within a single borough it would have likely failed due to a much less powerful network of support. The ability to bring a head teacher from Haringey to support a school in Tower Hamlets, or vice versa, was critical. The relative failure of attempted 'Challenge' programmes in Manchester and the Black Country was, in part, down to turf wars between local authorities and the teams running the programmes, something that was largely avoided in London.

In recent years, we have seen the development of mayoral combined authorities (MCAs) – with cross-party support. These typically cover city regions like Greater Manchester or Liverpool, so combine a greater scale than councils with a far more local approach than Whitehall could ever manage. Most are still in the early stages of development and fairly fragile; some have not worked well; but they undoubtedly have the ability to run much more contextually informed programmes. We have seen some initial evidence of this from the success of health and probation programmes in Manchester, which has been up and running the longest.

So far, most MCAs have done little on pre-18 education. It is not an area in which they have any statutory responsibilities or for which they receive any funding. But some – like Manchester and the North East – are keen to play a greater role, given the importance of education to regional economic growth and the broader success of an area. Labour should embrace this by allowing MCAs to lead, where they want to, on new regional school improvement programmes with Department for Education backing.

A first step would be to align Department for Education regional directors with MCAs to enable a closer working relationship, and then to use the department's intervention powers in coordination with the local school improvement initiative rather than as the only tool in the box. It would allow for that critical mix of collaboration and accountability.

A regional approach would breed a variety of different models that could be evaluated for effectiveness and adopted by other MCAs as they are established across the country. Some would not work, that is the nature of devolution, but within any given area it would have a better chance of success than any alternative.

The biggest challenge to this way of working would be finding local leaders who could balance encouragement and challenge, as Tim was able to do, but at least the structure would exist to replicate the model he made work so well.

References

Department for Education (2010). *The Importance of Teaching: The Schools White Paper* (November). Available at: https://www.gov.uk/government/publications/the-importance-of-teaching-the-schools-white-paper-2010.

Chapter 18

Dropping pebbles into ponds: promoting school collaboration in Northern Ireland

Tony Gallagher

Tony Gallagher is professor emeritus at Queen's University Belfast and was honoured to read the citation for Tim's honorary doctorate. Tony and Tim were appointed as academic advisers to the Review Body on Post-Primary Education in Northern Ireland (1999–2000), and Tim chaired the governing body of a school collaboration project led by Tony (2010–2013).

Tim was a regular visitor to Northern Ireland who always left inspiration and energy in his wake. One inspiration he left us with was the idea of collaboration, an idea that has become a central principle of our education system.

The school system in Northern Ireland is characterised by the 11+ and academic selection and the role of the churches in school governance. After the election of the Blair government in 1997, the new direct rule minister with responsibility for education in Northern Ireland commissioned research on the impact of selection to inform public debate. When the research was published (Gallagher and Smith, 2000), the Northern Ireland Assembly had been established with Sinn Fein leader Martin McGuinness as minister of education. He established a Review Body on Post-Primary Education to be chaired by former Ombudsman Gerry Burns, and with Tim and I appointed as two of five academic advisers.

The work of the review body sparked widespread interest – a response form was sent to every household in Northern Ireland and over 200,000 forms were completed and returned! In our early discussions, the main options seemed to be the retention of some form of academic selection or an all-ability or comprehensive system, but no one was convinced that either was entirely satisfactory. In our discussions, Tim offered the idea of a 'collegiate' system for consideration, in which groups of schools would work collaboratively. The analogy he used was the Oxford or Cambridge colleges, each with their own identity but working together for a common purpose.

Although facing initial scepticism, Tim's idea became more attractive the more we talked about it, not least because it seemed to provide a way for every child to have access to a full range of curricular options, while avoiding the divisive effects of academic selection. The idea of establishing collegiates, which schools would be obliged to join, became one of our three main recommendations in the Burns Report (2001). The others were the abolition of academic selection and the use of formative, rather than summative, assessment in primary schools. We identified 20 collegiates across Northern Ireland involving all the 234 grant-aided grammar and secondary schools at the time.

Views on the collegiate proposal were mixed, but the idea of collaboration took hold. A later Review Group, tasked with assessing the results of the consultation on the Burns Report, accepted the principle of collaboration, but suggested it should be voluntary, rather than statutory, and based on schools working together to provide a wider curriculum for all students.

A draft education bill in 2006 included a clause to abolish academic selection, but this was stymied by a deal between the UK government and the Democratic Unionist Party at the St Andrew's talks on restoring the Assembly (which had been suspended since 2002). The bill also included an 'entitlement framework' requiring all schools to provide a set minimum range of subjects at Key Stage 3 and post-16, with this delivered through collaboration with other schools. In order to facilitate collaboration, the Department of Education established area learning communities, which have had a measure of success, although the level of collaborative activity has tended to be bounded.

An opportunity to drive the agenda for collaboration further came through work on Shared Education partnerships. This addressed the issue of separate schools for Protestants and Catholics by promoting locally based collaborative networks involving schools from all sectors. Partnerships would run shared classes in which students from all the schools would participate and provide opportunities for the establishment of professional learning communities for teachers. Being locally based also meant there was a real prospect that school collaboration could be wide-ranging and sustainable.

Funding from the Atlantic Philanthropies and the International Fund for Ireland provided the opportunity to run large-scale pilot projects to test the idea and develop an effective model of collaboration. An independent governing body (IGP), involving representatives from educational and community stakeholders, was established to oversee the pilot projects. We were very pleased when Tim agreed to act as chair of the IGP between 2010 and 2013. His experience of promoting school collaboration in Birmingham and London was invaluable. He was also keen to visit school partnerships, both to see the work in action and to offer his own inspiration and encouragement to teachers.

Shared Education was adopted as a statutory responsibility for the Department of Education in 2016, and the organisation and support of Shared Education partnerships was mainstreamed. By 2020, almost two-thirds of all schools in Northern Ireland were part of a Shared Education partnership, and the idea of collaboration had become a central feature of our school system. Despite the legacy of a divided society, it is now commonplace to see students with different uniforms in classrooms and school corridors learning and socialising together. Where once separate uniforms were a symbol of our difficulty in dealing with difference, they have now become a mark of our capacity to transcend and engage with difference. Where once teachers would rarely, if ever, cross the threshold of schools from different sectors in their own area, now many have access to a network of friends and colleagues in neighbouring schools for advice and support.

Tim used to talk about the crucial role of 'energy providers' in schools, and used the analogy of the ripples set in motion when a pebble was dropped into a pond. His collegiate idea dropped a pebble into the pond that is Northern Ireland education, and the ripple effects have cascaded down the years to shift the axis of the way we work. Tim was the ultimate energy provider, and we will be forever grateful for the time he spent with us. We are equally determined that the ripples continue to spread and the spirit of collaboration extends even further in our education system.

References

Burns, G. (chair) (2001). *Education for the Twenty-First Century: Report of the Review Body on Post-Primary Education* [Burns Report]. Available at: https://www.education-ni.gov.uk/publications/report-review-body-post-primary-education-burns-report.

Gallagher, T. and Smith, A (2000). *The Effects of the Selective System of Secondary Education in Northern Ireland*. Bangor: Department of Education.

Chapter 19

Reclaiming accountability

Christine Gilbert

As teacher, head teacher, director of education and Her Majesty's Chief Inspector at Ofsted, Christine was inspired by Tim for over 30 years and is proud to have worked with him. An Honorary Fellow at UCL, Christine is chair of the Education Endowment Foundation and of Camden Learning, a school company.

The case for change

It is hard to imagine any debate about education reform in which the word 'accountability' would not be used. Usually, it is interpreted negatively as unhelpful pressure on schools and teachers. This is because it is associated with public accountability: results, league tables and inspection. The accountability agenda comes to a head in inspection. But accountability is broader and more important than that, and to focus on the reform of Ofsted is too narrow.

Real change will only occur when accountability has been reclaimed by schools and is seen as central to their work and to teachers' professionalism. This means leaders and teachers taking pride in their role as agents of professional accountability and working collaboratively within and across schools to strengthen it. Accountability can inspire professional growth, enhance teachers' expertise and, ultimately, better support pupils' learning. As such, it deserves to be championed as an essential and even energising element of our school system.

The shift in culture needed

Good leaders embrace both summative and formative accountability but with a working emphasis on the second. In aligning individual responsibility and collective expectations, they establish a culture that enables teachers to feel greater ownership of all forms of accountability. They encourage teachers to develop a strong sense of both individual and collective purpose, and to feel part of a professional learning community where a continuing process of review and dialogue about pedagogy and practice leads to change, innovation and better learning. Few leaders would use the word 'accountability' in describing such an environment, but placing 'professional' before 'accountability' reinforces ownership and pride.

It is teachers themselves who make the most difference to learning. Therefore, teachers should be at the centre of any internal accountability system. They have to own it and drive it, including making mistakes and using these to learn.

School leaders who take professional accountability seriously know it isn't a quick fix. They focus consistently on building the school's capacity for learning. This entails locating the learning as close as possible to the internal work of the school and establishing a culture of enquiry, innovation and exploration. This does not negate the need to look outwards. Professional accountability needs the sustenance gained through peer learning and the use of external research and evidence.

Good schools know themselves more deeply than analysis generated through the lens of an Ofsted inspection framework. Self-evaluation helps to redress the balance between summative and formative accountabilities. If it is to strengthen the professionalism of teachers, it should be undertaken as a collaborative exercise and a professional discipline. This provides the base for a professional and internal accountability system but also serves the demands of external accountability. The process of evaluation should operate at all levels, from interactions between teacher and pupil to whole-school benchmarking. It may well be professionally led, but it must engage others. Pupils have a key role in evaluating the quality of support for learning, and in helping to shape it too.

Accounting to parents and the public

The external accountability framework provides information for parents, but test results, league tables and inspection reports give a narrow view of the school's purposes. A Parentkind survey from 2023 indicates that just 24% of parents see Ofsted reports as useful to them.[1]

An annual school report card or record of achievement, perhaps assured and validated locally, has the potential to provide parents and external stakeholders with a broader and more balanced account of a school's achievements. Several interesting models are under development, often in collaboration with parents. Camden's model seeks to recognise:

● The value of the breadth of the education children experience.

● Achievements with pupils who do not show up well in exam league tables or with a more challenging journey ahead of them.

● Success in improving children and young people's health and wellbeing.

● The views of young people, parents and staff.

● The importance of young people's contribution to the community.[2]

The focus has shifted to a report telling the *real* story of a school. The Ofsted report is available as an additional piece of information, but it loses its primacy.

Inspection support for professional accountability

Inspection should be judged on how well it supports schools' systems for professional accountability and learning, as well as the quality and impact of its information to government and the public. Inspectors should be able to use their expertise and knowledge of practice, including using

---

1   See https://www.parentkind.org.uk/research-and-policy/parent-research/
    research-library/exams-and-assessment/school-inspections-parent-poll-
    july-2023.
2   See https://camdenlearning.org.uk.

the Ofsted database, to help schools respond to specific problems. This would provide practical encouragement for self-improvement. Greater insights would also enable Ofsted to identify schools that might be usefully selected for in-depth studies of particular aspects of education. This could strengthen learning within and across schools, but could also inform government about where in the system investment is needed and identify where more evidence is required to inform practice and decision-making.

If Ofsted were to take a different approach to the inspection of those schools that demonstrate strong professional accountability, change could be dramatic. Ofsted might test the rigour of the school's self-evaluation or, indeed, its public report card and the professional accountability processes that underpin it. If inspectors found them to be strong, they would give formal and public endorsement of these judgements. However, if inspectors had concerns, they would extend their time in the school to carry out a full inspection and produce a report. For schools with strong professional accountability, Ofsted would therefore be adopting a transparent, more cost-effective quality assurance role, which would not necessarily entail inspection reports.

Conclusion

Exam league tables, Ofsted and other high-stakes accountabilities have given a transparency that has helped to generate a significant improvement in education over the last 30 years. However, this has also encouraged a compliance culture and an accountability regime that many find negative and stressful.

A strong approach to professional accountability within and across schools should feed effortlessly into public accountability frameworks. Indeed, the two approaches should become mutually reinforcing, thereby strengthening learning, development and performance in all parts of the system.

Chapter 20

Governance of our schools: where next?

Emma Knights

Emma Knights was chief executive of the National Governance Association from 2010 to 2024, growing the organisation and the understanding of good governance. She had the privilege of representing the voices of school governors and academy trustees across England. It was through this national role that Emma knew Tim Brighouse.

We are all agreed that Tim Brighouse was a kind man, and that is particularly important in our gurus. Kindness is one of the seven virtues in the Framework for Ethical Leadership in Education,[1] but it can be in short supply with leaders who have succeeded in a big way.

I cannot think of any other education guru who came to sit in the National Governance Association's (NGA) office in Birmingham and commend what we were doing to improve governance in state schools in England, and to listen to our take on things. Tim started any conversation on governance by acknowledging the efforts of volunteers, as he did in *About Our Schools* (Brighouse and Waters, 2022b). Writing for the NGA's magazine, *Governing Matters*, the authors said: 'We cite governance as a vital part of the school system and highlight the importance of ensuring the local voice is heard' (Brighouse and Waters, 2022a: 20–22).

Those quarter of a million citizens who come forward and contribute to their schools and communities want to play a part in ensuring that children flourish, and it is almost always because they care about the place

---

1 See https://www.ascl.org.uk/ASCL/media/ASCL/Our%20view/Campaigns/Framework-for-Ethical-Leadership-in-Education.pdf.

where they live or work. After stepping up, governors and trustees soon realise that (yes, with some variation in structures) they are now responsible for ensuring that pupils receive the best possible education. This is achieved through strategic direction, support and challenge of the school and/or trust, leaders helping to embed values and a culture of learning and improvement, and listening to all voices.

Tim appreciated that I, despite being a governance geek, put people – not structures or processes – first. It was common ground. Good governance relies on people: their knowledge, their relationships, their values and behaviours, and their collective wisdom (see Figure 20.1). Good judgement is under-emphasised and yet it is crucial to good leadership. We make better decisions when we embrace diverse perspectives.

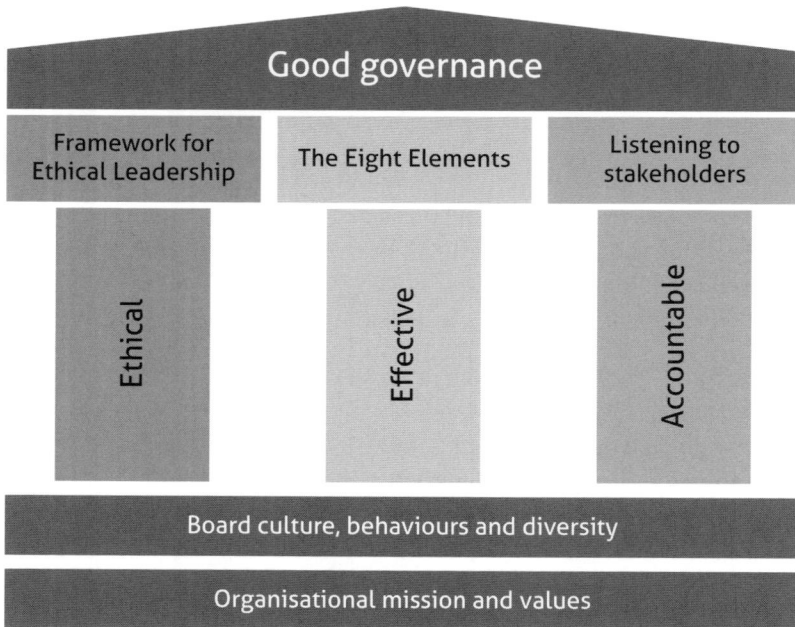

Figure 20.1. The elements of good governance

Source: National Governance Association (2023).

Hope, ambition and collaboration, which come across so strongly in *About Our Schools*, ring true with many who govern. Governance itself is a collaborative activity, both in terms of being around the board table with your fellows but also with school and trust leaders. That spirit of joint enterprise needs to be felt and embraced by leaders too.

The tremendous hope and ambition of all the parties involved will not be delivered without the capacity to do so. Resources are limited and there are distractions; in the swirl of the school day, many other things need doing. Will professional development be given the space it needs to make a difference? Governing boards need to ensure that it is, and for all.

Governance development

The NGA's data tells us that many volunteers take their own development seriously, but as the governance disasters reported in the press have diminished, the government's interest in supporting schools, trusts and individuals to improve governance has diminished correspondingly. This trend has continued to the point where the Department for Education now contributes nothing towards volunteer recruitment or governance development. It is left to the market, in which the NGA, a not-for-profit enterprise, plays a successful part. We have a huge array of relevant bespoke resources. However, the schools and trusts most in need of development can avoid doing anything. Just recently, I had a conversation about chairs who still do not realise it is their role to support the head teacher; however, this is the exception, I am pleased to say.

In 2023, the government abandoned the recently reformed National Leaders of Governance (NLG) programme solely on the basis that it could no longer afford the very limited funds. Conflict of interest declaration: the NGA successfully bid to run that NLG programme. Its removal leaves the regulator and others in the system with no quality-assured assessment of the state of school and trust governance and what exactly needs doing to improve it. The system must respect this knowledge, expertise and experience; that may seem blindingly obvious, but it is hard to achieve. If the sector culture is not supportive of good governance, and its leadership ambivalent on the issue, no amount of process design or quality frameworks will fix it.

Governance of trusts

As new volunteers join boards and new executive leaders and head teachers are appointed, establishing good governance continues. Multi-academy trusts (MATs) are no longer new; we understand what good looks like when governing a MAT.

In *MATs Moving Forward* (Collins et al., 2021), the NGA identified five debates:

1. Is too much power in the hands of too few people?

2. Is governance at the local tier being used effectively and meaningfully?

3. When is big just too big?

4. How best to support and develop the new forms of school leadership?

5. How best to promote the value and develop the supply of skilled governance professionals?

In *Shaping the Future of Multi-Academy Trusts* (Henson and Knights, 2024), we add at least two more:

6. Are MATs providing financial sustainability, especially pertinent in these times of tight resources?

7. Collaboration of schools within MATs is not enough: how do we ensure there is regular and effective collaboration by schools within MATs with other local schools in every place?

I am confident that local governance at academy level within MATs is here to stay; it is an important part of accountability and ensuring that trustees are aware of the views of pupils, parents, staff and communities. Confident but not complacent. We do need to keep making the case for governors, otherwise folk less wise than Tim will appear at intervals and think that the rest of us are stuck in our ways, and, in the guise of innovation and progress, overlook that we are in a people business and need the trust and support of our families and communities to provide the best possible education for their children. This will not change.

References

Brighouse, T. and Waters, M. (2022a). A New Age of Schooling. *Governing Matters* (June), 20–22.

Brighouse, T. and Waters, M. (2022b). *About Our Schools: Improving on Previous Best*. Carmarthen: Crown House Publishing.

Collins, C., Henson, S. and Knights, E. (2021). *MATs Moving Forward: The Power of Governance*. Birmingham: National Governance Association. Available at: https://www.nga.org.uk/knowledge-centre/mats-moving-forward.

Henson, S. and Knights, E. (2024). *Shaping the Future of Multi-Academy Trusts: The Power of Governance*. Birmingham: National Governance Association.

National Governance Association (2023). *Governing a Multi Academy Trust: A Handbook for Trustees*. Available at: https://www.nga.org.uk/governing-mat-handbook.

Chapter 21

Vertical slice teams: reversing the over-centralisation of decision-making

James Mannion

James Mannion is the director of Rethinking Education, a teacher training organisation specialising in self-regulated learning, implementation and improvement science. James is also the host of the Rethinking Education podcast, where he first met Tim, and the host of the Rethinking Education conference network, which hosted Tim as a keynote speaker in 2022.

What proportion of school improvement initiatives lead to improved pupil outcomes sustained over several years? Teacher Tapp, the teacher polling organisation, recently asked this question to around ten thousand teachers. Almost half of respondents estimated the success rate to be less than 20%, and more than seven in ten put the figure at less than 30%. This finding of a 70–80% failure rate is backed up by experts in change management and by the available evidence (Kotter, 2008; Bryk et al., 2015; Hill et al., 2017).[1]

In many schools, there are often several change initiatives happening at any one time. Indeed, it sometimes feels like the only constant is constant change, so this is not an insignificant problem. In fact, it is kind of huge. The same problem also exists at the national level. How many government

---

1   See also https://educationendowmentfoundation.org.uk/projects-and-evaluation/projects.

education policies lead to sustained, improved outcomes for children and young people? Space is limited, so let's consider this a rhetorical question.

Why is the success rate so low? I think there are two main reasons. First, school leaders (and government ministers) are not trained in how to implement change effectively. This is something of an oversight, because if you are a school leader or a government minister, implementing change is basically your job. The second reason is that in schools, as in government, we almost always implement change in a top-down way.

There are many reasons why top-down change is often ineffective, but I think the main reason is groupthink, the phenomenon whereby groups of like-minded individuals – even if those individuals are highly capable, intelligent and well-qualified – make terrible decisions because of dysfunctional group dynamics. According to Irving Janis, the psychologist who coined the term in the 1970s, members of 'prestige' decision-making teams often come to value the group, and their role within it, higher than anything else. This leads them to strive for conformity and unanimity on issues that the group faces, and to not think carefully enough about the implications of the decisions they make together (Janis, 1972).

When you are making decisions that affect many people's lives, it is a good idea to have highly capable, intelligent, well-qualified people in the room. What you *don't* want is to have *only* highly capable, intelligent, well-qualified people in the room. You also need people who are looking at the problem through fresh eyes. And you especially need people who aren't afraid to ask so-called 'stupid questions', because when someone says, 'Can I ask a stupid question?' what they often really mean is: 'Am I missing something, or is this a terrible idea?'

In recent years, I have had the great pleasure of interviewing Tim twice. The first was a long episode (three-and-a-half hours!) of the Rethinking Education podcast, along with Mick Waters, in which we took a deep dive into their magnum opus, *About Our Schools* (Brighouse and Waters, 2022; Rethinking Education, 2022). The second was 'In conversation with Sir Tim Brighouse', a video recording for the 2022 Rethinking Education conference (Mannion, 2022b).

On both occasions, Tim expressed profound concern about the marked shift towards greater centralisation of decision-making that has taken place in recent decades – a concern that I and many others share. Tim recognised that the only way to counter this is to bring more voices into the decision-making process. For example, in *About Our Schools*, Mick and Tim set out six 'foundation stones' for a better schooling system. The first of these is to establish a Schooling Framework Commission comprising representatives from a wide range of stakeholder groups.

Over the last five years or so, I have been immersed in (and increasingly obsessed with) implementation science and improvement science – two fields from healthcare that hold great potential for also improving educational outcomes . I have d scussed these ideas at length with Mick and Tim – they came to my session on 'implementing school improvement' at the Northern Rocks conference in 2022. Tim was even kind enough to suggest a name for the programme I have developed – 'Making Change Stick' – advice I have happily taken.

The Making Change Stick programme draws together tried-and-tested ideas from a range of sources to help schools improve the way they implement change (Mannion, 2024). But the big idea that drives the whole approach is this: *assemble a vertical slice team to design and implement the process of school improvement.*

In schools, a vertical slice team might comprise a senior leader, a middle leader, an early career teacher, a more experienced teacher, the special educational needs and disabilities coordinator, a learning support assistant, a parent/carer, a pupil or two, a member of support staff – all the people who have a useful perspective on the problem you are trying to solve. This is not just a consultation exercise; the slice team essentially becomes the executive, tasked with overseeing a particular area of school improvement.

Implementing change in this way is incredibly effective for two reasons. First, because you examine the problem from multiple perspectives, you get much better decision-making and much better policy. Second, people throughout the school community know that they are represented on the slice team – that there is someone like them who will represent their views and interests and with whom they can interact throughout the implementation period. And so you get buy-in like never before.

Recently, the Welsh Nationa. Academy for Educational Leadership ran a national pilot of the Making Change Stick programme. The feedback was astonishing (Rethinking Education, 2023), and the approach is taking root in schools in Wales and throughout the world. It is still early days, but emerging evidence suggests that this approach holds great potential to improve the educational and life outcomes of children and young people. I recently argued in a TEDx Talk that we should use the same approach to transform decision-making at the national level (Mannion, 2022a). What if we had vertical slice politics? I believe we owe it to Tim to find out.

References

Brighouse, T. and Waters, M. (2022). *About Our Schools: Improving on Previous Best.* Carmarthen: Crown House Publishing.

Bryk, A. S., Gomez, L. M., Grunow, A. and LeMahieu, P. G. (2015). *Learning to Improve: How America's Schools Can Get Better at Getting Better.* Cambridge, MA: Harvard Education Press.

Hill, A., Mellon, L., Laker, B. and Goddard, J. (2017). Research: How the Best School Leaders Create Enduring Change. *Harvard Business Review* (14 September). Available at: https://hbr.org/2017/09/research-how-the-best-school-leaders-create-enduring-change.

Janis, I. (1972). *Groupthink: Psychological Studies of Policy Decisions and Fiascos.* Boston, MA: Houghton Mifflin.

Kotter, J. (2008). *A Sense of Urgency.* Boston, MA: Harvard Business Press.

Mannion, J. (2022a). How to Change the World. *TEDx Brighton* [video] (13 December). Available at: https://www.youtube.com/watch?v=lvm9TYosmXo.

Mannion, J. (2022b). In Conversation with Sir Tim Brighouse: Time to Reset the English Schooling System – We Need to Trust Teachers More. Rethinking Education Conference [video]. Available at: https://www.rethinking-ed.org/speaker/sir-tim-brighouse.

Mannion, J. (2024). *Making Change Stick: A Practical Guide to Implementing School Improvement.* Woodbridge: John Catt Educational.

Rethinking Education (2022). Tim Brighouse and Mick Waters on 45 Years of Schools Reform, and Moving into an Age of Hope [podcast]. Available at: https://soundcloud.com/rethinking-ed-podcast/re37-tim-brighouse-mick-waters.

Rethinking Education (2023). The Impact of 'Making Change Stick': Video Testimonials [video] (11 August). Available at: https://www.youtube.com/watch?v=CvtN5seQIbl.

Chapter 22

School choice: tackling the pecking order

Fiona Millar

Fiona Millar is a writer and journalist specialising in education policy. She is also a school governor and campaigner for fairer school admissions. She first met Tim in 2003 and frequently spoke alongside him and interviewed him. They were also fellow members of the New Visions Group

---

I first met Tim Brighouse in the early noughties shortly after I had stopped working in Downing Street for the then Prime Minister Tony Blair. I was invited to speak at a conference where I had the daunting task of following Tim, who spoke without notes and held the audience rapt for half an hour with a passionate call to action on behalf of children and educators.

Tim was always positive and optimistic about people, seeing the good and potential in everyone. This was in stark contrast to the political rhetoric at the time, which seemed to have a vested interest in talking down a system that its leaders wanted to reform. It goes without saying that he was a hard act to follow.

In the intervening years we met frequently and usually agreed on everything apart from one issue – whether to campaign on school admissions. 'It will be a time and energy trap,' he would tell me. This was puzzling. Surely, campaigning for an end to selection and fairer school admissions was integral to the sort of inclusive education in which Tim so fervently believed? When I came to interview him, at the end of 2021, about the masterful book he wrote with Mick Waters (Brighouse and Waters, 2022), I was fascinated by one anecdote from his days as London schools commissioner.

Asked by Tony Blair if there was anything he wanted to add to the London Challenge prospectus, Tim's suggestion that they should do something about the chaotic state of secondary school admissions in the capital was 'greeted with an audible silence', after which he admits he backed off the subject.

It explained a lot and inevitably prompted me to ask if he had any regrets. 'I have no idea how often I spoke truth to power,' he told me. 'I didn't fight hard enough over admissions, and I am conscious now that I should have done more. I have never felt that I am pleased with what I have achieved because we didn't address the issue of admissions and exclusions, and you see the results of that now in the children who are effectively forgotten by the system.'

An unpalatable legacy of the 'market' reforms of the late 1980s is that they *have* left too many children forgotten by the system and created too many conflicting incentives for parents, schools and ministers.

Parents are urged to exercise choice and do the best for their own children. Schools are urged to be inclusive while doing the best for their reputations. Politicians are torn between pandering to those who have the means to colonise certain schools while doing the best for everyone else by narrowing gaps in outcomes.

As one of Michael Gove's favourite head teachers, the leader of a hugely oversubscribed (faith) secondary school, once explained to me: 'I am being asked to work in a market, so I am going to use the tools of the market to survive.'

Meanwhile, diminished local authority powers and resources, plus weak national regulation, mean it is all too easy for schools to use those tools to manipulate their intakes either by picking off the children most likely to succeed and/or off-rolling the most challenging.

The former catch-up tsar, Sir Kevan Collins, another towering figure in the education community, recently observed that admissions should be 'much more tightly managed to ensure that each school is serving ... the children of the community around it and not have these weird disconnects' (Roberts, 2024).

So, this is a pressing piece of unfinished business. Parent choice is undoubtedly here to stay, but the way it operates in this competitive market only exacerbates what Tim once memorably described as the 'giddyingly steep pecking order of secondary schools' (Brighouse, 2002).

The Brighouse/Waters suggestion of an Open School for the children who are currently out of school completely would be an innovative way of meeting some of this need, but the more fundamental change that is needed is for the incentives to be turned on their head, so that each school's success is defined by how inclusive rather than exclusive it is. Schools should be obliged to represent their local communities by taking in their fair share of pupils with additional needs or from certain backgrounds.

The best Ofsted grades, or whatever system follows the current model, should be conditional on this. No school should be outstanding if it isn't taking in the local proportion of children eligible for free school meals, for example. Governors should be required to act on local demographic data. Accountability measures could even judge schools in groups to give all leaders a vested interest in doing the best for their neighbours as well as themselves.

The long-discredited concept of an 11+ test of 'ability' should be phased out. Local authorities and the schools adjudicator should be empowered to ensure that poorer children aren't segregated into certain schools, so we can move towards the genuinely comprehensive system that international evidence suggests is the best way to achieve excellence *and* equity.

The response to these ideas would be predictable – accusations of 'anti-choice' social engineering would inevitably follow. But parents can't exercise choice fairly, and all education is a form of social engineering. You only have to read the Sutton Trust's reports into access to the professions to see that. What is Eton if not a form of social engineering? This one school has produced more prime ministers than the Labour Party.

It is tragic that Tim, with his calm, principled powers of persuasion, rooted in knowledge and experience, is no longer with us for this ongoing campaign. But it is one vital piece of unfinished business that the rest of us must take forward.

References

Brighouse, T. (2002). Part 1: Comprehensive Schools Then, Now and in the Future. *The Guardian* (28 September). Available at: https://www.theguardian.com/education/2002/sep/28/secondaryschools.

Brighouse, T. and Waters, M. (2022). *About Our Schools: Improving on Previous Best*. Carmarthen: Crown House Publishing.

Roberts, J. (2024). Sir Kevan: Tighten Rules So Top State Schools Take Poor Pupils. *TES* (12 March). Available at: https://www.tes.com/magazine/news/general/sir-kevan-tighten-rules-so-top-state-schools-take-poor-pupils.

Chapter 23
A learner from birth
Liz Robinson

Liz Robinson is a school and system leader who has worked with underserved communities across London. Liz's work focuses on challenging leaders to 'think big' about the purpose of school and has worked to radically reshape practices, based on a human-centred belief in the capacity of every child. Tim was a mentor and friend.

Interrupting history

As with many aspects of our education system, it is tempting to start with the old adage of the lost traveller asking for directions: 'Well, I wouldn't start from here ...'

No more acutely is that felt than in the 0–5 sector. Neuroscience shows unequivocally that these are the years when children have the greatest capacity to learn. 'Early plasticity means it's easier and more effective to influence a baby's developing brain architecture than to rewire parts of its circuitry in the adult years.'[1]

It also shows us that this is the most impactful time to intervene. What happens to children pre-5 is highly correlated with long-term outcomes: high-quality settings increase the likelihood of achieving five or more good GCSE passes by just under 20% (Kindred[2] et al., 2022: 5).

However, we have a system within which the state does not take responsibility for universal educational entitlement until the (fairly arbitrary) age of 5. It is a chaotic, underfunded, expensive to access and, consequently, vastly inequitable system.

---

1   See https://developingchild.harvard.edu/resources/inbrief-science-of-ecd.

You might expect me, as a former primary head teacher, to focus on the rich topic of early years pedagogy. However, we are at risk of rearranging the deckchairs on the *Titanic* to focus on the nuances of child-initiated learning, 'in-the-moment' planning and the relative merits of early phonics. The stark reality is a lack of access to affordable early years provision for many children, particularly those from underserved communities; many children are not getting any nursery experience at all.

The purpose of early years provision

There are competing agendas about the core purpose of provision for under 5s – educational and economic. As an educator, of course, I primarily bring a lens of learning. However, the 0–5 space is also driven by an economic agenda, enabling parents/carers to go back to work. Provision for 0–5-year-olds is seen as 'childcare' in a way that is just not the case for schools.

How might we start the thinking to bring the prominence and profile of learning to the fore for our youngest (and developmentally most influenceable) learners?

The relationship between the state and parents/carers

Successive governments have been reluctant to intervene more in early childhood. As the Times Education Commission (2022: 15) notes in *Bringing Out the Best*, there is a 'squeamishness' and a fear of being seen to 'interfere' in family life. There is a mix of statutory provision for under 5s (health visitors and GPs), but none has the status or reach of the school system.

At the age of 5, however, there is an (almost) universally accepted social contract. The state mandates that all children must attend school (or face legal consequences), the why, what and how of which are firmly in the purview of the government.

In contrast, the Scandinavian systems are underpinned by all children having access to free or (actually) affordable early years education from the age of 1 – a significant element of their sustained success across many metrics (including women's equality). Finland's 'baby boxes', providing a range of resources to new families as well as acting as the baby's first crib, are symbolic of a relationship between the state, parents/carers and their children from the beginning.

The challenging financial and logistical implications of reconsidering the relationship of the state to very young children and their families may put us off. However, reconceptualising the early years – creating parity of esteem in our thinking – would be a profound shift in bringing our statutory provision in line with scientific and social developments. Where are Tim's 'gaps in the hedges' here to galvanise us to be bold and follow both the logic and evidence base?

A new vision for early years – a learner from birth

Let us paint a picture of a system where we focus on *equity* for every young person. Yes, equity of access to high-quality provision for children regardless of parental circumstance, but also equity with themselves over time. When they reach 5, each child has the right to free, high-quality, local educational provision up to the age of 18 – a right that is not currently afforded to them before that age. How might we get there?

Some practical recommendations

- Key Stage 1 starts in Year 1 (i.e. age 5–6). Why? How about making our statutory learning phases start from birth to mirror the idea of a learner from birth. We might rename them: learning phase 1 (0–2 years old), learning phase 2 (2–4 years old) and so on. This would have conceptual, symbolic and structural implications, and provide the structure for other reforms.

- Agree and give statutory status to a 0–5 'curriculum' within the system. A set of developmentally appropriate milestones, building on the current 'red book' used by NHS colleagues, would be a powerful tool. This would allow for more coherent ways of assessing milestones across the range of aspects of child development, supporting early identification of those needing additional or specific support.

- Alongside this, invest in curating and targeting resources to parents/carers to support them in their role as primary educators. There is a role for technology to play here in tracking progress, with artificial intelligence-generated content to support parents/carers with resources and ideas that are developmentally appropriate.

- Assigning a unique pupil number from birth. Not a glamorous policy change, but a very significant one to line up the idea of a learner from birth and also to allow for data-tracking, early identification of concerns (missed milestones etc.) and support for appropriate intervention at an early stage.

- Increasing the pupil premium to match primary school rates, incentivising settings to take in underserved children, and giving local authorities greater resource to plan for and support provision at a local level.

Early childhood is a phase of life unparalleled in its significance. We must face the fact that our thinking and policies are out of date. It will take bold leadership and collective effort to shift the dial.

> Never doubt that a small group of thoughtful, committed citizens can change the world: indeed, it's the only thing that ever has. (Margaret Mead, quoted in Keys, 1982: 79)

References

Keys, D. (1982). *Earth at Omega: Passage to Planetization*. Boston, MA: Branden Press.

Kindred², ArkStart, Leyf Nurseries and British Association for Early Childhood Education (2022). *Solutions for an Improved Early Years System: A Discussion Document* (November). Available at: https://kindredsquared.org.uk/wp-content/uploads/2022/11/Solutions-for-an-Improved-Early-Years-System.pdf.

Times Education Commission (2022). *Bringing Out the Best: How to Transform Education and Unleash the Potential of Every Child*. London: The Times and The Sunday Times. Available at: https://nuk-tnl-editorial-prod-staticassets.s3.amazonaws.com/2022/education-commission/Times%20Education%20Commission%20final%20report.pdf.

Chapter 24
Breaking divides
Anthony Seldon

Anthony Seldon was head of Brighton College and then Wellington College and first came across Tim in both institutions. They shared a fascination with education in its broadest sense, and what gives meaning and purpose to life. They also shared an interest in politics. Anthony has written the inside books on every prime minister from Margaret Thatcher to Liz Truss.

'Typical public school prat. waste of space' was a nice version of what Tim Brighouse might have said about me when we first came across each other in the late 1990s. He had much to object to about me – public school educated, and then working in public schools and sounding off about them.

I remember our early conversations were quite sparky. Worse, I was writing a book about John Major at the time. And his education secretary, John Patten, had just described Tim as a 'madman ... wandering around the streets, frightening the children' (Crequer, 1994).

It didn't make for a happy meeting of minds. We came from different worlds, different parts of the country, different political tribes. This was the brave new world when state education, bolstered by new reserves of cash and with 'bog standard comprehensives' being consigned to the bin, would carry all before it. Tim was about to be appointed schools commissioner for London, at the peak of his illustrious and hugely influential career. We were on opposite sides of the barricades.

Yet, slowly, we discovered that what we shared was more important than our differences.

We came to agree that there was no merit in the two sectors tearing strips off each other or remaining in splendid isolation. Fundamentally, we accepted that all schools did the same job, trying to give students life-changing experiences which challenged and stretched them and which provided stimulating employment for staff.

'Partnership not paternalism' seemed to be the way ahead, and was the title I chose for my Institute for Public Policy Research booklet published in 2002, co-authored with Antony Edkins, head of a state school in Brighton. I had not met a state school teacher who wouldn't have benefited from spending a day or week in an independent school, nor an independent school teacher who wouldn't be immeasurably better for spending an equivalent time in a state school. Remaining aloof from the independent sector, as some state school teachers preferred to do, is virtue signalling, and helped neither their students nor their professional development. This applied the other way round too. I argued at the time that independent school teachers had more to learn from state schools; I now think that the quality of learning is equal on both sides.

I am not sure if Tim agreed with all my writing then, and if he regretted that he didn't involve independent schools in the London Challenge. Many independent schools would have been happy to contribute where they could; I wished I had pushed him harder on it.

In general, though, our thinking was becoming closer.

We realised that we were even more in accord about teaching well-being and character. Yes, rigorous academic teaching and standards are important, but they are not *all important*. By allowing them to become so and validating the success of teachers and schools based on exam performance alone was, we thought, a terrible error, with young people suffering the consequences. We agreed that it was shocking that almost one third of young people, already the most vulnerable and disadvantaged, were failing GCSEs because of this narrow academic focus. We were both worried and surprised by the seemingly inexorable rise in mental health problems among our young people, and indeed our staff.

More needed to be done urgently to sort out this mess. Tim published *The Joy of Teaching* with David Woods in 2008. Joy? There wasn't a huge pile of that in the brand spanking new Department for Education. Ideology was taking the place of evidence and good sense. Despite what we tried to argue, little has changed after 14 years of Conservative government and 10 education secretaries. Apart from Nicky Morgan, none wanted to prioritise the teaching of resilience and character or the skills of well-being.

Tim and I knew that doing so wasn't the enemy of exam success but the necessary corollary of it. Untold harm has been done to young people by the obtuse refusal of successive education secretaries to understand the essential role of good character in a rounded education. Aristotle knew it. But what did he know?

It is a great sadness to me that I never had that long conversation with Tim in latter years, which we promised to do when I was a proud contributor to his final volume with Mick Waters, *About Our Schools* (Brighouse and Waters, 2022). I think we would have agreed that, for all the gains in the first quarter of the 21st century, the losses have been greater. Social mobility is in decline, insufficient teachers of the right quality are being recruited and retained, and schools are still too far from being the places of delight and opportunity for all to learn how to live.

So, what needs to change? The current focus on well-being in schools is often about providing extra training and support staff and professionals to help diagnose and support students in difficulty. But this is only part of the story. In all my work on well-being in education over the last 20 years, as I discussed with Tim, I drew inspiration from Professor Martin Seligman (2012), the pioneer of 'positive psychology'.

He argues that, in addition to supporting those already suffering mental health problems, we should give equal attention to developing the skills, strengths and resilience in young people to cope with adversity and allow them to lead more rewarding and happy lives. He uses the analogy of the waterfall: current approaches focus very much on those who have fallen over the edge. What we need to do is focus on the top of the waterfall, thereby reducing the numbers of those who tip over the edge.

This is where we should devote our resources. The skills imparted in this approach will also help young people once they leave school (more so than their exam results). They will be able to thrive better in the workplace, in society and in life at large.

Perhaps the change in government will bring these changes. I certainly hope, and am sure, that Tim will be watching down with the keenest of interest.

References

Brighouse, T. and Waters, M. (2022). *About Our Schools: Improving on Previous Best.* Carmarthen: Crown House Publishing.

Brighouse, T. and Woods, D. (2008). *The Joy of Teaching.* London: RoutledgeFalmer.

Crequer, N. (1994). Patten Admits 'Nuttergate' Libel: Personal Bill for Damages and Costs Estimated at £50,000. *The Independent* (23 June). Available at: https://www.independent.co.uk/news/uk/patten-admits-nuttergate-libel-personal-bill-for-damages-and-costs-estimated-at-pounds-50-000-1424689.html.

Edkins, A. and Seldon, A. (2002). *Partnership not Paternalism.* London: Institute for Public Policy Research.

Seligman, M. E. P. (2012). *Flourish: A Visionary New Understanding of Happiness and Well-Being.* New York: Simon & Schuster.

Curriculum, pedagogy and assessment

Chapter 25

Education reform for a 21st-century curriculum

Kenneth Baker

Kenneth Baker is a former MP and cabinet minister. As education secretary, he introduced the national curriculum, city technology colleges and grant-maintained schools. He is the chair of Baker Dearing Educational Trust which promotes university technical colleges. Over the course of the last 40 years, he had several healthy debates with Tim about vital educational matters.

I got to know Tim Brighouse when I was the education secretary of state in the late 1980s. We did not always agree on everything, but I respected his enormous knowledge of education and his absolute lifelong devotion to trying to improve our national system, particularly to help disadvantaged children. When a few years ago Tim was working with Michael Waters on their 2022 book *About Our Schools*, we had a long talk and agreed entirely that a major change was necessary. If he were still alive, I am sure he would have welcomed with enormous enthusiasm the report by the House of Lords Select Committee on 11–16 Education published in December 2023.

The report finds that the English Baccalaureate (EBacc) curriculum imposed upon schools from 2010 to 2023 is word-for-word the same as 1904:

1904	2023
English	2 x English
Maths	Maths
Foreign language	Foreign language

1904	2023
Science	2 x Science
Geography	History
Drawing	or Geography

The EBacc curriculum was introduced to improve the life opportunities of disadvantaged children – it has failed. There were 300,000 disadvantaged children in 2010, and the number remains the same today.

This is a summary of the report's findings:

● Technical and creative subjects have been squeezed out (see Figures 25.1 and 25.2).

● Design technology has fallen by 70%. Creative subjects have fallen by 50%.

● The end of a broad and balanced curriculum.

● The acceptance by schools of the EBacc has stalled at 40% since 2014 (see Figure 25.3).

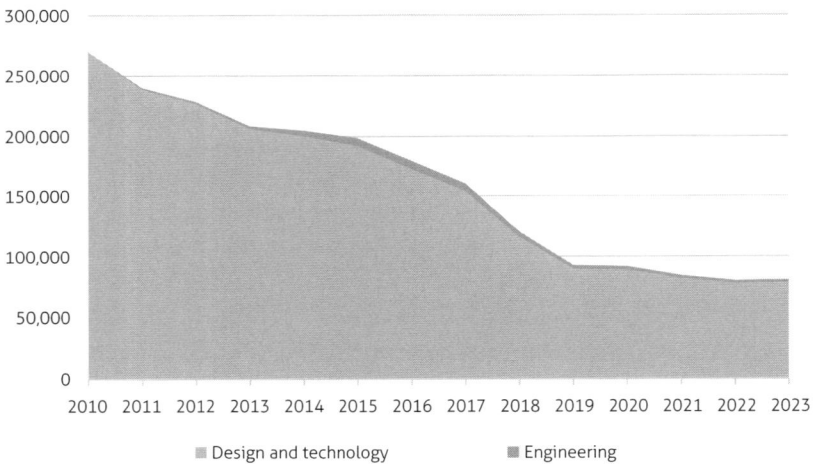

Design and technology   Engineering

Figure 25.1. Technical GCSE entries in England, 2010–2023

Source: House of Lords Education for 11–16 Year Olds Committee (2023: 51).

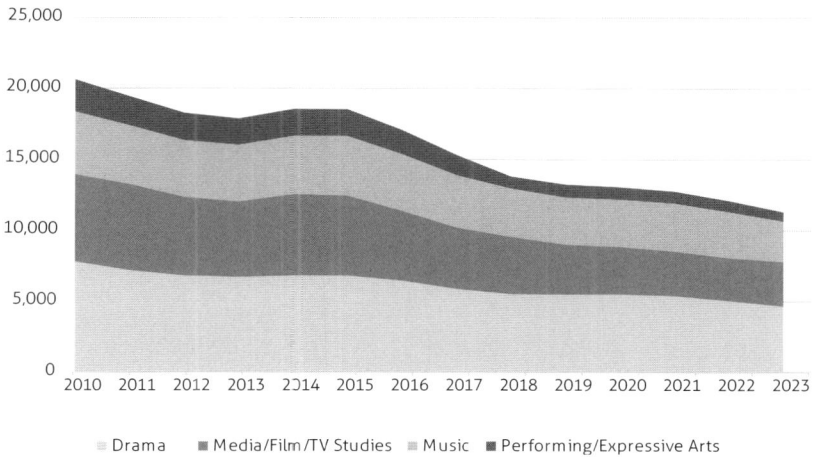

Figure 25.2: GCSE entries in creative subjects, 2010–2023

Source: House of Lords Education for 11–16 Year Olds Committee (2023: 46).

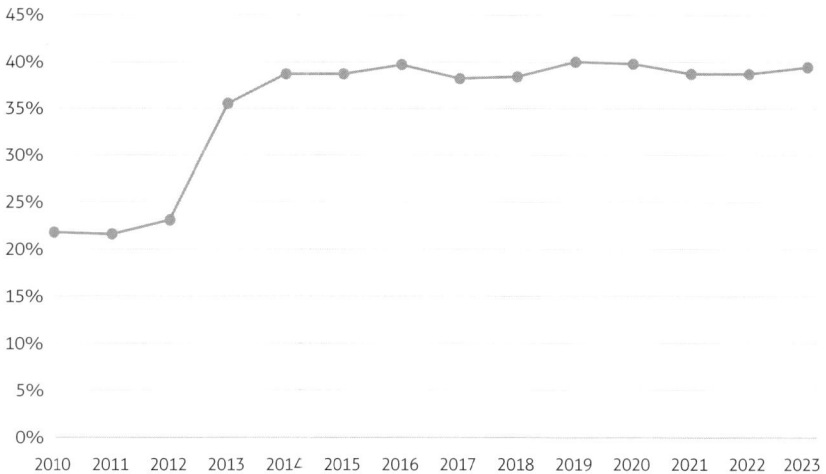

Figure 25.3. Percentage of pupils entering for the EBacc in state-funded schools following its introduction in 2010

Source: House of Lords Education for 11–16 Year Olds Committee (2023: 87).

The committee received much evidence about the 11–16 curriculum from students, student leavers, head teachers, teachers, parents, multi-academy trusts, university departments, senior educationalists, think-tanks, Department for Education, and representatives from industry and commerce both large and small.

Our conclusion is that there is an urgent need to reform the 11–16 curriculum to incorporate technical, digital, cultural and green areas of study. We recommend that the government should drop now the 90% target of schools offering the EBacc and remove all EBacc requirements on schools and Ofsted. This means Progress 8 will be replaced by the three key subjects of English, maths and science. This freedom will allow schools to offer a wider range of subjects with more teaching time:

- **Data skills.** We recommend a new GCSE on applied computing to cover graphics, business data processing and web design.

- **Digital literacy.** We recommend a new GCSE to be taught from 14 to cover the skills needed to complete everyday digital tasks and lead to a 21st-century career.

- **Climate change and sustainability subjects.** We recommend that all young people must have the skills and knowledge to live in a climate change world and to enable the take-up of opportunities that are emerging in the green industry. Many of these skills are cross-curricular, which must be recognised in teacher training.

- **Creative, cultural and artistic subjects.** We received evidence that the creative industries will create 900,000 new jobs in the next 10 years. One-fifth of all jobs in London are now in the entertainment industry. The Conservative government said it would produce a cultural education plan by the end of 2023. We recommend this plan which includes courses covering design, creativity, critical thinking, drama, dance and the performing arts.

- **Functional skills.** We recommend that a new curriculum is needed to teach functional skills in English and maths from Key Stage 4. Schools will be free to continue offering GCSEs in English and maths.

Assessment at 16

We also recommend that the GCSE assessment system should be fundamentally reformed by reducing its burden on students, teachers and parents through the following changes:

- Reduce the extent of knowledge required in GCSEs.

- Increase the number of GCSEs taken at 16 using non-exam assessment. This can be assisted with the development of a student profile starting at primary level and continuing to 18. Artificial intelligence can help teachers to maintain the profile.

- The Higher Project Qualification is impressive and more student uptake should be encouraged alongside GCSEs.

- Online assessment is already happening in some schools, and we were told that 70% of their teachers agree it is a more efficient means of student assessment. We recommend the government should take the lead in implementing it.

Fundamentally, the committee recommend that EBacc and Progress 8 should be abandoned immediately. All schools should offer English, maths and science GCSEs, and the school can then decide which extra subjects they want to teach. I believe this will lead to many practical, technical and cultural courses currently squeezed out of the curriculum – like economics, business studies, politics, photography, design technology, dance, drama, music and art – being reintroduced.

We also drew attention to a report from Latymer Upper School (in the private sector), which within three years will limit the number of sit-down GCSE exams to just two, English and maths. Other subjects will be provided but these will be subject to internal school assessment only. The change will increase teaching time by 40% because the spring and summer terms will no longer be devoted to revision and sitting exams. This will allow for the introduction of many wider subjects, such as psychology, anthropology, drama, history of popular music, classical culture, design and technology, photography and the cultures of South East Asia.

I feel certain that Tim Brighouse would have supported these recommendations.

References

Brighouse, T. and Waters, M. (2022). *About Our Schools: Improving on Previous Best*. Carmarthen: Crown House Publishing.

House of Lords Education for 11–16 Year Olds Committee (2023). *Requires Improvement: Urgent Change for 11–16 Education. Report of Session 2023–24.* HL Paper 17 (12 December). Available at: https://committees.parliament.uk/publications/42484/documents/211201/default.

Chapter 26

The system, the school, the class and the teacher: where real improvement happens

Adam Boxer

Adam Boxer is a science teacher, teacher trainer and education director of Carousel Learning. Although he never met Tim, Adam corresponded with him on a number of occasions, often on points they disagreed upon!

In 2015, an ambitious school improvement programme, coordinated by Huntington School in York, aimed to place a research lead (RL) in schools across the country. This RL would be specifically trained to articulate and disseminate findings from educational research in their school, aiming to improve GCSE outcomes.

As a policy, such a programme is extraordinarily attractive. Teachers need ready access to cutting-edge research, and using a colleague might help with buy-in and contextualisation. The schools involved were self-selecting, so likely to support the approach and foster an environment of research engagement.

Despite this, in 2019, the Education Endowment Foundation evaluated the programme and found that it 'did not have a positive impact on pupil attainment' (EEF, 2019). In this project, the stars seemed to be aligned – everything that should lead to success was present – but the result was failure.

In 2010, Michael Gove promised an 'academies revolution' which would 'drive up standards' (Harrison, 2010), but in 2015, John Hattie argued that this system-level change was a 'distraction', and, as yet, there is no clear objective evidence that academies are outperforming other types of school (Andrews et al., 2017). In allowing schools autonomy and the ability to self-direct and collaborate, the academies programme sounds attractive, but, as with the RL programme, we are yet to realise its promise.

Education is full of ideas. Unfortunately, a sector that is now used to reform and policy change isn't used to seeing those changes bear fruit. Grand ideas like spreading research knowledge or freeing schools from bureaucratic oversight sound plausible and exciting, but somewhere along the line there is a disconnect between 'idea' and 'improvement'. Even vaunted and celebrated innovations like assessment for learning have made nary a dent on educational outcomes (Coe et al., 2013; Wiliam, 2018).

In my work as a teacher and teacher trainer, I have seen the odd relationship between ideas and outcomes at a different level. Policy researchers work at the 'top' level of the system – which policy have we implemented at a large scale, and what difference has it made a number of years later? I work at the 'bottom' level of the system – what can I see being implemented in the classroom right now, and what difference does it make?

My level has advantages and disadvantages. One advantage is its immediacy. If I am in a classroom, and a teacher explains to students that diffusion is the movement of particles from a region of high concentration to a region of low concentration, I don't need to wait six months for research funding, another six months for experiment design, a further year to write a paper and another year to go through peer-review to know if what the teacher said was heard. I can ask a student some basic questions about diffusion and see what they answer. Often, I will simply ask students what their teacher just said – and, on a worrying number of occasions, the answer is 'I'm not sure.'

This approach also allows me to give straightforward corrective feedback. I don't need to refer to some grand idea about teaching or policy to explain to a teacher that the reason a student didn't hear the explanation is because they were finishing the previous activity whilst the teacher was talking. Next time, the teacher needs to ensure that all students have stopped working before beginning their explanation.

On the other hand, whilst research can tell us much about immediate understanding or participation, it cannot tell if learning has taken place in the moment. Without getting bogged down in defining the term, it is clear that there is a long-term component to learning (Kirschner et al., 2006), and if a student answers one of my questions correctly in the moment, I certainly cannot know if they will retain it later. If they can answer it, learning could happen. If they cannot, it definitely won't. Analytically, a student being able to answer basic questions about the content they are covering today is a necessary condition of long-term learning, but not a sufficient one.

To return to our theme, I suspect there is one conceptual reason and one practical reason why the top policy level fails to influence the bottom implementation level: why what is discussed *out there* seems to bear no relation to what is implemented *in here*.

Conceptually, it is important to note that any large-scale social infra-structure – like the education system – is not an easy thing to change. It consists of a vast array of different stakeholders, each with their own training and habits, not to mention occasionally competing agendas. In the busy day-to-day, inertia can take over and radical ideas remain unim-plemented. Those working within the education system – and perhaps the very system itself – are on a certain path, and changing those paths cannot be achieved by government diktat, think-tank policy paper or glossy pres-entation at a big-name conference. It requires years of painstaking effort and perseverance, and we shouldn't expect policy ideas to be magically and immediately implemented. Not only must the stars align, but they must stay aligned.

Practically, and here drawing on the bottom level, my most common observation across hundreds of lessons in dozens of schools is that students simply aren't listening. Not because they are being naughty, malicious or disruptive, but because they are children, and because atten-tion is a white whale that most teachers have not been trained to hunt. If students aren't listening, then it matters little how expert the teacher's subject knowledge, how well sequenced their curriculum, how strategic their assessment for learning or how evidence based their practice – the students will not learn.

Teacher, school and system improvement is a tremendously complicated problem (White, 2019). That is where I found common ground with Tim Brighouse. In *About Our Schools*, Tim and Mick Waters (2022) argued for the role of 'expert consultant teachers' to engage properly in research at classroom level and build teams with expertise about increasingly specific and specialised aspects of teaching. We share the acknowledgement that grand ideas have their place and help to set an agenda, but if history tells us anything, it is that we need to descend from such lofty realms and ensconce ourselves in a different reality – one that understands what is happening in real classrooms in real schools – and focus on a different kind of improvement. Regardless of his role and status, Tim Brighouse understood that.

References

Andrews, J., Perera, N., Eyles, A., Sahlgren, G. H., Machin, S., Sandi, M. and Silva, O. (2017). *The Impact of Academies on Educational Outcomes*. London: Education Policy Institute. Available at: https://epi.org.uk/wp-content/uploads/2017/07/EPI_-Impact_of_Academies_Consolidated_Report-.pdf.

Brighouse, T. and Waters, M. (2022). *About Our Schools: Improving on Previous Best*. Carmarthen: Crown House Publishing.

Coe, R., Aloisi, C., Higgins, S. and Major, L. E. (2013). *Improving Education: A Triumph of Hope Over Experience*. Cambridge: Centre for Evaluation and Monitoring. Available at: http://www.cem.org/attachments/publications/ImprovingEducation2013.pdf.

Education Endowment Foundation (EEF) (2019). The RISE Project: Evidence-Informed School Improvement. Available at: https://educationendowmentfoundation.org.uk/projects-and-evaluation/projects/the-rise-project-evidence-informed-school-improvement.

Harrison, A. (2010). Teacher Guidance Over Homework 'Dumbed Down'. *BBC News* (26 May). Available at: https://www.bbc.co.uk/news/10159448.

Hattie, J. (2015). *What Doesn't Work in Education: The Politics of Distraction*. London: Pearson. Available at: https://visible-learning.org/wp-content/uploads/2015/06/John-Hattie-Visible-Learning-creative-commons-book-free-PDF-download-What-doesn-t-work-in-education_the-politics-of-distraction-pearson-2015.pdf.

Kirschner, P. A., Sweller, J. and Clark, R. E. (2006). Why Minimal Guidance During Instruction Does Not Work: An Analysis of the Failure of Constructivist, Discovery, Problem-Based, Experiential, and Inquiry-Based Teaching. *Educational Psychologist*, 41(2), 75–86. https://doi.org/10.1207/s15326985ep4102_1

White, B. (2019). The Wicked Problem of School Improvement [blog] (25 July). Available at: https://benjamindwhite.wordpress.com/2019/07/25/the-wicked-problem-of-school-improvement.

Wiliam, D. (2018). AFL in Science – Dylan Wiliam Responds. *A Chemical Orthodoxy* [blog] (3 April). Available at: https://achemicalorthodoxy.co.uk/2018/04/03/afl-in-science-dylan-wiliam-responds.

Chapter 27
Where next?

Graham Donaldson

Graham Donaldson and Tim have shared platforms on many occasions. Tim's unassuming manner and gift for connecting with an audience were unfailingly impressive, and Graham's admiration for him has continued to grow. They shared a passion for education and for supporting unfashionable football teams. Tim will be a huge loss as an inspiration and a friend. His wise counsel will endure.

The first 15 years of the century have seen an intensifying debate about equity, the nature of the curriculum and the governance of education. That debate is now being given added impetus by disruptive forces that are posing fresh challenges for both education policy and professional practice.

Developments in digital technology, such as social media, generative artificial intelligence and large language models, are already having an impact on well-being and on how and where learning can take place. Young people increasingly have access to sources of instruction that can be independent of the school and the teacher. Disparities in access to these technologies are likely to accentuate existing, unacceptable educational inequality. The scope and pace of these developments are unlike anything we have seen before, posing significant and urgent questions about how policy and practice should respond.

Existential issues such as climate change, geopolitical conflict and the retreat of globalisation raise challenging questions about 21st-century employment and citizenship. Employability skills are changing dramatically; young people who compete with digital technologies will struggle to find work. And, perhaps for the first time since 1945, we are seeing hitherto unchallenged assumptions about democracy being contested. All of this places fresh responsibilities on schools to help young people not just to acquire necessary knowledge and skills but also to develop values and ethical understanding that will guide their approach to fundamental questions of personal well-being and citizenship. Yet, education policy consistently relegates such matters to the fringes of the curriculum.

And then there are the effects of the COVID-19 pandemic. As yet, we cannot be certain how far issues of learning loss, absence and behaviour will be long or short term in their impact. Indeed, the unwritten contract between schools and society may be weakening. What seems clear is that the vital interpersonal role of schools as safe communities of learning has never been more important.

Amidst this apparent turmoil, there are potential growth points. Around the turn of the century, several countries began to think differently about the curriculum. Northern Ireland and Scotland both went beyond a curriculum that focused on content to one that sought to better prepare young people for the future. Northern Ireland's Learning for Life and Work embodied wider skill development. Scotland's Curriculum for Excellence (CfE) went further in structuring the curriculum around the development of four capacities as the drivers of learning and teaching: successful learners, confident individuals, effective contributors and responsible citizens. These capacities were elaborated through an outline of their essential characteristics and by sets of experiences and outcomes at five levels. CfE did not specify content in detail, and gave schools and teachers considerable scope to shape the specifics of learning locally.

This move from content specification to a broader focus on young people's agency was taken forward in Wales from 2015. The Curriculum for Wales followed a fundamental review of the existing national curriculum (Donaldson, 2015) and moved to a framework designed to take forward four broad purposes. These purposes were in similar territory to Scotland's capacities but gave greater scope for schools to think creatively about how they might be realised in local contexts. The purposes were that young people should develop as: ambitious, capable learners, ready to learn throughout their lives; enterprising, creative contributors, ready to play a full part in life and work; ethical, informed citizens of Wales and the world; and healthy, confident individuals ready to lead fulfilling lives as valued members of society. They were elaborated in a broad framework encompassing six areas of learning and experience and three cross-curriculum responsibilities – literacy, numeracy and digital competence. Guidance on progression sought to direct attention towards the role of formative and ipsative assessment.

A striking feature of the Welsh development was its commitment to subsidiarity. The elaboration of the curriculum was undertaken by 'pioneer' schools drawn from across Wales, further entrenching a move away from a centrally driven delivery model of reform. The reform process included a fresh approach to professional learning and leadership and a significant move away from high-stakes accountability (Welsh Government, 2017).

Developments such as these may provide insights into innovative approaches in times of disruptive change. Their focus on the development of young people as rounded individuals goes beyond an over-emphasis on the acquisition of content to stress the importance of critical thinking and the ability to apply knowledge creatively. There is also a focus on health and well-being and citizenship as central components of the curriculum. Equally, there is a recognition that centrally driven change is too remote and slow to meet the need for agility and responsiveness, and that quality depends on sustained teachers' professional development (Chapman and Donaldson, 2024). This continuing commitment to professional growth is buttressed by mechanisms for collaboration and ongoing research about learning and well-being.

The final piece in the policy jigsaw relates to accountability. The period since the mid-1970s has seen increasing central direction of schooling, allied to a strengthened accountability culture. However, evidence suggests that an oppressive high-stakes environment can have serious negative, unintended consequences and fail to deliver the improvement that its proponents expected (Payne, 2008). In recognition of such evidence, Welsh reform seeks to create a more trust-based environment with significant changes to performance measurement and inspection.

Unprecedented levels of uncertainty about the future pose huge challenges for policy and practice. The emerging developments described here reflect much of the thinking of Tim Brighouse – be true to your values, build from the classroom, be ambitious and keep improving. The risk is that we focus on issues in isolation without an overall sense of purpose and a clear realisation strategy. Unfinished business certainly, but a philosophy whose time has come?

References

Chapman, C. and Donaldson, G. (2024). Where Next for Scottish Education: Learning is Scotland's Future (Part 2). Unpublished working paper, University of Glasgow.

Donaldson, G. (2015). *Successful Futures: Independent Review of Curriculum and Assessment Arrangements in Wales*. Cardiff: Welsh Government.

Payne, C. M. (2008). *So Much Reform, So Little Change: The Persistence of Failure in Urban Schools*. Boston, MA: Harvard Education Press.

Welsh Government (2017). *Education in Wales: Our National Mission Action Plan 2017–21*. Cardiff: Welsh Government.

Chapter 28
It's the little things

Ian Gilbert

Ian Gilbert is an educational author and speaker and the founder of Independent Thinking. Celebrating its 30th birthday in 2024, this organisation was in its infancy when Ian first saw Tim Brighouse speak at a head teacher conference in Oxford. It was an event that Ian still talks about to this day.

'If the look on the head's face first thing is miserable, stressed or even just blank, then learning is negatively affected across the school for the entire day.'

I remember hearing Tim Brighouse recounting this warning to a room full of head teachers many years ago. (He was top of the bill. I was much further down. Rightly so.)

Like much of what he said, it stayed with me.

Looking back, I think there are two main reasons why Tim's observation still resonates today but even louder.

From a neuroscientific perspective, a smile is a very powerful weapon. A growing baby will focus on close-up objects first, and if that is the smile of a loving adult, such an image stays with us. 'You can turn a class round with a smile,' as I have told educators for years. 'Take your least favourite group and pretend they're your favourite group.' Try it. The results will make you, well, you know …

In an educational landscape where certain school leaders appear to be 'out-stricting' each other, the simple act of smiling has become subversive – and, personally, I am all for that. Education is too important to be taken seriously anyway.

I interviewed two leading educational leaders during the COVID-19 pandemic lockdown, Vic Goddard of *Educating Essex* fame and Dave Whitaker whose book, *The Kindness Principle* (2021), shares leadership wisdom drawn from special school settings in some of the UK's most socio-economically challenged areas. They were recounting the abuse they had received on social media after a 2018 *Guardian* article (Halliday, 2018) highlighted their approach to supporting young people with 'unconditional positive regard'. 'How come,' queried Vic, '"Head teacher is kind to children" has become a headline?' He has a point. It takes us right back to Tim suggesting that head teachers can set the tone for the day across an entire school with a smile.

But then, as Churchill once said, 'Headmasters [*sic*] have powers at their disposal with which Prime Ministers have never yet been invested.'

Another reason Tim's words still echo is because what he described was the simplest of things, but one capable of such a profound impact. Educating children is a complex business, but it involves little things – actions that cost nothing, don't require a training course and have no real place in a tick list on a clipboard.

When you reflect on what our most challenging young people need ('kindness' – Dave Whitaker (2021)) and add to that what great teachers display ('botheredness' – Hywel Roberts (2023)), what is needed for our emotional health ('laughter' – Stephanie Davies (2013)), what we need from our head teachers ('bravery' – Dave Harris (2013)) and what the brain needs to develop in a healthy way ('love' – Dr Andrew Curran (2008)), you begin to understand that perhaps we are overthinking things.

Yes, go through your cog-sci checklist and tick off your principles of instruction, but never lose sight of the basics: everyone in every class-room is a person looking for safety, connection, belonging and challenge.

My own work in and around thinking skills reinforces how our thinking can be bigger when we focus on the little things. For example, before a session on 'Thunks' with young people (Gilbert, 2007), I always start with a few minutes of creative thinking. (For the uninitiated, Thunks are philo-sophically minded questions without answers that make your brain hurt. If you have ever wondered if a broken-down car is parked or whether a pregnant woman is one person or two, you will know what I mean.) This is because the 'guess what's in the teacher's head' game dominates our knowledge-rich classrooms, so when someone comes at young people with a different rule ('There are no right answers to this question'), they need a bit of help in adjusting.

Not only do creative thinking questions like, 'What is the biggest colour?' or 'Is there more love or hate in the world?' shift their brains from memorising and retrieval mode to actually thinking, but it also frees them from the fear of getting it wrong. A tiny change but one that is truly liberating. Five minutes spent playing, cognitively speaking, is time well spent when it comes to seeing what their brains are capable of with some great Thunking.

When we keep at least one eye on the notion that teaching young people to think is as important as teaching them to know, we spot opportunities – little things – to stretch their brains.

- Not 'What is the answer?' but 'How many answers can you think of?'

- Not 'What is one plus one?' but 'What else could one plus one be?'

- Not 'What comes next? but 'What would you do?'

- Not 'Do you remember what happened as a result' but 'What do you think might happen if ...?'

- Not 'Why did X take place?' but 'Why didn't Y take place?'

- Not only 'What do you know?' but also 'What do you think?'

You are still teaching children the curriculum material they need to play the game of school, but you are doing it in a way that moves beyond just learning and remembering to one that also involves thinking – thinking deeply, creatively, originally and, heaven forfend, independently.

As such, you begin to articulate an answer to that most provocative of all classroom questions: what are they learning while you are teaching them?

Getting to the heart of what education is all about, making it simple, having fun with it and keeping it human. There are many legacies to look for in Tim Brighouse's work, but these are probably as good a starting point as any. And there is plenty to smile about there.

References

Curran, A. (2008). *The Little Book of Big Stuff About the Brain: The True Story of Your Amazing Brain*. Carmarthen: Crown House Publishing.

Davies, S. (2013). *Laughology: Improve Your Life with the Science of Laughter*. Carmarthen: Crown House Publishing.

Gilbert, I. (2007). *The Little Book of Thunks: 260 Questions to Make Your Brain Go Ouch!* Carmarthen: Crown House Publishing.

Halliday, J. (2018). 'We Batter Them with Kindness': Schools That Reject Super-Strict Values. *The Guardian* (27 February). Available at: https://www.theguardian.com/education/2018/feb/27/schools-discipline-unconditional-positive-regard.

Harris, D. (2013). *Brave Heads: How to Lead a School Without Selling Your Soul*. Carmarthen: Independent Thinking Press.

Roberts, H. (2023). *Botheredness: Stories, Stance and Pedagogy*. Carmarthen: Independent Thinking Press.

Whitaker, D. (2021). *The Kindness Principle: Making Relational Behaviour Management Work in Schools*. Carmarthen: Independent Thinking Press.

Chapter 29

Cultivating flourishing schools in the land of my fathers

Ty Golding

Ty Golding was only able to hear Tim speak at a conference once, yet he was extremely grateful for a brief and memorable conversation at that event. It was from there that Ty began to read more about Tim's work, and his ideas began to influence Ty's thinking, leadership and, most recently, his role in the development of Curriculum for Wales.

Wales's education landscape has been dramatically evolving for almost a decade. In early 2015, the Welsh government focused their spotlight on the murky pits and irregularities of the system, providing a well-lit path towards what has become the Curriculum for Wales.

The origins of this lie in *Successful Futures*, a review document by Professor Graham Donaldson (2015). It was, and remains, brimming with astute observations, powerful ambitions and clear recommendations. Just as Wales's wide-reaching reforms have been sculpted by input from both policy and practice, you need not look much further than *Successful Futures* for resounding echoes of Tim Brighouse's ideas and ideals. For me, he both simplified the complex and embraced the paradoxical, something that we often find a struggle, all the way from system level to our classrooms.

However, three simple ideas sit at the very heart of my reflections of Tim, what he strived towards and how his ideals will continue to match my own beliefs and practices. Arguably, these ideas continue to serve as the bedrock of the Welsh reforms: subsidiarity over centralisation, a successful future relies on successful teachers establishing successful classrooms, and the importance of leadership and leading.

There is a sinewy tendril that has woven its way across our reform. From the outset, Wales's national curriculum design and development was driven through co-construction, involving pioneering practitioners, policy leads and researchers, which was integral to wider reform efficacy. This tendril is *subsidiarity* – the concept that a centralised authority should only provide what the local level cannot. Curriculum for Wales has been designed to deliver upon the ambitious notion of *subsidiarity by design*, to try to combat a narrowing of learning experiences and avoid a 'shrinking pedagogic repertoire' (Brighouse and Waters, 2022: 180).

Curriculum for Wales requires us to understand that a curriculum involves much more than centrally defined content – what is learned. It has been deliberately developed to provide greater practitioner agency, allowing those closest to the contextual challenges to make key decisions about how and what they teach – a key Brighouse principle.

Curriculum for Wales works on two distinct levels: a national-level framework and school-level design and planning. The ability to navigate between these two is a significant step and provides a necessary gully to stop excessive political tinkering with practice in schools. Education reform that seeks success through a new age of optimism and trust 'is a significant shift given several decades of policies that worked to de-professionalise teachers by taking agency away from them and replacing it with prescriptive curricula and oppressive regimes of testing and inspection' (Priestley et al., 2012: 2).

We, in Wales, are learning the hard way something that Tim long advocated – that increasing the trust in, and expectations of, our teachers must be accompanied by high-quality professional learning and development. It is here that Tim was explicit: the development of successful schools and practices grow from collaboration through planning, teaching and observing others teach. These should be rights and not luxuries, and must extend to all staff, as 'learning and achievement is everyone's business' (Brighouse, 2006: 23).

Teachers are responsible for establishing the climate of learning in their classrooms and creating the conditions for learners and practitioners to flourish. For me, and more importantly for Tim, how learning happens depends on the culture in classrooms, the beliefs and habits that underpin teachers' everyday practice. This starts with valuing relationships and builds through a relentless focus on being a learner – be that child, adolescent or adult. Tim often articulated the need for a curriculum that reflected the value of learner experiences, alongside opportunities to collaborate, be creative and enterprising. These are among the aspirations rooted in the pedagogical principles throughout Curriculum for Wales and blossom in its ambition for all 16-year-olds to become:

- ambitious, capable learners, ready to learn throughout their lives
- enterprising, creative contributors, ready to play a full part in life and work
- ethical, informed citizens of Wales and the world
- healthy, confident individuals, ready to lead fulfilling lives as valued members of society.[1]

My school's whole approach to improvement is awash with lessons from Tim's work. The Flourish Curriculum at Holton Primary School is built on working collaboratively on curriculum development with other schools and organisations; increasing learner engagement; developing the learning characteristics and capacities of our children; embedding authentic learning opportunities; building an awareness of the world beyond our school; giving learners a meaningful voice; providing enrichment opportunities beyond the typical school day or week; and understanding that *how* we learn is often more important than *what* we learn. We are at an early stage, but we have already recognised that sustained success will depend on developing leaders across our community – children and adults.

During my time as a school leader, I have seen a much greater emphasis on school leadership practices. As I have read and listened to Tim's reflections, it is his take on leadership that has influenced me most – in particular, the need to focus on both people and processes, especially in this age of accountability where process and end-product get much more attention when it comes to measures and expected behaviours. In terms of Wales's reforms, and indeed any other educational paradigm shifts,

---

1   See https://hwb.gov.wales/curriculum-for-wales/designing-your-curriculum/
     developing-a-vision-for-curriculum-design.

school leaders would do well to note Tim's stance on seeing change as a norm and for us to become more comfortable with being uncomfortable. He rarely referred to schools and school leadership without mentioning the need to be creative, either as a classroom practitioner or school leader.

If I were to distil my leadership journey and how it has resonated with Tim's influences, I would settle on these three simple ideas:

1. Start with the 'why'. When others have clarity on the purpose behind plans and actions they are much more likely to contribute positively. And always be prepared to revisit and sometimes refine the why.

2. Regularly look in the mirror. Question how your practices and those of others can be improved. A key to leadership is a relentless quest to build on previous best.

3. Never lose sight of your philosophy. There are many deliberate and inadvertent drivers of behaviours in education, but, as a leader, you need to adhere to your beliefs, expectations and values.

Given how Tim influenced my practice, and how his ideas ripple across reform in Wales, you may think that I saw him speak numerous times, followed him avidly and read all his works. This isn't the case. I have read several of his books, listened to him speak once and, unfortunately, only had the pleasure of meeting him briefly, but it is surely a testament to him as a person and to his ideas that I can contribute to this celebration. There are few people from any field of work that transcend their immediate expertise and place. There are fewer still who possess the ability to encourage others to flourish, to be able to influence and inspire at both a political and practitioner level. Tim Brighouse could do all of these, and did them with integrity and gusto. *Bob amser yn ddiolchgar – diolch yn fawr iawn.* (Always grateful – thank you very much.)

References

Brighouse, T. (2006). *Essential Pieces: The Jigsaw of a Successful School.* Abingdon: RM.

Brighouse, T. and Waters, M. (2022). *About Our Schools: Improving on Previous Best.* Carmarthen: Crown House Publishing.

Donaldson, G. (2015). *Successful Futures: Independent Review of Curriculum and Assessment Arrangements in Wales.* Cardiff: Welsh Government.

Priestley, M., Biesta, G. and Robinson, S. (2012). Teachers as Agents of Change: An Exploration of the Concept of Teacher Agency. Teacher Agency and Curriculum Change Working Paper no. 1. Available at: https://core.ac.uk/download/pdf/9549545.pdf.

Chapter 30

Assessment that matters
Louise Hayward

Louise Hayward has worked in practice, policy and research in Scotland and internationally to transform assessment experiences for all learners. Tim was a role model for her: a powerful educationalist who lived by the values he espoused and understood the potential for assessment to promote social justice.

At the 2024 International Congress on School Effectiveness and Improvement, many delegates expressed sadness that Tim Brighouse was gone. There were common themes. He represented the best of what it is to be a professional in education: open, informed, inclusive, compassionate and committed. He understood that education should encourage and support children and adults to thrive; everything else should serve that aspiration and that moral purpose.

More than anything, Tim understood connectedness. In a world that often looks at issues in isolation – curriculum or pedagogy or assessment or professional learning or leadership – he recognised these as intertwined and interdependent. His contribution to *Deep Leadership for Social Justice* (Brighouse, 2019) explored what that would mean in practice. For every person, and therefore society, to thrive, we need a clear, shared and well-informed idea of what matters to an educated citizen in the 21st century. That should then become the focus for curriculum, pedagogy, assessment, leadership and learning. Accountability should address that focus rather than what can be easily measured.

Few would disagree that assessment, qualifications and accountability are powerful drivers for learning. Too often, though, the power they exert is negative. Tests and examinations assess what they can, but not everything is so readily assessed. As a result, data that is easy to gather and what tests can measure drives what is determined as important in the curriculum. Schools are not held accountable for what matters – their moral purpose and what that means for the experiences of learners – but for how assessment evidence, related to limited aspects of their work, compares with other schools, often presented as league tables.

What might our education systems look like if the power of assessment were liberating and enabling rather than restricting and disabling?

Living ideas of moral purpose

We should not start from assessment. Each society needs to begin with a clear understanding of what matters. We should identify knowledge, skills and capacities that reflect what matters and articulate learning progression within, across and beyond different areas of the curriculum. A connected understanding of curriculum and progression leaves behind the arid debates of knowledge vs. skills or academic vs. vocational learning and describes flexibly how these elements interact to support progression in learning. These descriptions of what is important for progression become the basis for all aspects of education.

Deepening our understanding of learning progression

The pedagogy of how we develop learning progressions is crucial to their success. To be authentic, descriptions of progression must emerge from classrooms. There is some research evidence about progression in learning in different curricular areas (Hayward et al., 2018), but many national curricula are based on 'best guess'. Learners deserve more than that. Some countries have begun this task. Teachers, policymakers, researchers and learners in Wales have started to develop classroom-informed ideas of progression based on evidence of how children actually progress rather than how we think they progress.[1] These broad descriptions of what matters in learning will guide teachers and learners in assessment for learning.

---

1   See https://hwb.gov.wales/curriculum-for-wales/understanding-curriculum-in-practice-camau-ir-dyfodol/assessment-and-progression-in-a-purpose-led-curriculum.

Assessment focused on learning progression

Although assessment serves many purposes (Newton (2007) identified 22 purposes), ultimately, it serves two functions: learning and judgement. If an assessment process tries to serve both, judgement will dominate. When test or examination results are used to judge schools, the result is that schools teach to the tests used for evaluation. Tim knew this and was a powerful advocate of sample surveys. Both England (Children, Schools and Families Select Committee, 2008) and Scotland (Dockrell, 1987) have a long tradition of national surveys. However, both have stopped using surveys, perhaps because their purpose was insufficiently clear.

Sample surveys provide evidence to policymakers and governments about education systems without the negative impact of our current account-ability systems. For example, the Survey of Scottish Achievement (SSA) provided information on literacy and numeracy in different areas of the curriculum on a rolling programme. Yet, schools commonly argued that they invested effort for little reward. Perhaps naming the scheme Save Scotland from Accountability would have made the point. Future account-ability systems should be sample based to avoid the negativity evident in our current systems. Wales is currently investigating this approach (Welsh Government, 2023).

Qualifications that are fit for the future

The final connection required for moral purpose to remain strongly aligned with classroom practice lies in the design of qualification systems. Stobart (2021) argues that the UK is almost exam obsessed, seeing that form of assessment as the quality standard. Future systems should also reflect achievements in learners' knowledge, skills and capacities when using and applying knowledge in and across individual subject areas in purposeful projects.

The purpose of education extends beyond the timetabled curriculum. The wider experiences learners have in sport or the arts, in leadership roles or in their involvement with their communities contribute powerfully to their learning. Through these experiences learners can demonstrate achievements of a different kind – for example, the ability to work independently or within a team, interpersonal skills, leadership and compassion. Future qualifications should provide a broader range of evidence of learning linked to who they are. Qualifications reflect what learners have achieved in schools and colleges, but they are also used for progression in life, to further or higher education, to employment or the voluntary sector. Scotland is currently considering such an approach to qualifications (IRG, 2023).

To realise Tim's vision of a fairer and more equitable society, we need assessment systems aligned with what really matters in education, and we need ways to gather evidence for accountability that support, not interfere, with moral purpose.

References

Brighouse, T. (2019). How We Have Arrived At Our Current System of Schooling. In S. Williamson (ed.), *Deep Leadership for Social Justice*. London: SSAT, pp. 18–33.

Children, Schools and Families Select Committee (2008). National Monitoring by Cohort Sampling: How It Works. Minutes of Evidence, Appendix 3. Available at: https://publications.parliament.uk/pa/cm200708/cmselect/cmchilsch/169/8011410.htm.

Dockrell, W. B. (1987). The Impact of Scottish National Surveys of Achievement on Policy and Practice. *Educational Evaluation and Policy Analysis*, 9(3), 274–282. https://doi.org/10.2307/1163614

Hayward, L., Jones, D. E., Waters, J., Makara, K., Morrison-Love, D., Spencer, E. et al. (2018). *CAMAU Project: Research Report (April 2018). Project Report*. Glasgow: University of Glasgow. Available at: https://papers.ssrn.com/sol3/papers.cfm?abstract_id=3806612.

Newton, P. E. (2007). Clarifying the Purposes of Educational Assessment. *Assessment in Education: Principles, Policy & Practice*, 14(2), 149–170.

Independent Review Group (IRG) (2023). *It's Our Future: Report of the Independent Review of Qualifications and Assessment*. Edinburgh: Scottish Government. Available at: https://www.gov.scot/publications/future-report-independent-review-qualifications-assessment.

Stobart, G. (2021). *Upper-Secondary Education Student Assessment in Scotland: A Comparative Perspective*. OECD Education Working Papers, No. 253. Paris: OECD Publishing. Available at: https://www.oecdilibrary.org/education/ upper-secondary-education-student-assessment-inscotland_d8785ddf-en.

Welsh Government (2023). *Curriculum for Wales Evaluation Plan 2023*. Available at: https://www.gov.wales/sites/default/files/publications/2023-07/ cfw-evaluation-plan-v2_0.pdf.

Chapter 31

Placing joy and wonder at the heart of learning

Debra Kidd

Debra Kidd is leader of learning and teaching at the British School of Brussels and an author and teacher trainer. As co-founder of Northern Rocks, she was grateful to benefit from the wise contributions of Tim Brighouse and proud to contribute to his and Mick Waters' book, *About Our Schools*.

Year 5 are presenting their responses to their enquiry into the Stone Age – 'How did human beings move from surviving to thriving?' Some have chosen to present posters, some have made models, others have created oral presentations. All demonstrate a deep understanding of the changes from nomadic lifestyles to settlements and from hunting and gathering to farming. They understand the changes to humans, both physically and socially, and enjoy choosing how to demonstrate this knowledge.

One child stands thoughtfully to one side. She has made a poster which accurately charts the changes we have asked them to consider, but, as she explains her understanding, she says: 'You know, at first I thought that I would rather have lived in the Neolithic period where it was easier to get food and you had a home, but now I'm thinking that those things brought problems. Maybe I would have preferred to live in the Palaeolithic period. It was harder to survive, but there's no evidence of war in that period. I would rather live in a world without war.'

We might have chosen to assess the children's learning with a series of questions testing their knowledge. She would have passed with flying colours. But, by giving them the opportunity to find their own medium of communication and to explain their thinking process, we have opened the door to much more than knowledge. There is deep contemplation, reflection, imagination, empathy and a regret that carries the seeds of possibility, which can be explored in a subsequent unit, 'Stand Up for Your Rights!' It seems oxymoronic to think of hopeful regret, but that is what education should seek to achieve – to get us to think deeply about the state of the world, both past and present, and seek better ways of living. For me, and for Tim, seeking better ways of living sits at the heart of good schooling.

To wonder is to question, to think deeply, to be curious about the world. It is also to seek solutions, test possibilities and consider alternatives, and these modes of thinking demand more than the simple acquisition of knowledge. They demand that we test that knowledge, view it from multiple perspectives and contexts, and use it. Wondering deeply brings joy to learning; joy can exist within conflicting emotions if the resulting thought/experience leads to hopeful action.

Tim called one of his books *The Joy of Teaching* (Brighouse and Woods, 2008), and the word 'joy' is also present in the teaching and learning principles of our school in which we aim to:

● Provoke joy and wonder in learning.

● Build and nurture strong relationships and know our learners well.

● Be experts in our field, engaging learners to discover more to make a difference.

● Create inspiring and supportive environments that promote creativity and enable ownership of learning.

● Develop knowledge and skills for life and learning.[1]

Joy is not about simply having fun or being wholly positive and happy. True joy is more complex, and there is no one agreed definition, although the Good Life project at Yale University is moving towards a broad consensus that joy is:

● Agential (what you do)

● Circumstantial (how the world is for you, both materially and culturally)

---

1   See https://www.britishschool.be/early-years-and-primary-at-bsb/key-stage-1-5-7/how-we-teach.

- **Affective (how you feel) (Yale Center for Faith and Culture, 2018)**

This hypothesis of joy tallies well with psychologist Martin Seligman's definitions of happiness. He states that true joy exists when life is both good and meaningful – namely, that you feel good, you have a good standard of living and you do good (Seligman, 2002). Teachers would understandably argue that there is little they can do about a child's standard of living, and recent rises in poverty rates in the UK show a society failing to provide that basic condition for children's well-being.

However, teachers can create the three elements of joy/happiness in their classrooms. They can attend to children's feelings, the circumstances in which they learn (safe, secure and loving classroom environments) and to their sense of purpose and agency in learning. The Yale researchers describe the modern world, in which the removal of the consideration of joy in our lives has had the consequence of 'a "flattening out," a "graying," of human life and communities – abundance of entertainment notwithstanding – and a sharp bloom of individual and communal dysfunction' (Yale Center for Faith and Culture, 2018). I suspect that this flattening out and graying occurs in many children's experiences of school where how they feel and what they do is considered as less important than what they can reproduce for tests.

Yet it is perfectly possible to create conditions, regardless of deprivation, where learning can be joyful. At Barrowford Primary School in Lancashire, children 'learn to love, love to learn', and the curriculum is founded on the principle that children should be 'rounded and grounded' – that whatever their personal circumstances, there is an opportunity to be part of an active and ethical community that seeks to do good in the world.[2] Built around the United Nations Sustainable Development Goals,[3] the curriculum is both ethical (doing good) and playful (feeling good), and staff are well trained in creating conditions for thriving in class (the standard of living in the class is good). This is despite the school having an above average number of children with emotional and developmental learning needs. In their 'be curious, not furious' approach to behaviour, the staff ensure that the children feel secure, safe and rooted in their school community, and this forms the foundation from which deep learning can emerge.

---

2   See http://barrowford.lancs.sch.uk.
3   See https://sdgs.un.org/goals.

The fact that two schools with vastly different intakes, and in different countries, can achieve both joy and wonder in learning demonstrates that it is not what we have but who we are that creates the conditions for joyful learning. Let's have more of it!

References

Brighouse, T. and Woods, D. (2008). *The Joy of Teaching*. London: RoutledgeFalmer.

Yale Center for Faith and Culture (2018). The Theology of Joy and the Good Life. Available at: https://faith.yale.edu/legacy-projects/theology-of-joy.

Seligman, M. E. P. (2002). *Authentic Happiness: Using the New Positive Psychology to Realize Your Potential for Lasting Fulfillment*. New York: Free Press.

Chapter 32

Teaching about the climate crisis in Wales: what we learnt from our students

Lucy Kirkham

Lucy Kirkham teaches geography at Bassaleg School, Newport, South Wales. Lucy met Tim when she hosted a discussion into young people's views on climate change. Lucy and her students went on to organise a climate education conference in June 2023 where Tim's speech was a highlight of the day.

They won't thank us for keeping quiet about it now and not helping them understand the implications for reshaping how people live. (Brighouse, 2023: 11)

At Bassaleg School, an 11–18 comprehensive in Newport, South Wales, our students prompted us to explore how we can embrace learning about climate change in a productive way. When the young people explained their frustration and loneliness around a lack of climate education and action, it hit home.

We found the dialogue between students and teachers very powerful and, with Tim's encouragement, we broadened that discussion through a climate education conference at Cardiff University in June 2023. Over one hundred Year 10 and Year 12 students and their teachers from 13 schools across South Wales attended this incredible day, full of energy and purpose, including Tim's unforgettable address.

Through the workshop sessions, delegates worked collaboratively to explore our key question. 'How can we recognise and build young people's skills to navigate the multidimensional climate emergency?'

The ideas from the summer conference were discussed and refined further at a follow-up conference, six months later. From this, the Bassaleg students created a climate education entitlement, summarised below:

In order to learn to navigate the climate emergency, students in Wales should be entitled to:

- **Involvement with actions to tackle the climate crisis.** Doing something builds hope, agency and tackles eco-grief. Schools should support students in identifying and carrying out meaningful actions both individually and collectively.

- **Engagement with confident and informed educators on the different dimensions of the climate crisis.** Teachers in schools should be carbon-literate in the widest sense: informed about how their students are and will be affected, both in terms of the mental stresses put on young people as well as the extent of the effects of climate change.

- **A continuum of developing climate education beginning in the early years.** A gradual introduction is important and this should strike a balance between not overloading young children with stressful details and not sugar-coating the magnitude and severity of the problem.

- **Opportunities to develop skills for independently responding to the evolving climate crisis.** Opportunities to further knowledge and skills about actions should be through a range of educational contexts, from regular lessons to drop-down days and conferences.

- **Up-to-date and reliable resources about the climate crisis.** Learning should involve the latest research and teach students to be critical thinkers in the process. All schools could collaborate with researchers and universities and take part in projects such as citizen science.

- **A range of contexts for learning about and responding to the climate crisis: individual, local, community, national, global.** Climate education should encompass all scales from individual to global. However, the community/neighbourhood is identified as a particularly useful context, where people can see changes in place and where they have the opportunity to contribute.

- **Education on how the climate crisis will influence their futures, including career opportunities.** Students want engagement with and visits to and from employers to see how the workplace is evolving in response to the climate crisis, and how careers in various industries are changing.

- **Opportunities to constructively express and explore ideas, opinions and feelings about the climate crisis.** At the conferences, students and teachers found it extremely valuable to share their thoughts on the climate emergency. Opportunities should include small-group conversations and wider debates across and within schools.

- **Learning about the climate crisis across, between and beyond all subjects.** The climate crisis is multidimensional; it will need everyone to find ways of navigating the challenges – from writers to engineers, health workers to artists, financiers to scientists.

- **First-hand learning and access to outdoor and non-school settings.** Giving students access to first-hand experiences and bringing learning outside of the classroom will result in better understanding and engagement.

These 10 statements represent a view directly from the classroom: the ideas of secondary students and their teachers from a diverse range of settings. The process of discussing the complex matter of teaching about the climate crisis was extremely positive for all involved. Students felt heard and realised their concerns were shared. Teachers were impressed and felt supported to bring in changes to their lessons right away.

The Bassaleg School conference team of students have been central to this whole process. Students, then in Year 10 and Year 12, along with a student who left the school in 2019, worked together to plan the June conference programme, choose and meet with speakers, organise workshops and chair the conference itself. Their responsibility increased with the follow-up December event where the students facilitated the workshops.

This involvement has kept students' ideas and concerns at the heart of what we are trying to achieve. The team have also been ambassadors, reaching out to audiences within and beyond Wales, disseminating the outcomes through presentations at other events, both in person and via webinars.

Now, the growing student team has all of Bassaleg School's staff in their sights. Next academic year they will run a whole-school training day on how the climate crisis affects them, why climate education is important and what schools can be doing to engage and act.

These informed young voices are powerful and cut through much of the cynicism, apathy and fatigue of stretched education staff. All teachers, and the wider school community, have a part to play in helping us to mitigate and adapt to the social, economic and ethical challenges posed by the climate crisis. Students working with teachers raises awareness and empowers everyone – whether in a classroom, workshop, studio or forest school – and is a vital step in helping us all to navigate this existential change.

References

Brighouse, T. (2023). Should Schools Teach About Climate Change? *Elephant Times* (March). Available at: https://www.tidegloballearning.net/files/2023-03/ET%203.2%20Tim%20Brighouse%20reflects.pdf.

Chapter 33

Agency: the person and purpose of the teacher in learning

Bridget Knight

Bridget Knight is a teaching head, CEO of Values-based Education and editor of *On the Subject of Values ... and the Value of Subjects* (2022). Tim Brighouse has been a standard bearer through her whole career. With him, we knew that teaching could be about educating the whole person.

What is agency in teaching?

Teacher agency is about feeling essential to teaching and learning – about feeling we have a say. It emanates from our sense of purpose and authority, and it resides in the relationships we build with our students.

A common definition of education is 'an enlightening experience' – something that makes us more fully human. Isn't that wonderful?

Yet, the reality is that the sincere quest to improve schools is putting a premium on conformity above all else. Consistency is one thing, but when taken too far it kills the spirit of learning. Teachers who feel crushed become deskilled and cannot enlighten learners.

No teacher expects – or probably wants – unfettered freedom, but nor do they want to be automatons. And nor should they.

Agency through purpose

I propose that education should be rooted in deeply considered, values-based principles. As a nation, we need to think: what kind of people do we want to grow? What kind of world do we want to build? This should be the bedrock of, and motivation for, our work.

Even in the absence of any such supra-structure, values-based schools work according to shared principles and ethics. They highly value their unique workforce, placing a premium on the teacher. They explicitly promote affirming and supportive relationships – teacher to teacher, teacher to child. This creates and realises the human potential for high function. Individual skill sets are noticed and promoted, as are innovation and dynamism. Action research and collaboration are encouraged, and teachers see their role as one of continuous enquiry.

The rewards are implicit. Success breeds success. This is real professional well-being, bringing purpose and energy.

Agency through relationships – the person of the teacher

Who was your favourite teacher? Oprah Winfrey attributes her success to Mary Duncan: 'I always ... felt I could take on the world. [She] did exactly what teachers are supposed to do, they create a spark for learning that lives with you from then.'[1] Ex-professional footballer Ian Wright equates his teacher, Mr Pigden, with transformation: 'He really opened up the world to me ... he was the first man who showed me any kind of love' (Wright, 2018).

We respond to something in our stand-out teachers. They are, at least partly, why we are who we are today. Moreover, research shows that a relationship with one trusted adult can mitigate the effects of childhood trauma and adverse childhood experiences (Couper and Mackie, 2016).

---

1   See https://www.oprah.com/oprahshow/the-teachers-who-changed-oprahs-life/all.

As a teacher, you could be that one person. Education needs to value and illuminate the person – both the adult and the child – creating a vital spark.

A culture and ethos of agency

This spark, though, is elusive and delicate, and requires the right conditions to flourish. Teachers and students thrive in a positive climate, one that is motivating and psychologically safe, inducing a sense of interconnectedness. Space is necessary for this spirit to come into play.

The best schools create safe structures that positively encourage teachers to make their classrooms their own and to bring to bear their own personalities, inclinations and interests on learning. This creates purpose, well-being and meaning – and leads to success.

Agency through subject disciplines

Teachers have always taught a syllabus and followed a curriculum. In present times, though, there is a strong imperative to play it safe through following published schemes.

When we are attuned to our students, we look at learning through the eyes of the child and, in turn, we learn how to be better teachers. Contributors to *On the Subject of Values .. and the Value of Subjects* (Knight et al., 2022) demonstrate how subject disciplines are deepened and illuminated when the teacher draws out the inherent quality of values. This leads learning into an even more productive, memorable and meaningful arena. However, it depends on the teacher feeling empowered and supported within the ethos of the school.

Agency through pedagogy

Teacher agency is about how we see ourselves as teachers, and how our contribution shapes our work. It is about how we bring critical thinking to everything we do.

Good teachers are passionate for their students; they are on a learning journey with their class. They notice what works and what doesn't. They are curious and relentless in their analyses and evaluations of their own performance and its outcomes for their children. They don't solely rely on formal feedback; they engage in rich conversations with colleagues, reflect on research and want to solve the challenges they unearth. They are intrigued by the mysteries of their profession. The energy is unmistakable, creating a contagious vitality.

Concluding thoughts

In developing a new path for education, we need to ensure a shift in focus to teacher agency. In *About Our Schools*, Tim Brighouse and Mick Waters (2022: 571) argue powerfully that, if politicians are serious about our education system, 'we cannot afford the human waste we have tolerated in the past'. Unlocking teacher talent will affect the future of our society. We ignore it at our peril. It is about honouring our children. It is about dignifying our profession. It is about making a better world.

So, what can you do to retain agency in your role?

- Consider which values you want to shape your life. Which ones will give you good foundations for your life's work? Which are the values that you will become known for by your students and colleagues?

- Keep at the forefront of your mind the South African concept of *ubuntu* – the idea of reciprocal relationships: I am because of you. If we can realise it, our children can be our teachers as much as we are theirs. Honour and enjoy the relationships – all of them.

- Keep a diary of things that work.

- Keep thinking and wondering. Try out new ways of working. Develop a mode of action-based research in your own classroom.

References

Brighouse, T. and Waters, M. (2022). *About Our Schools: Improving on Previous Best*. Carmarthen: Crown House Publishing.

Couper, S. and Mackie, P. (2016). *'Polishing the Diamonds': Addressing Adverse Childhood Experiences in Scotland*. Glasgow: Scottish Public Health Network. Available at: https://www.scotphn.net/wp-content/uploads/2016/06/2016_05_26-ACE-Report-Final-AF.pdf.

Knight, B. (ed.) with Chater, M., Hawkes, N. and Waters, M. (2022). *On the Subject of Values ... and the Value of Subjects: New Thinking to Guide Schools Through the Curriculum*. Woodbridge: John Catt Educational.

Wright, I. (2018). Earning My Smile. *The Players Tribune* (26 November). Available at: https://www.theplayerstribune.com/articles/ian-wright-earning-my-smile.

Chapter 34

Rethinking assessment in schools to value the whole range of young people's skills

Bill Lucas

Bill Lucas is professor of learning at the University of Winchester, co-founder of Rethinking Assessment and an acclaimed education reformer. At the start of his career, Tim seconded Bill to develop the Oxford Certificate of Achievement, and Bill taught at Peers School where Tim's son, Harry, was a student.

Early in my teaching career in the 1980s, I was seconded by Tim to help develop his idea of a new kind of assessment, the Oxford Certificate of Educational Achievement (OCEA). Ahead of its time, as were so many of Tim's ideas, OCEA was a forerunner of the portfolios and profiles that many countries are currently introducing today.

Students, as Tim always argued, are so much more than a clutch of grades or marks, and Rethinking Assessment's focus on the development of digital learner profiles for all students clearly caught his imagination. What was simply not possible for OCEA in the 1980s is technologically achievable today, enabling us to go beyond the limitations of GCSEs, A levels and BTECs.

A vision of a more expansive school system

Imagine a world in which schools teach a broad mix of subjects, gradually encouraging specialisation over time. Some subjects are studied at depth for several years, others in less detail for less time. Distinctions such as 'academic' or 'practical' have ceased to be used as schools seek to develop head, heart and hands in equal measure. Once the core concepts are mastered, much of school life is framed by engaging questions requiring disciplined investigation. Sometimes these explorations will have a global flavour, other times more locally focused. Always they will promote deeper, more real-world learning (Lucas et al., 2013).

Systematically infused within the curriculum are opportunities to develop important dispositions – thinking creatively, collaboration, being reflective and developing tenacity. Residential trips, high-quality work experience and meaningful community activities form a core part of the curriculum.

It is axiomatic that, in this imaginary school, students take great pride in what they do, with their beautiful work displayed extensively. Teachers have a wide repertoire of assessment methods to ensure that the focus is always on knowing where learners are on their journey and what they can do next to improve. Threaded through all of this are the twin objectives of helping students to develop into better people (developing character) and become more powerful learners (metacognition). And integrated throughout is an expectation that students will take increasing responsibility for their learning with support, encouragement and challenge from their teachers, peers and external mentors.

Far from being radical, such a vision has considerable global consensus (see Figure 34.1).

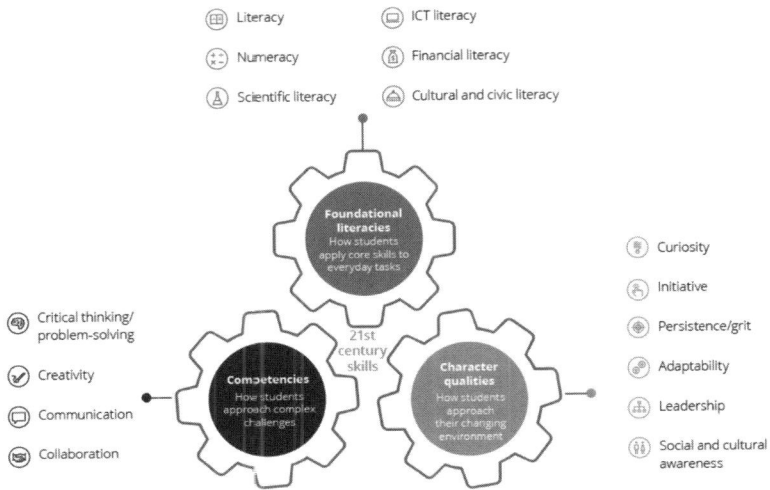

Figure 34.1. A vision of a contemporary curriculum

Source: Adapted from World Economic Forum (2015: 3).

Tim would have endorsed this kind of curriculum thinking. But, in the spirit of the critical thinking which forms part of the World Economic Forum's suggested competencies. I suggest that the branding of '21st century skills' isn't helpful (Lucas, 2019). It suggests a crusading evangelism which can undermine the deep love of knowledge that I want to see encouraged *alongside* competencies and character. It is also hubristically silly to suggest that we can predict the skills that will be needed in a few years' time, let alone 70 years from now.

Realigning curriculum intentions with assessment practices

For the kind of world I have just described to be a reality, we must change the way we assess young people in schools. There are exciting developments currently taking place in countries as disparate as Australia, the United States, Portugal and Scotland, and a number of clear trends are emerging internationally (see Figure 34.2).

1. Shallow, narrow, solo	**1. Nature of learning**	Deep, wide, collaborative
2. Dominated by head-work	**2. Range of strengths**	Head, heart and hand
3. Number or grade	**3. Style of credential**	Evidenced narrative
4. Single body	**4. Source of credential**	Broad consortium
5. Predominantly summative	**5. Focus of assessment**	Predominantly formative
6. High-stakes, standardised	**6. Integration**	Ongoing, authentic
7. National/State norms	**7. Personalisation**	Individual progression
8. Employers/HE/FE	**8. Ownership**	For learners and for others
9. Largely for accountability	**9. Strategic intent**	Mainly for improvement
10. Formulaic, mechanistic	**10. Approach**	Carefully evidencing capability

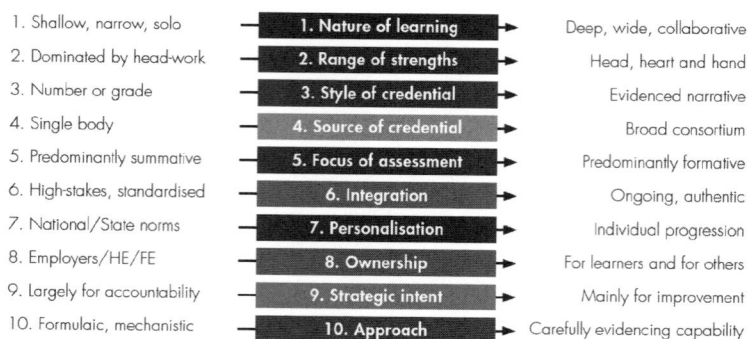

Figure 34.2. Global trends in assessment

Source: Lucas (2021: 36).

In England, our focus at Rethinking Assessment is on strategically changing the way that we mark the end of formal schooling, for it is this 'hinge point' that drives so much behaviour in education. Universities, colleges and employers use exams as a sifting mechanism. Parents use it as a yardstick by which to judge school performance. And teachers teach to it.

The power of digital learner profiles

There is a growing consensus that upper-secondary education in England should be more expansive (Lucas, 2023), and that the endpoint of a more rounded post-16 education should be a digital learner profile (see Figure 34.3). Learner profiles provide a space for capturing a broad range of a young person's strengths, qualifications and achievements rather than merely a set of grades. They enable students to create a full picture of themselves and then share this with different audiences.

A levels, BTECs and other formal qualifications could be part of any profile, as would existing alternatives such as the Extended Project Qualification (EPQ) and Higher Project Qualification (HPQ). Both EPQ and HPQ provide an opportunity for students to gain credit for their investigations. Awards that currently have Universities and Colleges Admissions Service (UCAS) tariff points (such as music grades) as well as those that don't (such as the Duke of Edinburgh's Award) could be included.

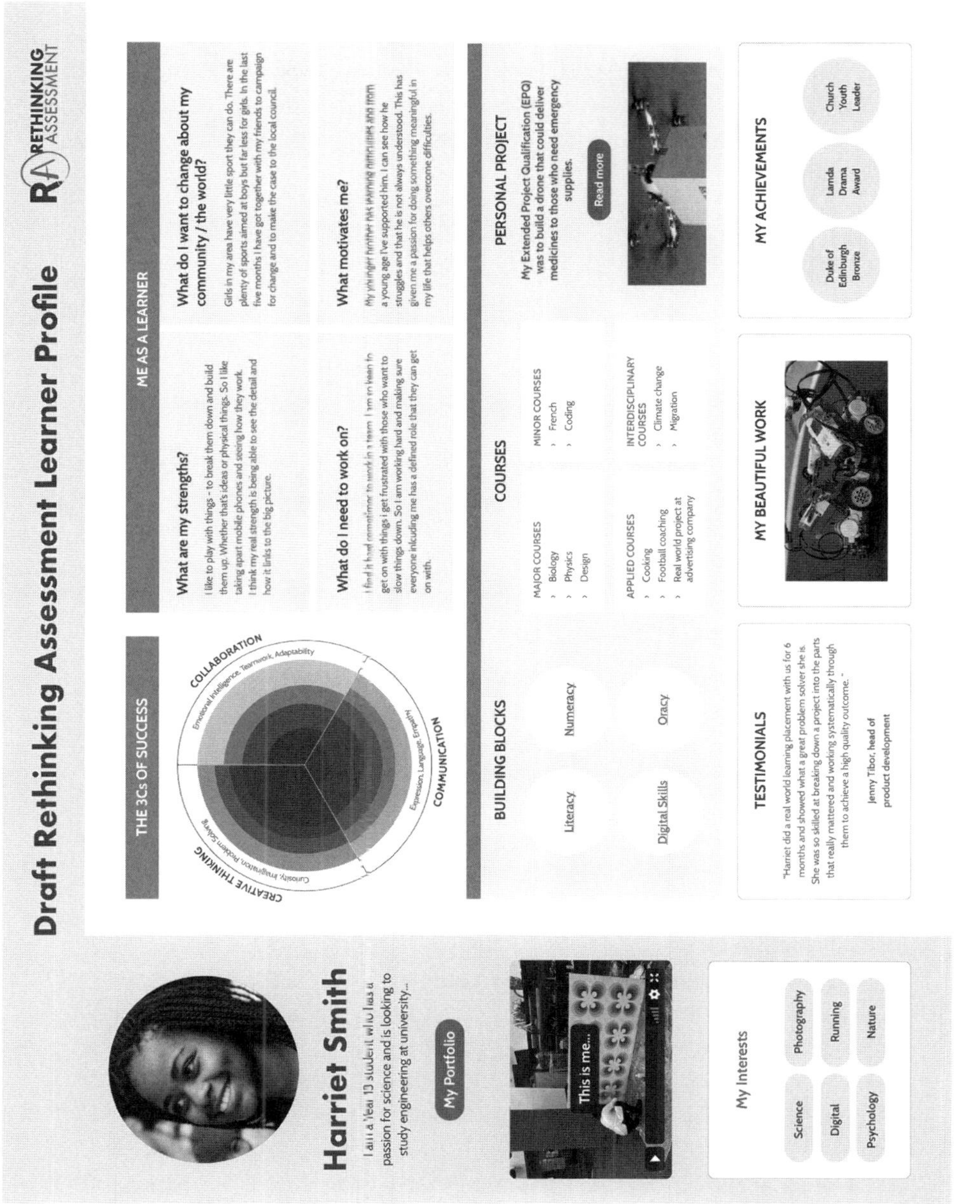

Figure 34.3. Rethinking Assessment's prototype learner profile

Source: Lucas (2023: 81).

There are other ways in which learners might demonstrate their achievements – for example, witness statements, annotated photographs, certificates, newspaper clippings, posters, designs, scripts, log books and journals. Along the way, these could be included in portfolios or e portfolios and act as a focus for discussions with teachers, parents and others.

Three key competencies, creative thinking, collaboration and communication, can be evidenced within the profile, and an area exploring metacognition, Myself as a Learner, is being piloted in schools now. Students are encouraged to celebrate their best work, to summarise their achievements to date and, just as they might in the world of YouTube or TikTok, communicate the essence of themselves in short films.

As I write, the RA Learner Profile is being piloted in more than four hundred schools in more than six countries across the world. OCEA, an idea in the head of a visionary educationalist, has paved the way for a revolution in assessment for a world in which students will learn throughout their lives and be valued for the full range of their strengths. Learning profiles, I have no doubt, will be the Learning LinkedIn of the future, a personal URL for life.

References

Lucas, B. (2019). *Why We Need to Stop Talking About Twenty-First Century Skills.* Melbourne: Centre for Strategic Education.

Lucas, B. (2021). *Rethinking Assessment in Education: The Case for Change.* Melbourne: Centre for Strategic Education.

Lucas, B. (2023). Rethinking Sixth Form Education. In N. Csogor and B. Watkin (eds), *Sixth Form Matters: A Collection of Essays and Case Studies.* London: Sixth Form Colleges Association, pp. 70–85.

Lucas, B., Claxton, G. and Spencer, E. (2013). *Expansive Education: Teaching Learners for the Real World.* Melbourne: Australian Council for Educational Research.

World Economic Forum (2015). *New Vision for Education: Unlocking the Potential of Technology.* Geneva: World Economic Forum. Available at: https://www3. weforum.org/docs/WEFUSA_NewVisionforEducation_Report2015.pdf.

Chapter 35
Unfinished business: the curriculum

Mary Myatt

Mary Myatt is an education adviser, writer and speaker. She trained as an RE teacher and is a former local authority adviser and inspector. She engages with pupils, teachers and leaders about learning, leadership and the curriculum. Her work has been informed by the wisdom, insights and humanity of Sir Tim Brighouse.

In the spirit of Tim's deeply human way of conducting business, I want to make the case that we echo Tim's humanity in the way we tackle the curriculum. Tim's way of working was to honour the preciousness of every child and of every educator, and I would like to foreground this with a few thoughts on the curriculum.

The first is that the curriculum is truly inclusive for every child. That we reject the diminished diet which is the fare for some of our pupils who are deemed unable to cope with more demanding material. If we listen to what pupils and students themselves say about the curriculum, it can be summarised as a desire for demanding work that makes them think. Alongside this, there needs to be deliberate and intentional development to create the conditions for high challenge accompanied by low threat. Interesting, low-threat work means that no one is made to feel stupid.

The second is that the materials we offer our pupils and students are connected to the great themes and achievements of human endeavour. That they draw on the particular to elucidate the general, that they cut across stereotypes, biases and misconceptions, and that they leave our pupils and students both fascinated by the deep stories and jewels of the material they encounter and equipped to do something with it.

The third is that, whenever possible, the curriculum needs to be brought to life with teachers having the chance to talk with colleagues about how to unpack the content that needs to be taught. This is a big ask and we cannot do it all in one go; it is a matter of pacing ourselves and thinking through what this looks like over time. Tim said that you know you are working in a good school when teachers and leaders are talking about teaching and learning. And it is this element of curriculum development that is underappreciated. Deliberate planning is required to make these conversations and this way of working happen, an obligation that I believe lies with leaders first because communities of curriculum practice do not come about by chance.

A neat example of this: one leader had identified that his colleagues did not have a wide knowledge and understanding of children's literature beyond a diet of Dahl and Walliams. He was concerned about this, but instead of nagging colleagues and getting stressed himself, he decided to use one of the weekly staff meetings to get the ball rolling. Instead of the usual agenda, colleagues came into the staffroom to find a pile of children's books on the table. He said, 'Instead of the usual staff meeting, pick up one of the books that takes your fancy, spend the next half an hour skimming or reading it and we'll come together to talk about what we think.' By the end of that half hour, everyone was buzzing and excited to talk about what they had read, and many of them wanted to take their book home. He had created the time, invested some resources, and created the conditions where teachers and leaders were talking about teaching and learning.

The fourth is that the content to be taught comes from authentic sources, as opposed to being mediated through third-rate providers, and is not only faithful to the domain but is also communicated in a way that does not patronise pupils. Young people deserve to be treated as though they are intelligent human beings, which is what they are.

The final principle is that the content offered to pupils and students should be beautiful. Not in the sense that the resources are covered in sparkly butterflies, but in the spirt of William Morris who said that we should not have anything in our homes unless we know them to be useful or believe them to be beautiful. In a curriculum context, this means that the resources we select should be useful for learning in that they help young people to engage deeply, and they should be beautiful in that they are well designed and draw on the domain. This might mean selecting an image of a mosque, such as the Süleymaniye Mosque in Istanbul, rather than a poorly sketched worksheet with none of the beauty or symbolism of a real mosque.

A second example, if I am teaching a Year 6 science unit about the theory of evolution, I have the choice to download a resource, which might or might not be beautiful, which might or might not be presented in a tone that speaks to my class as though they are intelligent human beings, or which might or might not be full of the luscious vocabulary that will open up this fascinating unit for my class. Or I could use the exquisite text by Sabina Radeva, *Charles Darwin's On the Origin of Species* (2019). I have confidence that this will be accurate because Sabina trained as a scientist and retrained as an artist; the images are beautiful, and that is what my class deserve; the tone is appropriate; and the text contains elegant vocabulary, which is a gateway to the domain.

My hope is that we collectively find the joy and humanity in the curriculum, and in turn are in a position to offer this feast to our young people.

References

Radeva, S. (2019). *Charles Darwin's On the Origin of Species*. London: Puffin.

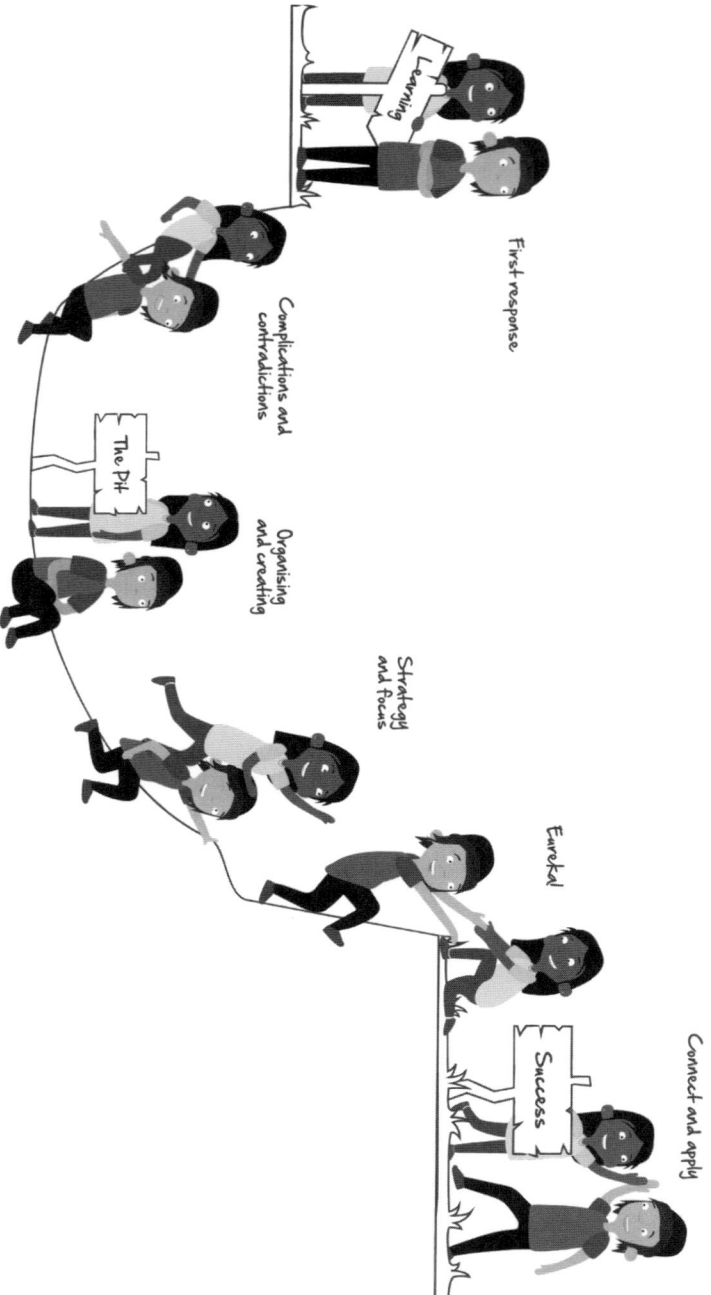

First response

Complications and contradictions

The Pit

Organising and creating

Strategy and focus

Eureka!

Success

Connect and apply

Learning

Figure 36.1. The Learning Pit by James Nottingham

Chapter 36

Travelling through the Learning Pit

James Nottingham

James Nottingham is a teacher, consultant and author of 12 books. He leads demonstration lessons and creates commissioned videos for schools. A highlight of his career has been the many pinch-me-now moments as a second keynote speaker to Sir Tim's headline presentations at education conferences across the UK.

Success is not straightforward. If it were, every dream, whatever it was, would become a reality.

The inconvenient truth is that becoming successful means growing our talents towards a goal, and that means leaving our comfort zone. This inevitably leads to a dip in performance.

Here is an example: pick up a pen and write your name. Now switch hands and write it again. See how much more effort and determination the second attempt took than the first. As for outcome, it is likely there is a performance dip etched on the paper in front of you right now!

The discomfort we experience – both in terms of process *and* outcome – is what leads many people to give up. 'Why do I need to be ambidextrous anyway?' goes the self-talk. 'My handwriting is already decent enough using my dominant hand. Who even writes these days? Even typing is on its way out.'

It is a similar story with every challenging goal. Perhaps you want to deepen your understanding of an event in history, a novel or a play. What you have read so far seems straightforward enough, but then you come across some contradictory ideas or arguments; you discover examples that don't fit your theory; you begin to realise that you don't know as much as you thought. It is confusing and frustrating. Your grumbling self-talk kicks in again: 'This is a silly endeavour; surely there's a better way? Maybe I can wing it and hope nobody notices.'

There are examples in every curriculum area. 'Learn French? Why? It's too hard! I'll just use a translator app.' 'Do PE? What's the point? The sporty kids already do lots of exercise and the rest of us feel inadequate or out of shape.' Art is for the arty kids; computing is for the nerds ...

Not that performance dips are the *only* reason students won't engage, but they are amongst the most significant. Notice how even the most disinterested of students will come alive in the areas in which they excel. Better to show off their talents than to struggle developing others.

Develop, though, we must if we are to grow and be more successful.

That is why I developed the Learning Pit (Nottingham, 2007): so that I can better prepare my students for the journey ahead. Not to frighten them but to forewarn (and, indeed, forearm) them. Let them know that building talents means stepping out of their comfort zone, which then means going through performance dips. Expecting to feel confusion and encounter complication along the way. Being prepared to go backwards before going forwards; to move from knowing something to realising that that something conflicts with another thing – and that both can exist at the same time. Finding better ways to collaborate, strategise, focus, rearrange and construct, so they are more able to climb out of the Learning Pit and reach a more thorough understanding or accomplished skill.

The Learning Pit (Figure 36.1) offers students a shared reference to think and talk about the progress they are making. 'I feel like I'm stuck in the pit – can you help?' 'It's OK to be frustrated – learning is like that. You're just in the pit right now.' 'I feel I'm climbing out of the pit at last. Things are starting to make sense ...' These are some of the phrases I hear from students familiar with the pit.

In some ways, the Learning Pit is a student-friendly version of theories such as Vygotsky's zone of proximal development (1978) or Piaget's theory of cognitive development (Huitt and Hummel, 2003) in that learning begins at the edge of challenge. Other theories and research that influenced me in the development of the model include Dewey (1916), Bruner (1957), Montessori (1967), Lipman (1987) and Feuerstein et al. (2006).

Interestingly, after speaking at a conference with Sir Tim some years ago, he, Mick Waters and I had a fascinating conversation around Tim's opening question: 'Do you think the Learning Pit applies as much to adults as to kids?' 'Yes,' says I – after all, whenever anyone – old or young – seeks to improve knowledge, habits or skills, they will step out of their comfort zone and find themselves in the pit. 'Might we seek out Learning Pit opportunities?', 'How does the Learning Pit apply to teacher development?' and 'Can the Learning Pit become addictive?' were subsequent questions that Tim asked.

Doing a quick search online, the number of references to the Learning Pit (400+ million) would suggest that it is an idea that fits multiple contexts. What I loved about Tim's questions, though, wasn't just his enjoyment of the model – which was deeply encouraging – but that he also wanted to understand how this might benefit everyone. Not just our students but ourselves and our colleagues.

That was the mark of the man: always encouraging and forever wondering. It was a deep honour, and one I will never forget, to have met Sir Tim Brighouse.

References

Bruner, J. S. (1957). On Perceptual Readiness. *Psychological Review*, 64(2), 123–152.

Dewey, J. (1916). *Democracy and Education: An Introduction to the Philosophy of Education*. Toronto: Collier-Macmillan.

Feuerstein, R., Feuerstein, R. S., Falik, L. and Rand, Y. (2006). *Creating and Enhancing Cognitive Modifiability: The Feuerstein Instrumental Enrichment Program*. Jerusalem: ICELP.

Huitt, W. and Hummel, J. (2003). Piaget's Theory of Cognitive Development. *Educational Psychology Interactive*, 3(2), 1–5.

Lipman, M. (1987). Critical Thinking: What Can It Be? *Analytic Teaching*, 8(1), 5–12.

Montessori, M. (1967). *The Absorbent Mind*, tr. C. A. Claremont. New York: Henry Holt.

Nottingham, J. A. (2007). Exploring the Learning Pit. *Teaching Thinking and Creativity*, 8:2(23), 64–68.

Vygotsky, L. S. (1978). *Mind in Society: The Development of Higher Psychological Processes*. Cambridge, MA: Harvard University Press.

Chapter 37

Curriculum realms of botheredness

Hywel Roberts

Hywel Roberts is a teacher, writer, bassist and brewer. His books include *Oops! Helping Children Learn Accidentally* (2012), *Uncharted Territories* (with Debra Kidd) (2018) and *Botheredness* (2022). Hywel worked alongside Sir Tim at conferences where he would be found nodding his head a lot. He hasn't had enough of experts.

> The people in this country have had enough of experts.
>
> **Michael Gove**[1]

I am clueless in early years, but I want to be there. I am a secondary teacher who has found himself there by mistake.[2] The joy of teaching and learning rushes around the space like some ancient campfire spirit, illuminating the world and all its foibles for everyone to see, particularly these little ones.

I am in the chair.

We are immersed in a forest of bears.

Now, dear reader, bears, as you know, can be grumpy. How do I know this? I know this because Blane, all two feet of him, tells me. In his words – his

---

1   This was the first part of a sentence in an interview with Faisal Islam on *Sky News* on 3 June 2016, which you can watch here: https://www.youtube.com/watch?v=GGgiGtJk7MA. In a later interview at the European Think Tank Summit (Farrar, 2017), Gove explains that he was expertly interrupted by Islam and the comment became the headline.
2   To paraphrase *Withnail and I* (Robinson, 1987).

small, well-formed and articulate reaction to iterative play and imagination – 'They are well grumpy.'

'How can I be safe?' I ask Blane, and he shakes his head, as if there is no hope. He even looks me up and down whilst considering this.

Angela, reading the room, steps in to help me. She has turned 4 and has a colourful, starry sticker that reads 'Mentor'. I am in safe hands.

'The bears are asleep, so it's okay,' she reassures me.

'What if they wake up?' I ask. 'I'm worried about their claws.'

Angela grins and takes my hand as if the paw of a bear.

'Don't worry, Mr Blowbats.[3] The claws are kind.'

The session finished and the children left, each a little better versed in what it means to have care for something. They have also felt like experts.

There is a lot to smile about here. It is joyful, momentary and perhaps un-assessable. Blane and Angela are my guides through this experience, and I am absolutely assessing as I go. But let us park that and return to the whole idea of what the Center for Research on Education, Diversity and Excellence calls 'joint productive activity'.[4]

Joint productive activity does exactly that. It is where the teacher works alongside the children – the science teacher modelling the experiment, the PE teacher demonstrating the skill, the English/drama teacher in role as Banquo, the Year 1 teacher leading the enquiry on how to protect the beach from plastic. It is not a rallying cry against other pedagogies; rather it is an antidote to lifeless aspects of curriculum delivery that dehumanise learning and encourage professional withdrawal from active, enactive teaching.

In the spirit of direct instruction,[5] sometimes we just need to tell kids stuff and that is it. Most high school kids are hardwired to believe that being passengers in the classroom, rather than participants within it, is just how it is in school, as if they have forgotten what it was like when they were younger. How many of us during our own secondary education sat back

---

3   Blowbats = Roberts.
4   See https://manoa.hawaii.edu/coe/credenational.
5   A worthy pedagogy for sure, but not the only one.

and let the teacher ramble as we daydreamed of better times? So, direct instruction is fantastic for some. But, if we rely on it as our sole pedagogy, we ignore much that teaching can be.

If you are a leader, walking around your setting, what are you seeing the children do in class? Where do you see the children up and doing? Where do you see the teacher up and doing with the children? It might be easier in some subjects, but I have seen the delivery of drama reduced to a corporate PowerPoint rather than a human exploration of our world.

As teachers, what sets us apart from being mere content providers (and therefore replaceable by cheaper professionals or AI) is the fact that we are sherpas, sharers, sense-makers and negotiators. We all operate in the ultimate human endeavour: equipping the next generation with what they need to thrive. We want them to be literate, numerate, curious, creative, compassionate and positive contributors to their world. Any curriculum we create needs to do this. And the delivery of such a curriculum should be as alive and optimistic as this aim.

Consider these three realms of what a curriculum is:

1. **Should.** This is what you might publish on your website. Some of your fantastic colleagues have worked hard to create this document. It is a selling point for your school and a focus for the inspectorate, but not for the children who never express an interest in this version of curriculum. It is *academic*.

2. **Could.** This is the lived aspect of curriculum. It is the 'should' realm brought to life. I cannot help but think of Ted Lasso dancing with his team.[6] It is the home of joint productive activity, where every ounce of professional learning around delivery, engagement and investment is realised. It is *social*.

3. **Must.** This is the hidden curriculum. It is where lives are enhanced because children haven't just done geography, they have done geography with you. We are all thriving, not just professionally surviving. The 'must' realm of curriculum is *human*.

---

6 You need to watch *Ted Lasso* (2020–2023) if you have missed it. I recommend it in the same way that you need to see *Kes* (Loach, 1969) and *Dead Poets Society* (Weir, 1990).

Put these realms together and you approach a textured understanding of what a rich curriculum experience might be – the opposite of what Martin Haberman (1991) called 'the pedagogy of poverty', rather a pedagogy of hope, celebration and community.

For us as teachers, it is an invitation to work together, eyes and ears from within and beyond our institutions, in a mass productive activity that places children and young people at the heart of what we do, whilst also protecting them from bears.

References

Farrar, T. (2017). Michael Gove on the Trouble with Experts [interview]. *Chatham House* (March). Available at: https://www.chathamhouse.org/2017/03/michael-gove-trouble-experts.

Haberman, M. (1991). The Pedagogy of Poverty Versus Good Teaching. *Phi Delta Kappan*, 73, 290–294.

Loach, K. (dir.) (1969). *Kes* [film]. Woodfall Film Productions and Kestrel Films.

Robinson, B. (dir.) (1987). *Withnail and I* [film]. HandMade Films.

Weir, P. (dir.) (1989). *Dead Poets Society* [film]. Touchstone Pictures and Silver Screen Partners.

Chapter 38
Finding the invisible child
Rachel Sylvester

Rachel Sylvester is a journalist at *The Times* and chair of the Times Education Commission. Tim gave evidence to the Commission.

Socrates said that education was 'the kindling of a flame, not the filling of a vessel'. The film director Sir Steve McQueen put it slightly differently. 'All kids need is a spark, or half a spark, just a little light. They think, "Mmm, that's interesting,"' he told the Times Education Commission (2022: 6). 'We're not creating robots, we want to create great human beings who can actually contribute.'

For Tim Brighouse, the secret of great teaching was 'about being human' and 'finding the invisible child' (Bates, 2023). He was right, but too often the creativity, inspiration, individuality and curiosity have been drummed out of an education system fixated on narrow metrics and grades.

The current one-size-fits-all approach appears increasingly outdated and flawed. It is not working for the 'forgotten third' of pupils who effectively fail all their GCSEs, and it is failing to stretch the most academic children who are frustrated by formulaic rote learning. Young people are forced to make choices too early, narrowing their options for the future before they have had a chance to explore and develop their interests.

Meanwhile, there is a mismatch between the capabilities being developed in school and those that the economy needs. Businesses complain that the education system is not preparing young people for the world of work, let alone the jobs of the future. Parents worry about the epidemic of mental ill health, driven at least partly by the pressure of exams, which has left many children struggling. Teachers are being infantilised by an education system that has become more about perspiration than inspiration.

Schools need to rediscover their human side, both for the sake of pupils, who are growing up in the age of the robots and need to acquire the skills that the machines cannot learn, and to tackle the recruitment and retention crisis among teachers, who feel disempowered by an over-prescriptive curriculum and demoralised by the requirements of teaching to the test.

The knowledge-rich curriculum is necessary but it is not sufficient. Business leaders, scientists and cultural figures all agree that it does not meet the needs of the modern world or provide young people with the tools to flourish. The focus on traditional academic subjects has squeezed out creative, design and practical work.

High-stakes assessment has become the tail that wags the dog, then wraps itself around the creature's neck and strangles it nearly to death. Exams are important – both as a way of measuring pupils' progress and of holding schools to account – but they have become too dominant. The single-minded focus on grades has undermined the broad and balanced education that should be offered to all young people and is leaving too many categorised as failures. There are all sorts of perverse incentives, and the accountability system and the assessment process have become muddled up.

If Britain is to create the inventors, entrepreneurs and scientists that will help the country to thrive in the future, then schools need to get better at encouraging innovation and individuality. Education should be about character as well as qualifications. We need a new curriculum and a transformed assessment system to encourage greater breadth and to break down the barriers that have been set up between humanities and sciences, vocational and academic qualifications, knowledge and skills.

The Times Education Commission proposed a British Baccalaureate, an equally rigorous but broader qualification than A levels, with academic and vocational options under the same umbrella. Children would study a wider range of subjects up to 18 and take a slimmed down set of exams at 16. Rishi Sunak recognised this with his outline support (there is a dispute about his commitment) to replace A levels with a new qualification called the Advanced British Standard, which would involve more subjects, both academic and vocational. This does not go far enough, but it does open up the possibility of the wider reform that is needed to bring the curriculum and assessment system into the 21st century. Technology must be fully integrated into the education system to personalise learning for pupils, reduce paperwork for teachers and make school fun.

Education should leave children with a lifelong curiosity about the world around them rather than an ability to tick the right boxes and regurgitate the correct phrases to pass exams. At a time when conspiracy theories and fake news are becoming increasingly prevalent, children need to learn how to question and interrogate information rather than just remembering facts. School should be engaging, with hands-on experience as well as desk work. Sport, music, drama, art, debating and dance must be an integral part of the timetable for all children, not an optional extracurricular add-on.

The Harvard education professor Howard Gardner argues that human beings have a variety of different intelligences – emotional and practical as well as academic – and the purpose of education is to develop them all rather than just focusing on one. He likes to ask not how intelligent a child is, but rather in which way the child is intelligent. In Estonia, which has the best education system in Europe, according to the Organisation for Economic Co-operation and Development, they understand the importance of individuality and creativity in education. Teachers have a high degree of autonomy and the curriculum is based around what the government calls '21st century competencies', including problem-solving, critical thinking, citizenship, collaboration, communication, entrepreneurship and digital skills.

Children learn robotics from the age of 7 and technology is fully integrated into the education system. All pupils study humanities and sciences throughout their school career, and only a small part of the timetable is taken up with preparing for national tests. At the Viimsi Gymnasium, a secondary school near Tallinn, the auditorium is dominated by a painting of a butterfly emerging from a chrysalis. 'It's about the stages of development,' the principal Karmen Paul explained to me. 'If you help open the chrysalis, it might become the butterfly that cannot fly. As a teacher you can be there and instruct and listen, but you cannot do the work for the pupils. They have to be active learners.'

References

Bates, S. (2023). Sir Tim Brighouse Obituary. *The Guardian* (20 December). Available at: https://www.theguardian.com/education/2023/dec/20/sir-tim-brighouse-obituary.

Times Education Commission (2022). *Bringing Out the Best: How to Transform Education and Unleash the Potential of Every Child.* London: The Times and The Sunday Times. Available at: https://nuk-tnl-editorial-prod-staticassets.s3.amazonaws.com/2022/education-commission/Times%20Education%20Commission%20final%20report.pdf.

Chapter 39

Making educational assessment fit for purpose

Mick Walker

Mick Walker is a former executive director of education at the Qualifications and Curriculum Development Agency and Honorary Research Fellow at the University of Leeds. Mick first met Tim Brighouse in 2006 when he was an adviser to the Expert Group on Assessment of which Tim was a member.

The launch of the 'Great Debate' on education (Callaghan, 1976) signalled the demise of what Lawton (1980: 22) called the 'golden age of teacher control' and greater external control and surveillance (Foucault, 1991 [1977]; Ball, 2003). Arguably, the two main tools of control and surveillance are school inspections and educational assessment. This chapter focuses on the latter, with educational assessment defined as: 'all those activities that involve eliciting evidence of student learning and drawing inferences as the basis for decisions' (James, 2010: 162).

Before Callaghan's speech and some years following, assessment was largely unproblematic: general qualifications bobbled along with consummate ease until the Education Reform Act 1988 and the national curriculum hit the airways. A graded qualification at the end of compulsory schooling was no longer the only assessment kid on the block. The national curriculum introduced statutory assessments at the end of the first three of four key stages, with the GCSE providing an assessment crescendo at Key Stage 4 – although assessment at this point has never been statutory.

The initial statutory assessment framework was 'based exclusively on teacher assessment with a system of externally set Standard Assessment Tasks (SATs), administered and marked by teachers and externally moderated' (Walker, 2020: 41). Following objections over workload and teacher boycotts – and the Dearing Report (1994) – tasks morphed into externally set and marked tests. The warning that 'external tests will impose *arbitrary restrictions on teachers' own work* ... and devalue their professional role' (Department of Education and Science and the Welsh Office, 1988, para. 16; original emphasis) went unheeded. Of equal if not more significance, school performance tables were introduced in 1992, making public the outcomes of end-of-schooling examinations with the addition of statutory tests in 1996.

Historically, general qualifications have included teachers in the assessment process, but over time this has diminished and all but disappeared, more often than not over issues of trust in what has been described as 'teachers marking their own homework', prompting calls for an end to coursework (Major, 1991; QCA, 2005, 2006; Colwill, 2007). More recently, the NAHT Commission on Assessment (2014: 14) raised concerns over what it called 'a worrying lack of trust' in teacher-based assessment.

But why are teachers attracting such criticism and suspicion at a level that undermines their professional status? One key issue is grounded in the regime of accountability. Up until the introduction of statutory assessments and performance tables, there was little concern over the efficacy of teachers' involvement in assessment, at any level; the entrance of league tables into the educational lexicon proved to be a game-changer.

Interest in internal assessment largely remains within the teaching profession, yet even here the discourse often degenerates to redundant and impoverished summative versus formative debates (Newton, 2007) rather than focusing on validity. This raises a second key issue: the level of assessment expertise amongst the teaching profession. Many of the so-called formative assessment practices used in schools are more theatre than science, as teachers perform the assessment for learning dance around purple pens, lollipop sticks and cold calling, with subsequent 'data drops', 'flight paths' and 'pupil tracking' operating at industrial proportions. These flight paths are based on unwarranted assumptions working towards foregone conclusions and should be confined to air-traffic control, with tracking left to people delivering packages.

Unfortunately, students do not learn everything we teach; if they did, we wouldn't need assessment (Wiliam, 2013). So, assessment is important. It is the best tool we have to gauge learning, inform teaching and recognise achievement; it stands in 'dynamic interaction' with teaching and learning (Gipps, 1994). Consequently, we should put more emphasis on building teachers' understanding of assessment. To increase the validity of educational assessments at school level, teachers need high-quality initial and ongoing training. At present, this is not the case as there are 'significant gaps in both the capacity of schools and ITT [initial teacher training] providers in the theoretical and technical aspects of assessment' (Carter, 2015: 9; see also McIntosh, 2015).

School leadership teams cover all aspects of school life, but how many have an assessment lead? And not someone responsible for data drops but someone specifically qualified for the post. Tim Brighouse long advocated for a lead assessor in every school and, ultimately, a chartered educational assessor (DCSF, 2009; Brighouse and Waters, 2022; CIEA, 2024; NAHT, 2024). These professionals support and advise colleagues and quality assure assessment practice across the school. And for anyone suggesting this increases workload, think again. A professional and considered approach to assessment will rid time spent entering baseless data into spreadsheets, generating meaningless charts and triple marking using various coloured pens until the school runs out of ink, or the will to live – and all without any trace of measuring the impact on learning (Department for Education, 2016a, 2016b).

Schooling is complex, often driven by politics as much as altruistic goals and practicalities. Yet, at the heart of every school sit three interrelated dimensions – curriculum, pedagogy and assessment – with assessment the poor relation, an imposed evil rather than a core skill of the profession. Assessment is not the work of the devil, and, in fairness, our qualification system is well regulated; yet, even here, the fallibility of assessment is recognised (Meadows and Billington, 2005: Rhead et al., 2018). Formal qualifications are fundamental in any education and training system, but they need to be valid. Users want to know that pilots can fly a plane – and land it – not because they received a grade squeezed into the symmetry of the bell curve (an approach despised by Tim Brighouse) but because they met the required criteria.

Assessment has many purposes (Newton, 2007), but those purposes need to be clear, with specifically designed assessment instruments and defensible inferences. All assessments involving children's learning are high stakes (Popham, 2010), and teachers are wholly capable of producing valid educational assessments. However, regaining trust in their judgements and re-establishing their professional status will only be achieved through appropriate training, qualifications and ongoing professional development.

References

Ball, S. J. (2003). The Teacher's Soul and the Terrors of Performativity. *Journal of Education Policy.* 18(2), 215–228. DOI: 10.1080/0268093022000043065

Brighouse, T. and Waters, M. (2022). *About Our Schools: Improving on Previous Best.* Carmarthen: Crown House Publishing.

Callaghan, J. (1976). A Rational Debate Based on the Facts. Speech delivered at Ruskin College, Oxford (18 October). Available at: https://education-uk.org/documents/speeches/1976ruskin.html.

Carter, A. (chair) (2015). *Carter Review of Initial Teacher Training (ITT).* London: Department for Education. Available at: https://www.gov.uk/government/publications/carter-review-of-initial-teacher-training.

Chartered Institute of Educational Assessors (CIEA) (2024). Lead Assessor Support Programme. Available at: https://www.herts.ac.uk/ciea/lead-assessor-support-programme.

Colwill, I. (2007). *Improving GCSE: Internal and Controlled Assessment. Recommendations on the Nature of Controls Needed for Internal and Controlled Assessment in Future GCSE Specifications* (March). London: Qualifications and Curriculum Authority. Available at: https://assets.publishing.service.gov.uk/media/5a81e6aeed915d74e3400a9a/0307_IanColwill_qca_Improving_GCSE_internal_and_controlled_assessment.pdf.

Dearing, R. (chair) (1994). *The National Curriculum and Its Assessment: Final Report* [Dearing Report]. London: School Curriculum and Assessment Authority. Available at: http://www.educationengland.org.uk/documents/dearing1994/dearing1994.html.

Department for Children, Schools and Families (DCSF) (2009). *Report of the Expert Group on Assessment.* Available at: https://www.education-uk.org/documents/pdfs/2009-expert-group-assessment.pdf.

Department for Education (2016a). *Eliminating Unnecessary Workload Around Marking. Report of the Independent Teacher Workload Review Group* (March). Available at: https://www.gov.uk/government/publications/reducing-teacher-workload-marking-policy-review-group-report.

Department for Education (2016b). *Eliminating Unnecessary Workload Associated with Data Management. Report of the Independent Teacher Workload Review Group* (March). Available at: https://www.gov.uk/government/publications/ reducing-teacher-workload-data-management-review-group-report.

Department of Education and Science and the Welsh Office (1988). *National Curriculum Task Group on Assessment and Testing: A Report.* Available at: https:// education-uk.org/documents/pdfs/1988-TGAT-report.pdf.

Foucault, M. (1991 [1977]). *Discipline and Punish: The Birth of the Prison.* Harmondsworth: Penguin.

Gipps. C. V. (1994). *Beyond Testing: Towards a Theory of Educational Assessment.* London: Falmer.

James, M. (2010). An Overview of Educational Assessment. In P. Peterson, E. Baker and B. McGaw (eds), *International Encyclopedia of Education: Vol. 3*, 3rd edn. Oxford: Elsevier, pp. 161–171.

Lawton, D. (1980). *The Politics of the School Curriculum.* London: Routledge & Kegan Paul.

Major, J. (1991). Education – All Our Futures. Speech made to the Centre for Policy Studies at the Café Royal, London, 3 July. Available at: http://www.johnmajorarchive.org.uk/1991/ mr-majors-speech-on-education-to-centre-for- policy-studies-3-july-1991.

McIntosh, J. (chair) (2015). *Final Report of the Commission on Assessment Without Levels* (September). London: Department for Education and Standards and Testing Agency. Available at: https://www.gov.uk/government/publications/ commission-on-assessment–without-levels-final-report.

Meadows, M. and Billington, L. (2005). *A Review of the Literature on Marking Reliability.* Manchester: AQA. Available at: https://filestore.aqa.org.uk/content/ research/CERP_RP_MM_01052005.pdf.

NAHT (2014). *Report of the NAHT Commission on Assessment.* Available at: https://www.stem.org.uk/system/files/elibrary-resources/2016/04/ Assessment%20commission%20report%20document%20%282%29.pdf.

NAHT (2024). Lead Assessor Support Programme. Available at: https:// www.naht.org.uk/Membership/Special-partner-offers-for-members/ Services-for-schools/Lead-Assessor-Support-Programme.

Newton, P. E. (2007). Clarifying the Purposes of Educational Assessment. *Assessment in Education: Principles, Policy & Practice*, 14(2), 149–170. DOI: 10.1080/09695940701478321

Popham, W. J. (2010). *Everything School Leaders Need to Know About Assessment.* London: SAGE.

Qualifications and Curriculum Authority (QCA) (2005). *A Review of GCE and GCSE Coursework Arrangements*. Available at: https://assets.publishing.service.gov.uk/media/5a74fbe1ed915d3c7d5297bd/0105_QCA_a-review-of-GCE-GCSE-courswork.pdf.

Qualifications and Curriculum Authority (QCA) (2006). *A Review of GCSE Coursework*. Available at: https://assets.publishing.service.gov.uk/media/5a822c58ed915d74e34021fa/0106_QCA_courseworkreport.pdf.

Rhead, S., Black, B and Pinot de Moira, A. (2018). *Marking Consistency Metrics: An Update*. Coventry: Ofqual. Available at: https://assets.publishing.service.gov.uk/media/5bfbfd70e5274a0fb775cca3/Marking_consistency_metrics_-_an_update_-_FINAL64492.pdf.

Walker, M. G. (2020). Whither Teachers' Assessment: Trust in Teachers' Assessment since the Norwood Review of 1943. Unpublished PhD thesis. Available at: https://etheses.whiterose.ac.uk/28335.

Wiliam, D. (2013). Assessment: The Bridge Between Teaching and Learning. *Voices from the Middle*, 21(2), 15–20. DOI: 10.58680/vm201324461

School improvement, leadership and technology

Chapter 40

Let's tear down some hedges!

Amjad Ali

Amjad Ali is a teacher, trainer, TEDx speaker, author and senior leader. He has a background in challenging, diverse schools and young offender prisons, and co-founded the BAMEed Network. Amjad has delivered continuing professional development at events alongside Sir Tim and was fortunate to have been informally mentored and supported by him.

On 28 June 2013, I attended TeachMeet Oxford where I delivered a short presentation to many attendees, including Sir Tim Brighouse. I had never met Tim before, but, at the end of the evening, he called me over and introduced me to the then head teacher of the host school.

In September 2013, I started my first assistant head teacher role at the tender age of 29 as the director of inclusion. (I always tell people that Tim recommended me directly for this job!) Whilst at the school, I went on to create the biggest annual TeachMeets in the South East by inviting some of the leading voices in education to come together for food, prizes and pedagogy. I am fairly certain that it was in one of Tim's keynotes (I always asked him to keynote) that I first heard the phrase 'cognitive science', and I am sure it would have been the first time for many others too.

Tim was a governor at the school, and he made himself available to me whenever I needed it. He did this with many people. He reminded me of my all-time favourite teacher, Mr Wickens; he had this special skill of making every single student feel like they were the most important person in the classroom – without anybody else knowing! My relationship with Sir Tim extended to him mentoring me as a new assistant head teacher in a large city secondary school. Again, he was always available to answer the many questions I had.

I watched Tim speak at an event alongside John Hattie and Ron Berger. I watched him at other TeachMeets, leadership breakfasts and school events. Every time I met him, he shared a story with me; a simple anecdote to him but career defining to me.

Tim spoke of the butterfly effect, which stems from chaos theory, a lot – about how small changes in one place can have a massive effect in others. I was blown away by the examples he provided:

- Ask teachers to provide revision sessions in exam locations – for example, the school assembly hall or gym. Then ask teachers to use everyday objects to link to key concepts from their examination specification, such as the exam hall clock, basketball nets and so on.

- Get a student's work marked by a teacher from another school, and then discuss the difference in marking styles and feedback.

He encouraged me to choose my words wisely and insist on the best for everyone for whom I had responsibility. This included staff as well as students.

He taught me about 'energy creators' and how, in really great schools, teachers talk to each other about teaching and learning, they plan together and they learn from one another. As a former advanced skills teacher in teaching and learning, I deliver continuing professional development one day a week and I have applied Tim's theory for years.

I always recommend that schools and organisations give their staff an hour or so to simply talk about the ideas I have shared, and then to bring them back as a group and talk further. This simple idea of giving teachers time enables schools to increase the number of energy creators. I have extended this to sharing ideas on staff shout-out boards too.

We also talked about immersion. Tim told me, as a new leader, don't get fixed in your own silo but immerse yourself for two weeks (minimum) in other areas of the school. Read, listen, watch carefully, learn and engage because, in doing so, you will improve your own area. Initially, I must admit, I thought, how can I make the time for this? But I realised that all experienced leaders need to know about the interconnected aspects of our responsibilities.

Another hot topic we often discussed was change management and 'adopters' and 'resisters'. He instilled in me the need for clear and effective induction. I still don't believe that schools have this right, yet. He taught me that if we show new staff, this is the way we do things, then it is the only way they know and it will filter across the school.

I also spoke to him candidly about the risks of self-promotion. I was wary of tweeting, showing off and making it seem like 'me, me, me'. Tim was excellent in explaining that there will be many teachers who cannot translate my enthusiasm from reading my posts or will be unable to replicate the practice I am trying to transfer via writing alone. However, there will be many who can read about an activity or an idea, see the sense in it, adapt it for their groups and carry it through brilliantly. Even if they aren't successful the first time, they will work on it and try again. He told me to continue doing what I am doing. From this I have adapted the phrase, 'try, refine, ditch'.

Writing this chapter has made me realise how much Tim has impacted on my career and growth. It is thanks in huge part to him that I have written a book, which is underpinned by Tim's views on teaching and change (Ali, 2024). I have borrowed his phrase 'low effort, high impact', which he referred to as his 'butterflies'. I have woven in what Tim has taught me by trying to make the ideas I share of benefit to everybody.

Let me end with this: there aren't many educationalists who have had such a profound impact on education who are so inclusive in their approach. Tim told us to 'teach the child you expect, not the child you think you have'. He told us that we shouldn't try to get rid of the gaps in education by creeping through the hedges, but we should start a revolution and tear down those hedges.

So, who is with Tim? Let's tear down those hedges!

References

Ali, A. (2024). *A Little Guide for Teachers: SEND in Schools*. London: Corwin.

Chapter 41
Tim's sixth-form sustainability conferences

Anna Bush

Anna Bush has worked in education for 20 years and currently works for United Learning. A role on the London Challenge meant working closely with Tim Brighouse and getting behind the efforts of the capital's most challenging schools. Anna is known for her passion and commitment – or, in Tim's words, 'Anna is easy to work with and gets things done.'

I first met Tim in 2003 when I was a civil servant on the London Challenge team; Tim was commissioner for London schools. We worked closely on our Keys to Success schools – the lowest performing, most deprived schools in the capital. He said if we could crack it there, breaking the link between deprivation and underachievement, we would show it was possible anywhere. Very different from the government's 'secret hitlist' of schools which ran on the front page of the *Standard* (Miles, 2012). It was a pleasure to work with Tim and watch his skill and magic turn the most difficult meeting into consensus and a clear way forward.

I saw Tim sporadically after that, read his work and always felt huge warmth and admiration. I am incredibly grateful for the opportunity I had so early in my career to work with him.

In summer 2023, Tim reached out to my boss and his dear friend, Jon Coles, CEO of United Learning, about a climate conference that was happening in Cardiff, led by a passionate and wonderful teacher, Lucy Kirkham (see Chapter 32). Tim was going and wanted one of us to attend; unfortunately we couldn't manage it. We were keen to hear about it, though, and Tim thought the idea had potential.

I met Tim online in the summer holidays. He was at home, having been in and out of hospital. It was lovely to reconnect; it felt like we had been working together yesterday, not 20 years ago. He didn't want to talk about his health, rather how great the Cardiff conference had been and how he thought we could get a movement going, with students entitled to be involved in discussing an important global issue, bigger than themselves: climate change. We made a plan, which involved Tim sending lots of emails and me convening a meeting.

Tim's vision

Tim understood the fundamental importance of students experiencing learning beyond the classroom. He had the greatest respect for young people. He believed in them, optimistic that, in the right conditions, all could thrive. In this final unfinished project, he combined that with his concerns about the climate emergency and was passionate about how that context could enhance students' learning experiences.

Tim's vision was for young people aged 16–17 to be involved in an issue that was bigger than themselves. He recognised that many young people feel passionately and are worried about climate change, and saw that as the obvious place to start a bottom-up movement for an enriched experience. A movement that could grow, with more conferences held each year, until it built to become an entitlement for all young people.

Tim's idea: regional student-led events

One of Tim's early thoughts for the project was that we aim for eight to ten regional conferences as near to midsummer's day as possible. He envisaged them being hosted by universities for Year 12 students. His ambition was that all young people not only experience a conference but 'own' it.

Tim's attendance at the Teens and Teachers Conference had been formative. Lucy Kirkham and her students designed and delivered this at Cardiff University in 2023 for 100 students from 13 schools. It had been an extremely positive experience for the young people who had made the event happen and for all those who attended.

Drawing on the expertise of those involved, Tim was clear that the content would need to be developed by the young people locally and interwoven with common aspects to unify the events, such as a recording of an excellent keynote speaker and a shared logo.

The students would be integral to the design of the conferences, helping to shape the agenda, participating on the day and taking subsequent action. Media students could help to publicise the events, while others could record the day's activities, actions and commitments.

The materials we produced as a result have formed a toolkit for conference organisers and young people to draw on as they pull their local conferences together. The teachers and students using them are making Tim's vision a vibrant reality.

We sought national sponsors to fund the events: students for whom travel costs would be prohibitive, speakers, refreshments and technical equipment. Even from his hospital bed, Tim drew on his impressive array of contacts: the *Guardian*, the Paul Hamlyn Foundation and even David Attenborough's cousin. Universities were lined up to be venues. We are grateful for the support we have secured from the Paul Hamlyn Foundation and Let's Go Zero, as well as to the universities that are kindly hosting.

As usual, Tim's aspirations were limitless, aiming to secure none other than David Attenborough to record a message about the importance of the next generation in tackling climate change to open all the conferences. Unfortunately, we haven't been able to fulfil this ambition, but Tim gave it a good try!

Tim's plan realised: the conferences

After Tim's passing in December 2023, it was unanimously agreed that we would continue with our plans and aim to realise his vision with the conferences happening in 2024. We are hugely grateful for the energy and commitment of colleagues across the country in making these happen in the following locations:

- South West: Cabot Learning Foundation in Bristol for 400 young people.

- South East: Avonbourne Academy at Southampton University for up to 250 young people.

- West Midlands: Arthur Terry School and Windsor Academy Trust at Keele University for up to 300 young people.

- Yorkshire and Humberside: Greenhead College at Huddersfield University for approximately 150 young people.

- London: Paddington Academy at UCL for up to 250 students; Walthamstow Academy at King's College London; Mulberry Trust details to be confirmed.

- Wales: Two conferences at Bangor University and at Swansea University.

Around 2,000 young people are likely to benefit from Tim's vision through this experience and the action that follows.

Continuing Tim's legacy

We lost Tim's shining light, but all we have learned from his brilliance and huge heart remains. His passion for sixth-form conferences on climate change will benefit hundreds of young people in 2024 alone.

We would love to grow this idea and build towards his vision. We are exploring the possibility of making it an annual series of events, reaching more young people each year and building towards participation as an entitlement.

Anyone reading this who feels they have something to offer to keep this unfinished business alive, then please do get in touch. It is a genuine piece of unfinished business that we must now continue for Tim, for the students and for the planet.

References

Miles, T. (2012). London Schools on Secret Hit-List. *Evening Standard* (12 April). Available at: https://www.standard.co.uk/hp/front/london-schools-on-secret-hitlist-6351346.html.

Chapter 42

We can be heroes ...

Lena Carter

Lena Carter started her career in Cambridgeshire in 1992. She is currently a shared head teacher of two rural Scottish primary schools. In 2017, she had the good fortune to spend a weekend with Tim and educators from across the UK, exploring how our four countries can learn from one another.

Growing up as the daughter of two teachers, Ted Wragg's was the name that punctuated dinner-table conversations around education. Having studied under his tutelage at Exeter, my mum had been strongly influenced by the Prof's strong and passionate convictions about education and his passion for teaching as a higher calling that would enable children to make sense of the intriguing, beautiful and awful world around them.

Ted was mum's educational hero and therefore, by default, mine. I am not aware of ever having met him, but his wisdom and vast knowledge became part of my schema as a teacher.

I can remember no such hero figure during my time studying for a PGCE at Cambridge. Paul Dix and I were there as contemporaries but, at that point, I hero-worshipped him from afar for his singing voice and talents as an actor rather than his then latent skill as a teacher.

As I progressed through my career, there were several teachers and mentors with whom I connected through shared values or who made me consider whether I needed to re-examine my values and convictions. It is certainly true that the established beliefs and habits of a teacher can sometimes be shaken up for the benefit of learners through an encounter with someone who believes or thinks differently. Just like the children we teach, we all need to have human mirrors around us who reflect our beliefs and help to give us confidence that our values are shared and based on deep connection, reflection and learning. However, we also need those who act as human windows, who respectfully and supportively help us to look out on vistas where alternative possibilities are made visible to us.

Most of those who supported me professionally in this way would be names that never made it onto the pages of the *TES*, let alone onto the relatively new platforms created by social media. Social media has only played a part in the last decade of my 30-year career in education. Most of my educational heroes were not and now never will be on social media, and nor would they be comfortable with me mentioning them here.

My connection with Tim started through the pages of print copies of the *TES*. It was a guilty pleasure of mine, on a Friday night throughout the 1990s, to treat myself by finding a quiet corner where I could devour the pages of the *TES* and the two sections of a coconut-filled chocolate bar. I remember Tim's words and thinking having a huge influence within those pages. I was also greatly influenced, as I began to take on leadership roles, by his book, *How to Improve Your School* (Brighouse and Woods, 2005).

And then, finally, in November 2016 and March 2017, I got to spend time with Tim at two events organised up here in Scotland. I wrote about each one in posts that are available on my blog (Carter, 2016, 2017). Many others have spoken and written about Tim's heroic qualities, and there has even been the suggestion that by cloning Tim we could have sorted education across the UK – and perhaps even the world – in one fell swoop. And whilst I have been tempted to agree, and have at times fallen into the hero-worship and fan-girl behaviour that has also been triggered in me by meeting, amongst others, Dylan Wiliam, Suzanne Zeedyk, David Cameron and Norman Drummond, I also know that Tim, along with any number of clones in his army, would not have been the answer.

The answer is that Tim, although he probably never knew it at the time, spoke words and shared wisdom that helped reawaken the hero in me. Mine is a reluctant hero; the one who was with me at birth but who somewhere along the line put on the wrong suit of armour and has spent several years trying to get out of it again. And my reluctant hero connected with Tim's when, on that snowy November night in Glasgow, he talked about the sad school-phobic pupil (him) from 67 years ago who changed schools and moved from a black-and-white world to a world in colour because of a skilled and empathetic teacher.

We sadly lost Tim and the iconic Tina Turner in the same year, both aged 83. They were both heroes but, in their passing, I have become more aware than ever that we don't need another hero in education with a title or a pedestal. Tim reminded me that, as a school leader, I need to bring out the hero inside every child and adult in my care. My role as head teacher is not about me, my title or the power that I think I might have to bring about 'improvements'. It is about the privilege that I hold in working with all the adults in our children's lives, so that these children experience, through a well-planned curriculum and within safe and loving environments, a world in colour.

References

Brighouse, T. and Woods, D. (2005). *How to Improve Your School.* Abingdon and New York: Routledge.

Carter, L. (2016). Professor Sir Tim Comes to Scotland. *Lenabellina* [blog] (18 November). Available at: https://lenabellina.wordpress.com/2016/11/18/professor-sir-tim-comes-to-scotland.

Carter, L. (2017). Four Countries. *Lenabellina* [blog] (3 March). Available at: https://lenabellina.wordpress.com/2017/03/03/four-countries.

Chapter 43

School trusts as civic institutions

Leora Cruddas

Leora Cruddas is the founding chief executive of the Confederation of School Trusts – the national organisation and sector body for school trusts in England. She had a feisty relationship with Tim founded on mutual respect. She is visiting professor at UCL Institute of Education. Leora was awarded a CBE in the New Year's Honours in 2022.

In February 2019, the Civic University Commission launched its final report, *Truly Civic: Strengthening the Connection Between Universities and Their Places*. The report sets out how universities have the capability, opportunity and responsibility to be civic partners and support the places where they are based to solve some of their most pressing problems (UPP Foundation, 2019).

The late Lord Kerslake, then chair of the Civic University Commission, commented: 'The deep economic and social changes that are happening in Britain today have, alongside Brexit, made the civic role of universities even more vital to the places they are located in' (Brabner, 2019).

In England, school trusts are organisations with the sole purpose of advancing education for public benefit. The trust is a group of schools working in deep and purposeful collaboration in a single legal entity under strong strategic governance.

School trusts are also well set up to play a civic role. I first made the case for school trusts as a new form of civic structure in *Systems of Meaning: Three Nested Leadership Narratives for School Trusts* (Cruddas, 2020). Since then, we have had a global pandemic followed by a period of geopolitical tensions and economic challenges. This has had an enormous detrimental impact on some of our children and communities.

One of the things Sir Tim Brighouse believed was that we should regard crises as the norm and complexity as fun. I think he was right. He also believed that we need a bottomless well of intellectual curiosity, a complete absence of paranoia and self-pity, and unwarranted optimism.

This is a leadership mindset. I think one expression of this leadership mindset is the civic mindset. No single individual or institution is going to solve the problems that we face on our own. We need to engage with other civic actors for a wider common good. We also need to think in terms that are longer than the short-termism of political cycles. This is because we are building public institutions.

I recently read Alex Hill's insightful book, *Centennials: The 12 Habits of Great, Enduring Organisations* (2023). Hill offers a fascinating set of insights into organisations that have lasted a hundred years or more. He argues that their strategies for maintaining excellence and success frequently fly in the face of conventional wisdom.

A key premise of the book is 'stable core' and 'disruptive edge'. The trust sector grew from a disruptive mindset, and a key part of our success has been the ability to innovate. Now that more than half of pupils in England are educated in school trusts, it is perhaps easy (and desirable) to argue that trusts are part of the establishment. We are. We should hold on to this. And we should make the powerful, evidence-informed, values-driven case for all schools to be part of a strong and sustainable group working together in deep and purposeful collaboration.

So, yes, we want a stable core, but we also need to continue to innovate. We need a disruptive edge.

Hill quotes Paul Thompson, the vice-chancellor of the Royal College of Art, who says that the college is 'radically traditional': 'Out of this balance emerges the energy that propels them forward and a stability that ensures that no one loses sight of what each Centennial is there to achieve or forgets what has led to success in the past' (2023: xv).

An interesting feature of Hill's disruptive edge is the habit of 'get better, not bigger'. This is perhaps controversial in our sector. Growth for most trusts is a priority. Hill says that growth for centennials is something to be cautious about: 'They worry that the pursuit of growth at all costs can all too easily be a distraction from core goals and values. Excellence can change the world. Growth on its own won't' (2023: 132). He adds: '[Centennials] look at the whole of society, and every possibility, and ask themselves: How can we shape how society thinks, and behaves, not only today, but for the next twenty to thirty years?' (2023: 7).

We know that trust and confidence in public institutions is a concern right now. We see this in our schools through the problems with pupil attendance, behaviour and the exponential rise in parental complaints.

We also know that the legitimacy of public institutions is crucial for building peaceful and inclusive societies. Trust is integral to the functioning of any society. Trust in each other, in our public institutions and in our leaders are all essential ingredients for social and economic progress, allowing people to cooperate with and express solidarity for one another.

So, it is essential that, as public leaders, we work with our parents and communities to repair the social contract and to rebuild trust in schools as public institutions.

It is worth returning to Lord Kerslake's prescient words from 2019. The situation he described then is even more complex now with greater implications for our public services and public institutions. The deep economic and social changes that are happening in Britain today have made the civic role of public institutions even more vital, not just to the places they are located in but in leading a response to the renewal of our communities and of civic life.

This requires something different of public leaders; it requires us to think in longer term horizons and to build school trusts as public institutions. This is how we will build the resilience of our school system. It is how we will build back.

References

Brabner, R. (2019). Over 30 Universities Sign New 'Civic University Agreement' to Reaffirm Local Role. *UPP Foundation* (11 February). Available at: https://upp-foundation.org/leading-universities-pledge-commitment-to-local-communities.

Cruddas, L. (2020). *Systems of Meaning: Three Nested Leadership Narratives for School Trusts*. Nottingham: Confederation of School Trusts. Available at: https://cstuk.org.uk/knowledge/discussion-and-policy-papers/systems-of-meaning-three-nested-leadership-narratives-for-school-trusts.

Hill, A. (2023). *Centennials: The 12 Habits of Great, Enduring Organisations*. London: Cornerstone Press.

UPP Foundation (2019). *Truly Civic: Strengthening the Connection Between Universities and Their Places. Final Report of the UPP Foundation Civic University Commission*. Available at: https://www.upp-foundation.org/wp-content/uploads/2019/02/Civic-University-Commission-Final-Report.pdf.

Chapter 44

Sometimes it is the messages you don't want to hear

Ben Davis

Ben Davis is the head teacher at St Ambrose Barlow RC High School in Salford. Prior to this he worked as a head in Scotland, where he first encountered Tim through David Cameron, an association that continued after his move to England in 2015.

I was fortunate to encounter Tim several times, but I can't claim him as a friend. Rather, I felt his influence, experienced his impact on education and on those around him, and always found his Audenesque countenance convivial, deeply engaged and curious.

Early in my current headship, I realised that it might demand more than I had anticipated – possibly more than I could give. Having met Tim previously, I was keen to renew the acquaintance (perhaps imbibe some of the magic) and attended a meeting about human resources in Salford Quays. It was as unprepossessing as it sounds, except for Tim.

Two gems stand out, both delivered with the kind of genial, conversational freestyling that few can pull off in a formal presentation. Both were preceded by, 'And please tell me you're not still ...' which most of us were, and many still are, underlining his determination to challenge and go beyond received wisdom: progress cannot be achieved by cleaving to the old ways. He was not slavishly refashioning convention but thoughtfully undoing and reshaping established ways of leading.

These twin bright jewels of insight were simply this: don't distinguish between teaching and non-teaching staff – they are all teachers and should be accorded that status; and don't publish job descriptions that state 'and any other tasks as required by the head teacher'. I didn't want to hear either of these things, sitting anxiously in the audience and emanating the lacerating fear that only a school leader on the verge of an unfavourable Ofsted can know. They were, however, what I needed: principles of humane, warm, sustaining leadership. I was hoping for a panacea for immediate school improvement; instead, what Tim offered has stayed with me, less because of what they mean for recruitment and professional development, and more because they say so much about his ethos of leadership. I arrived hoping for the short-term fix; I left reminded of the nourishing and transformational power of relationships.

Later, during the claustrophobic, chaotic COVID-19 spring of 2021, I had become the chair of our local head teachers' association and invited Tim to speak to all 23 of us. It was an online session, and he had just published *About Our Schools* with Mick Waters. The remote nature of the forum proved irksome for Tim, who seemed to want to explode out of our screens and reinvigorate our pandemic-weary souls. Nevertheless, for an hour or so, he careened through his thoughts on where we were, what education needed to recover from the pandemic and, specifically, on inclusion. There was nothing aimless about his peregrinations; sagacity resonated in the sincerity and depth of his knowledge, cut through with an eloquent humility and without magisterial overstatement or hubris. It seemed that with each new experience in his career, he simply saw a little more of the vastness there was to understand. That did not stop him from setting us a task: reduce and then eliminate exclusions.

In raising this issue, he was motivated by the experience of a family member. He knew this was a topic that could elicit considerable antipathy from many in the meeting, but he had the foresight to spot that exclusions would rocket as the pandemic retreated. Again, by two years, he pre-empted the crisis in attendance, well-being and exclusion that we now flail at with such visceral panic.

I am ashamed to say that we failed him. Our exclusions soared. He probably knew they would, but he also knew that, given the opportunity to speak to 20 secondary head teachers, he had to confront us about it, albeit with humour and empathy. He did so with the eminence of long experience (even if, as he acknowledged, a different experience) and with the certainty that not trying to reduce exclusion would risk failing to serve the young. Tim's presentation fizzed with intensity, his wholehearted respect and concern for the experience of young people sharpening into focus as it progressed. It is surprisingly rare to hear this articulated with such raw clarity by others of comparable status.

From what I know of him, this impulse came from years of granular as well as strategic leadership, peering into the nooks and crannies of schools. He frustrated politicians for many reasons, but one was that he could influence what happened in educational institutions in a way they could not. They were thwarted by their bludgeoning; he forged trust by bolstering. His appreciative nature was characterised by being an excellent listener, a natural conduit for ideas and conversation, for gathering perspectives and skill from disparate people and directing them in the service of the young. That so many from across the spectrum of often fractious education debate lay claim to some degree of alignment with his vision shows his expansive and generous character. In the days following his death, he achieved something unheard of on edu-X by appearing to unite those who usually exist in a state of animus in their respect for his leadership and achievements.

Tim's legacy is to remind serving head teachers to be what he practised. Good leadership is collaborative and liberating, not directive and fussy. It is relational, not in thrall to routine and procedure, and usually tangled rather than neatly ordered. Furthermore, attractive false dichotomies are anathema to good leadership; teams cannot be cohesive if they are striated into roles of different status. What staff feel about their roles and their value can be undone in seconds through careless nomenclature or monarchical proclamations about what each staff member is expected to do. Ultimately, what matters is how young people in our care feel, not just what they learn and achieve. It shapes their lives in ways that knowledge cannot because it lingers long in the memory.

Tim's singular commitment to those who learnt and worked in schools meant he was more attuned than most leaders at his level to the hidden places of schools, with his quiet reverence for the complex art of classrooms and their messy complexity. In the length and variety of his service, he embodied the truth that real, enduring change takes time, discernment and, more often than not, relies on consensus. We are easily misdirected by the fleeting and superficial or drawn to shallow rhetoric rather than committing to the longer slog of building relationships and thinking things through. There was profound experience and compassion in those short sentences in Salford Quays – messages that, as the education system convulses once again, we would do well to heed.

References

Brighouse, T. and Waters, M. (2022). *About Our Schools: Improving on Previous Best.* Carmarthen: Crown House Publishing.

Chapter 45

Developing tomorrow's leaders today

Maggie Farrar

Maggie Farrar first worked with Tim when she set up the University of the First Age in Birmingham. Since then he has provided support and inspiration as a mentor and friend through her time as a director at the National College for School Leadership and now as a leadership coach.

An unanswered question

Sadly, when someone dies, we often think about the question we always wanted to ask them but somehow never did. So it was with Tim. Given his extraordinary gift for leadership, I always wanted to know about his own leadership development. How did he grow into the leader we knew and admired?

I do know that he never participated in any formal leadership development programmes. Instead, he read widely, was deeply curious and loved debating ideas. This is not to imply that programmes are ineffective in growing leaders. Many jurisdictions, including England, think they are effective, and have introduced suites of nationally recognised and accredited programmes.

It is a start, but they can be overly prescriptive and, when funded by government, ideologically driven. As Liz Robinson stated at the launch of the Big Education report *Rethinking Leadership* (Robinson and Hallgarten, 2024), 'national professional qualifications are necessary, but not sufficient, if we are to equip leaders with the knowledge and skills they need'.

Exploring our ambition

Tim was never caught in an ideology trap. His leadership was enacted through his philosophical beliefs about what it means to live a good life, committed to something bigger than oneself. This was the mark of his leadership. How might we learn from his lifetime of leading to reset our ambitions for developing leaders?

Tim believed that in order to extend our vision of what is possible, we act as both historians and futurologists (Brighouse, 2007: 11). We retain the best of the past whilst building a better path to the future.

What might this look like for leadership development? I am curious about the warp and weft of leadership development – the warp being the vertical programmatic experiences and the weft the horizontal opportunities woven through the daily lives of leaders.

What might this look like?

- Leaders access the significant body of knowledge about what they should know and be able to do *and* creatively apply their learning through adaptive and reflective practice.

- Leaders learn from experts *and* cultivate an insatiable curiosity about the adaptive nature of leading in their own context.

- Leaders engage in episodic planned experiences *and* see leadership development as a daily practice by asking for help, inviting feedback and reflecting with a skilled mentor or coach.

- Leaders learn individually, attending to reading and assignments *and* with peers, confronting long-standing issues and solving challenges that no one leader could address alone.

- Leaders manage the outer world of school leadership *and* have the skills to build a strong relationship with their inner world through cultivating greater self-awareness.

- Leaders learn to be tough on issues *and* kind on people, including themselves, demonstrating generosity of spirit, compassion and respect for those they lead.

- Leaders create a climate in which they can attend to the task of getting the job done *and* their relationships with staff through building capacity, confidence and a sense of belonging.

Leadership guarantees

However, extending the experience of leadership development beyond programmes and weaving it into the daily practice of leaders presents a challenge. Access can depend on who you know, where you work and for whom you work. Opportunities can feel serendipitous.

Just as programmes are insufficient in developing leaders, Tim knew that an individual school experience is insufficient for children. Whilst in Birmingham, he introduced the notion of 'guarantees'. Children and young people across the city were guaranteed a set of experiences, regardless of where they went to school. They helped to craft them. Schools across the city got behind them.

The masterstroke Tim played was that the guarantees were so ambitious that no one school was able to offer them alone. They could be offered only through collaboration between schools and other organisations.

Could we create something similar for leaders? Could we define a broad set of experiences that leaders might thrive on, whatever their career stage or context? Perhaps an opportunity to shadow someone in the next stage of leadership? Or the chance to take part in a research study of their choice with others? Or to be trained as a coach or mentored by someone from a different sector?

Leaders helping other schools to improve or mentoring newly appointed heads has long been part of school systems. Multi-academy trusts, in particular, are seeing the notion of a specific 'guarantee of professional learning' as a pathway to becoming an employer of choice. But a broad menu of guarantees crafted by leaders, for leaders, is not yet available to all.

Could we honour Tim's legacy by reshaping his notion of guarantees into an approach to leadership development that is more likely to not only retain head teachers in post but to help them thrive and flourish in it? Guarantees that embody the values and core principles that defined his own leadership and are testimony to the demanding and complex job of school leadership. A set of experiences that encourage leaders to heed his clarion call in Birmingham of 'always improving on previous best'. A tapestry of opportunities available to all.

A personal insight

I met with Tim when I became the interim CEO of the National College for School Leadership. 'How are you going to handle it?' he asked. 'Well,' I responded, 'I think I have a choice. I could live every day pretending I know how to do a job for which I feel wholly unprepared, or I could treat it like a Harvard Leadership MBA on which I have a front-row seat.' Tim chuckled and said, 'So start building your own peer group, find your own tutors and sort out your own assessment as well. Bloody hell, give yourself a pass mark now and just get on with it!'

There was a gleam in his eye. He knew that the best leadership learning comes from embracing our messy world and its ambiguities, being comfortable with our own inadequacies, asking for help, grasping the challenge and having a group of leaders we respect around us.

Perhaps that is his answer to the question I never asked.

References

Brighouse, T. (2007). *How Successful Head Teachers Survive and Thrive.* Abingdon: RM.

Robinson, L. and Hallgarten, J. (2024). *Rethinking Leadership: What Else? What Next? What If?* London: Big Education and Centre for Education and Youth. Available at: https://bigeducation.org/wp-content/uploads/2024/01/Big_Education_Rethinking_Leadership.pdf.

Chapter 46

A hopeful future for all teachers and leaders

Evelyn Forde

Evelyn Forde was head teacher of Copthall School in Mill Hill, North London from 2016 to 2023, during which time she led the school to achieve significant improved outcomes and worked with staff to secure a range of accolades for the school. In 2022, Tim and Evelyn contributed to the Commission on Teacher Retention.

I met Tim when we both contributed to the Commission on Teacher Retention in 2023, and whilst his reputation had, of course, gone before him and I was fully aware of his work, I was still a star-struck leader who listened intently to his words of wisdom on what he felt was needed to retain teachers in the profession. Indeed, Tim wrote a paper on the recruitment challenges in 2005, but at that point he noted: 'Nationally, the peak of the "crisis" in terms of teacher vacancies has passed' (Brighouse, 2005: 1). It is an indictment of our education system that nearly 20 years later, we have come full circle and are back in crisis.

It is with this in mind that I reflect on what the future for school leadership is, as we navigate a system that is crying out for adequate funding and better provision for our most vulnerable young people, alongside child poverty, a widening of the disadvantage gap, an increase in mental health concerns faced by young people, and a system that fails to pay due attention to the exodus of brilliant teachers and schools leaders from the profession.

For schools to have great leaders and teachers, it may well be up to those leaders in our schools to find the solutions. At the Association of School and College Leaders conference in 2023, I encouraged leaders to get stroppy and to feel empowered to wrestle back some of the decision-making from ministers. I believe this will have to be the future of school leadership, where our voices are heard loud and clear, where we are respected as a profession, and where we are given agency to lead our schools with precision and autonomy.

First and foremost, it is my strongly held belief that every head teacher should be assigned a coach as part of their development and well-being. How can it be that you are a deputy head teacher on 31 August and then on 1 September you are expected to 'know it all'? It is just not possible. Therefore, to support a head teacher's growth and to retain them in the profession, a coach/mentor should be mandatory and feature as part of the future of school leadership.

Over time, even within multi-academy trusts, school leaders often operate in silos, in competition with each other for school places, for the best exam results and for better Ofsted outcomes, but, in doing so, we forget that great leaders lead others, not just within their own settings but beyond. After all, 'it takes a village to raise a child'. We need to create opportunities for leaders to collaborate with other leaders, whether that is nationally or internationally, so they can work together to solve common problems and thus drive change through a shared moral purpose of sustaining and improving the system for all children. We need to create safe spaces for school leaders to support each other and benefit from the wisdom and experience of other leaders through peer-to-peer development.

I also see the future of school leadership as one which reflects our diverse communities because currently they don't. A recent report by the National Foundation for Educational Research (Sharp and Aston, 2024) found that 'Barriers to recruitment, retention and progression coalesce around the unequal treatment of teachers of colour in a system that was not designed to support either ethnic or intersectional diversity. An anti-racist school culture is a key enabler of progression. Therefore, action should focus on ensuring a positive working environment for teachers and leaders from diverse ethnic backgrounds.'[1]

In 2003, the UCL Institute of Education ran an Investing in Diversity initiative, which was a groundbreaking programme for people of colour, and led to many, including me, becoming successful leaders. This

---

1   See https://www.nfer.ac.uk/publications/ethnic-diversity-in-the-teaching-workforce-evidence-review.

programme closed, and whilst Diversity Hubs made a brief appearance back in 2014, no real investment or commitment to addressing the lack of diversity in our teaching workforce has been made.

Finally, I write this having stepped down from headship in the summer of 2023. I know that having a break – time to reflect, time to read, time to connect and just time to be – has meant that I now feel more energised and ready to go back into the sector and continue to make a difference. The future of school leadership has got to be one where we recognise that the role of head teachers and leaders has changed. We have become the fourth emergency service, supporting our parents with housing, accessing healthcare, liaising with social services and much more, all of which is not sustainable.

Giving school leaders, specifically head teachers, a paid sabbatical every seven years (which feels like a natural cycle for schools) would go a long way towards recognising that the work they do requires time away from the coalface, and it could potentially help with the retention drain. I heard murmurs of a government strapline – recruitment, retention, return. However, it feels to me that the landscape has got to change if we are to entice teachers and leaders to return to a system they dearly love but has not adapted to the increased expectations and high-stakes accountability.

My ask is for the future of school leadership to be one where we have the agency to lead our schools, where there is significant investment in a system that is currently under immense pressure, and where we carve out some time and space to think about the substance of education. If we could do all this, we might get back to the situation in 2005 when Tim spoke about the retention crisis having passed.

References

Brighouse, T. (2005). *Choice and Equity in Teacher Supply*. London: Institute for Public Policy Research.

Commission on Teacher Retention (2023). *1970s Working Conditions in the 2020s: Modernising the Professional Lives of Teachers for the 21st Century*. London: Education Support and Public First. Available at: https://www.educationsupport.org.uk/media/bn2bk5a3/1970s-working-conditions-in-the-2020s.pdf.

Sharp, C. and Aston, K. (2024). *Ethnic Diversity in the Teaching Workforce: Evidence Review*. Slough: National Foundation for Educational Research. Available at: https://www.nfer.ac.uk/publications/ethnic-diversity-in-the-teaching-workforce-evidence-review.

Chapter 47

Technology in schools

Mark Grundy

Mark Grundy has been associated with Shireland Collegiate Academy for over 25 years, initially as principal and more recently as CEO of the trust. Over the years, Tim was a frequent visitor, looking at the use of technology to support school improvement and the innovations in curriculum delivery across the trust's primary and secondary schools.

Arriving at Shireland High School as head teacher in 1997, there was the typical profile of technology: a small number of BBC computers, a few personal computers and a pile of overhead projectors, basic photocopiers and the odd piece of recording equipment. This is not what I had been used to in my previous schools where we had used technology to level the playing field. So, the mission began to try and move Shireland into the next millennium. I had worked with a company called Systems Integrated Research who had developed an integrated learning system and had been part of a national trial involving their solution and a competitive one from the United States.

We had used an integrated learning system at Wodensborough High School to provide a study support wrapper, so that our students could learn before and after school and have a different level of support during lessons. I remember hosting Tim at Wodensborough and explaining to him the potential of the integrated learning system. He was particularly interested in the way that we could potentially change the dynamic in lessons and create a previously unavailable extra pair of 'digital hands' in the classroom. This has been one of the repeated focus areas in our deployment of technology at Shireland over the last three decades – how we can add capacity without adding complexity. Our mission in our use of technology has always been not to replace but to reduce the amount of pressure on staff. Our aim is to make world-class resources available to everyone irrespective of an individual student's context. I genuinely believe that technology could help with our desire to leave no child behind.

As we pushed towards the year 2000 and received, at times, some interesting reactions to our growing profile around the use of technology, we also attracted some interesting publicity. When Tim asked if Shireland could be his ninth Birmingham school at a national conference, I agreed. This would have been fine – if Shireland had been in Birmingham (it is actually based within Sandwell local authority)! The local elected members of Sandwell and the director of education weren't entirely happy with me moving Shireland four hundred metres across the border, but we took it as a massive compliment that Tim looked at what we were doing and felt that we represented his vision for what he wanted for young people.

Years passed and our growing use of technology became ever more sophisticated. By the early 2000s, Shireland was one of the few schools in the country trialling a Microsoft SharePoint environment, we had half of our teaching force developing content and a team of developers turning that into live resources for our youngsters to use not only in school but also at home. Home access had started! Asking staff to create storyboarded resources that would be reproduced digitally changed the level of scrutiny that was applied to the delivery of our curriculum. Staff had to think about intent, implementation and impact years ahead of the requirements of an Ofsted framework.

By the time we got to the latter part of the 2000s, our school-based company provided a learning platform for 130 schools up and down the country. We developed an architecture for school improvement using Microsoft's technology which has served us for over 20 years. My wife, Kirsty Grundy, led on the embedding of our learning platforms in the schools across Sandwell, and, to this day, school staff reminisce about how for once in their career they had something that allowed them to collaborate, communicate and coordinate their delivery of resources to the young people in their care.

Today, our schools use an architectural approach to technology that is based on a combination of SharePoint and Office 365. Our structural approach to technology differentiates us in lots of ways from so many of the other institutions that do equally wonderful things. The difference is that our use of technology has always been mundanely clever, not heroically focused. This evolution has meant that our staff look at how they can build a process around a technological helper, not determine a process by the purchase of technology. As we have continued to grow, we have inevitably broadened our technology solutions, looking at the increasing use of machine code-based solutions, artificial intelligence and solutions such as Century learning, which have found a place in our framework. Century has allowed numerous of our young people to access courses and resources that support the programmes they are studying, even allowing them to diversify their study. Our students and staff just assume that all schools have this technological backbone and that the processes and practice in other schools is similar. But that this were true.

As we move forward in the fragmented world of multi-academy trusts and skeletal local authorities, something needs to act as a glue. Our glue has always been, in part, our use of technology. Not only can technology give me an extra pair of hands in class, but it can also link schools together to reduce the replication of solutions and, most importantly, reduce the workload on staff. Our main focus, though, has always been to provide access to resources for our children to level the increasingly skewed playing field.

I had the enormous good fortune of working with Mick Waters and Tim Brighouse throughout my career, and we have remained friends for many years. I would like to think that is because we have continually strived to enable the young people in our care to have the roundest, richest and most effective experience. We have never shied away from doing something different if we feel that it can make a profound difference for our children and our staff. The principles that Tim relentlessly pursued, irrespective of where he was based, can be seen across all our schools. Tim taught me to be brave and not to take no for an answer, and I would like to think that those coaching tips have served all the young people and the staff in my care well for the last few decades.

Chapter 48

Including student perspectives on school effectiveness and improvement

John Hattie

John Hattie is emeritus laureate professor at the University of Melbourne and previously chair of the board of the Australian Institute for Teaching and School Leadership. Like Tim, he has worked within and outside government, been a critic and developer, and Tim and John have shared many conundrums about how to make a system work more effectively for educators and students.

Too often, 'school effectiveness' is seen from the educator's viewpoint. Robinson et al. (2008), for example, identified five major indicators of effective schools on student achievement: leaders promoting and participating in teacher learning and development (d = 0.91); planning, coordinating and evaluating teaching and the curriculum (d = 0.74); strategic resourcing (d = 0.60); establishing goals and expectations (d = 0.54); and ensuring an orderly and supportive environment, such as protecting time for teaching and learning by reducing external pressures and interruptions and establishing an orderly and supportive environment both inside and outside classrooms (d = 0.49). 'The more leaders focus their influence, their learning, and their relationships with teachers on the core business of teaching and learning, the greater their likely influence on student outcomes' (Robinson, 2007: 15). We know so much about school effectiveness and improvement that such findings have been replicated many times.

So many of these claims, however, are based on a limited notion of effectiveness – achievement scores are usually measured by scores from tests. There is an overwhelming current imperative to 'increase achievement'. This presupposes a black box model of teachers adopting the most impactful methods leading to higher test scores – and the students become the problem, the fodder or the exchangeable unit in the middle.

Imagine if we asked the question about schools' effectiveness and included the students' viewpoint. There have been a few studies that have asked about school effectiveness from the students' point of view. Gentilucci (2004: 136) concluded that 'Much to the chagrin of those who blame poor learning on students' general disinterest in all things academic, this study found that elementary students are genuinely inter-ested in learning.' Although nearly all students in his sample thought learning was important, 91% reported that their schools were not chal-lenging, 74% noted teacher misbehavior (being angry, embarrassing them, not caring), 72% did not like the overuse of cooperative learning, 72% said they felt frustrated and 82% claimed they were bored, and 72% noted that inadequate instruction frequently hindered their learn-ing (teachers talk too much, didn't explain things well, were not strict enough with those who disrupted lessons).

Egeberg and McConney (2018) found that students argued that 'good' teachers establish caring relationships with students, ensure they hear the students' voices, exercise authority without being rigid (i.e. they main-tain control and order), challenge students to learn more and better, and made learning fun.

More recently, the Organisation for Economic Co-operation and Development (OECD, 2024) noted that across member countries, almost 40% of students reported that, in most lessons, the teacher did not show an interest in every student's learning or did not continue to teach until students understood the material.

A robust debate is needed about collecting evidence about students' per-ceptions of the quality of their learning: their sense of whether the class and school are inviting them to learn; their enjoyment of the challenges of learning; and asking them to elaborate on their learning strategies, especially their skills at error management, whether it is safe to not know, make errors and learn from mistakes. Such indicators could supplement the usual educator concepts of school effectiveness and may lead to different conceptions of what it means to be a great school.

The challenge is to consider the effectiveness of schools from the viewpoint of both the educators (how to maximise their impact on the learning lives of students) and the students (how to teach them to become the drivers of their learning and become their own teachers). This would lead to much more than the current over-focus on achievement, and it would necessarily involve indicators of the climate and culture from the students' perspectives relating to whether they feel invited to come and learn, their sense of belonging and engagement to drive their learning, and their opportunities to learn.

The current focus on the educator's perspective has led to the current mantra of words such as 'autonomy', 'choice', 'diversity' and 'accountability', as though they are uncontested and mutually reconcilable desirables (see Brighouse and Waters, 2022: 19). In addition, there has emerged a massive 'labelling' of children so that funding follows them, and the emergence of the appalling notion that certain groups of the population are 'underachieving' (as if all these students are underachieving and that teachers continue to be ineffective with many of these students). The Australian Government Productivity Commission (2022: 104) noted that more than 50% of underperforming students do not belong to any of the proclaimed 'equity groups', and 85% of students in the priority equity cohorts achieve at or above national minimum standards.

We may need new terms – such as challenge, learning, engagement, inviting, fun and exciting – to force central government to reconsider its excessive role in determining what happens in schools. As Brighouse and Waters (2022: 529) noted, prior to 1988, the secretary of state for England had only three powers (the removal of wartime air-raid shelters from school playing fields and playgrounds, the determination of the numbers in teacher training and where they would be taught, and the approval of the opening and closure of schools and the size of the school building programme), but now the powers are measured in the thousands.

In the United States, it was the first Bush who proclaimed national outcomes for schools. Previously, local districts had more say over the nature, climate and outcomes of schooling. Brighouse (2011) noted how such centralism in education is inherently unhealthy, induces a sense of powerlessness (which is the enemy of democracy and undermines teachers' professionalism), and that it is beyond the competence of central government to manage schools effectively – especially when the perspective of students is excluded other than their scores on achievement tests.

This massive centralisation of accountability has happened over the past 20 to 30 years, and while power taken is hard to retrieve, there must be hope. It is possible to cite many examples of local excellence, from the London Challenge to the many where all students are making more than a year's growth for a year's input. The argument is that accountability needs to become a broad basket of goods, including progress to achievement, the invitational nature of the school and the extent to which students can learn alone and with peers. Along with the usual indicators of school effectiveness from the educator's perspective, there is an imperative to add indicators from the students' perspective.

References

Australian Government Productivity Commission (2022). *Review of the National School Reform Agreement: Study Report*. Available at: https://www.pc.gov.au/inquiries/completed/school-agreement/report.

Brighouse, T. (2011). Decline and Fall: Are State Schools and Universities on the Point of Collapse? Lecture at Oxford Education Society, 16 September.

Brighouse, T. and Waters, M. (2022). *About Our Schools: Improving on Previous Best*. Carmarthen: Crown House Publishing.

Egeberg, H. and McConney, A. (2018). What Do Students Believe About Effective Classroom Management? A Mixed-Methods Investigation in Western Australian High Schools. *Australian Educational Researcher*, 45(2), 195–216.

Gentilucci, J. L. (2004). Improving School Learning: The Student Perspective. *The Educational Forum*, 68(2), 133–143.

Organisation for Economic Co-operation and Development (OECD) (2024). *PISA 2022 Results (Volume I): The State of Learning and Equity in Education*. Paris: OECD Publishing.

Robinson, V. (2007). The Impact of Leadership on Student Outcomes: Making Sense of the Evidence. Paper presented at The Leadership Challenge: Improving Learning in Schools conference, Melbourne, 12–14 August. Available at: https://research.acer.edu.au/research_conference_2007/5.

Robinson, V. M., Lloyd, C. A. a⁻d Rowe, K. J. (2008). The Impact of Leadership on Student Outcomes: An Analysis of the Differential Effects of Leadership Types. *Educational Administration Quarterly*, 44(5), 635–674.

Chapter 49
More human in an AI world

Jim Knight

Jim Knight chairs the boards of E-Act Multi-Academy Trust, the Council of British International Schools, Century-Tech and Educate Ventures Research. He worked with Tim as schools minister before serving as employment minister in the cabinet and joining the Lords in 2010. His continued work in education included regular discussions with Tim.

School leaders are facing several urgent challenges, all of which make it harder for schools to be the human places that Tim Brighouse knew they need to be. Recruitment and retention, Ofsted, funding, staff and pupil well-being, the state of the buildings and attendance are all priorities, so what room is there to think about technology? More profoundly, how can technology help school leaders to lead better and more human schools?

Whilst edtech has struggled to deliver a return on the investment, I believe that artificial intelligence (AI) will be very different. In his book, *The Coming Wave*, Mustafa Suleyman (2023) persuasively sets out how AI will quickly become a general-purpose technology that will be so widely adopted that we will no longer notice it, like the smartphones everyone is glued to on the Tube. It will alter how everyone lives and works – including teachers and learners.

Like any other technology, there are choices about how to use these new tools. There are valid fears that this technology will replace teachers for all but the richest; for everyone else, the big tech platforms will deliver online instruction and assessment in isolation, whilst sucking up children's data to train ever more profitable algorithmic machines.

This is a real danger.

We could react by trying to ban AI from schools, or we could make it work for the good of teachers and learners. We can choose to adopt this technology in the service of teachers.

The recruitment and retention of teachers is possibly the biggest challenge facing our education system. We spend a lot of money on controlling and de-professionalising teachers. The cost of distrust is huge and could be re-prioritised towards supporting teachers. This, in turn, means giving teachers more control over technology and how it is used in their classrooms. That requires training them to understand AI, giving them an appreciation of the opportunities and threats, making them aware of what tools are out there and allowing them to adopt them in their context.

The context is changing fast. Teachers need to be freed up to respond and, in doing so, to redefine the job of being a teacher.

Work will change as many language-based tasks get replaced by generative AI. Some jobs will disappear and new ones will emerge. Adults will need the resilience to change careers multiple times by being good at self-directed learning and by having the core skills of critical thinking, creativity, collaboration and emotional intelligence.

Humans will out-compete intelligent machines by being more human. We therefore need teachers to be able to develop people to think outside the box, to care for each other and the planet, and to be wonderfully unpredictable.

This is what we now need schools to deliver for young people. It needs a new curriculum, new pedagogy and new assessment.

Knowledge acquisition will remain vital for intellectual development. Literacy, numeracy and oracy will always be core skills. We already are good at teaching these things, but we might choose to use adaptive instructional learning platforms to teach some of the knowledge at home to free up time for more human, social learning at school.

Problem-based learning has felt much harder to teach and to relate back to the curriculum. What if AI could help? What if it could analyse the content of the learning in a project and map it back to the curriculum for you? What if it offered suggestions of other problems that similar learners had tackled that covered foundational aspects of the curriculum that learners might want to do next? Would that make teaching in this way more possible, more interesting and more engaging for the learner?

Under appropriate ethical constraints, machine learning could then start to learn more about you as a teacher and your learners. It could spot when children are struggling early on, identify what is engaging individuals and what is turning them off.

The technology already exists to give teachers feedback on their lessons. This should be in the control of the teacher, not managers, but it can allow for continuous coaching and improvement if the teacher wants that. Teachers can then feel the intrinsic benefit of more engaged pupils sharing their passion for learning.

The other great possibility is in assessment. AI has the potential to be used to assess individuals' contributions to group work by quickly learning to recognise the different voices and faces in a conversation. Assessment by observation is subjective and expensive, but this too could become more feasible by AI transcribing and analysing performance to improve the productivity and objectivity of expert assessors.

In turn, portfolios for employers and university admissions are now on the horizon. Qualifications are a blunt instrument and are often too slow to adapt to a dynamic future. However, new tools could easily crawl through the content of qualifications and other micro credentials an individual has acquired in their portfolio to present a much richer insight into the potential of a candidate.

This can also feel like an overwhelming amount of change for an already overburdened profession. It is therefore crucial that teachers are empowered to use technology to change their own jobs. It will be possible for teachers to work flexibly, potentially work from home and certainly work part time if they want to do so. Work–life balance is within reach.

These are possibilities that could happen very quickly. There is much more that I cannot conceive of yet or haven't heard about. But I can get excited and hopeful for this future.

Imagine that we embrace the possibility of learning anywhere and everywhere using technology, and then coming into school for the human exchange that brings that learning to life. School then nurtures in us the joy of learning from and with each other, led by properly supported teachers. I would vote for that!

References

Suleyman, M. with Bhaskar, M. (2023). *The Coming Wave: AI, Power and the 21st Century's Greatest Dilemma*. London: Viking.

Chapter 50

The powerful perspective of data in education

Laura McInerney

Laura McInerney is the CEO of Teacher Tapp, a daily survey of over 10,000 teachers. As a former journalist for *Schools Week* and the *Guardian*, Laura had the pleasure of interviewing Tim Brighouse on several occasions and chaired a set of events alongside him at the Education Festival in 2023.

Let me tell you a story about the power of education data. Only 59% of teachers intend to stay in the profession for longer than three years (Teacher Tapp, 2023).

Wait. That's not a story! Let me try again ...

Meet Jane – an experienced classroom teacher in England. On any given school day, her life follows a familiar rhythm: wake at 5.30am, commute to arrive by 7am, teach five lessons, break duties, mentor colleagues over lunch while prepping for afternoon classes. After the students leave at 3.15pm, she has meetings until 4.15pm and then tackles the influx of emails – safeguarding, behaviour issues, upset parents.

Around 5pm, Jane finally heads home, battling traffic before summoning enough energy to be present with her family over dinner. But the workday isn't done. At 8pm, she joins legions of teachers marking books in front of the TV, often until bedtime. Rinse and repeat. Weekends offer little relief, with time spent planning upcoming lessons and catching up on emails.

Finally, one afternoon, a researcher asks if Jane still intends to teach in three years' time. She pauses, considering the grind ... then taps 'Disagree'. And just like that, a statistic is born.

Reading this tale one might think the moral is that data is impersonal while a full story is compelling. But stories are single anecdotes. Jane's day doesn't tell us what is happening everywhere, which means it can be written off as unique.

Luckily, after seven years of working on Teacher Tapp, a daily survey of over ten thousand teachers, I can confidently say that Jane's day is normal. Most teachers *do* wake pre-dawn and log 10+ hour days. They juggle multiple weekly duties and meetings. And, yes, around 40% are marking every evening.

When I recount these findings, some teachers tear up. Hearing their reality mirrored is powerful validation. In that recognition they also often see breathing room. Must books be marked nightly? Can meetings be streamlined? Is arriving at 7am truly essential? There are many teachers who don't do these things and yet are excited about their work. Who are they, and what can we learn from them?

Our data echoes much of what I have learned about how data can be used overall to ensure better outcomes for everyone in education – students and teachers. Specifically, that it can (1) identify core issues (and potential solutions), (2) pinpoint solutions to fit a specific context and (3) facilitate more productive disagreements.

I. Identify core issues (and potential solutions)

Sometimes, we only spot problems when digging into the data. Take John Snow, the physician who traced London's 1854 cholera outbreak to a contaminated water pump on Broad Street using meticulous case-mapping. Removing the pump handle swiftly halted the epidemic. Data made the invisible threat visible (London School of Hygiene and Tropical Medicine, 2019).

A century later, data exposed hidden inequities in access to education. Post-war assessments of young men entering National Service revealed top-scoring working-class teens were seven times less likely to have O levels compared to their equally intelligent middle-class peers. This shocking statistic, published in the *Half Our Future* report (Newsom, 1963), galvanised politicians to push for comprehensive schooling until age 16.

Data also tackles smaller problems. One school I worked with analysed playground incident data and identified that fights frequently started over football-sharing. Leadership implemented a 'school football only' policy, with rules around who could play, drastically reducing conflicts. Not as world-changing as John Snow's discovery, but not a small thing for the children involved.

2. Pinpoint solutions to fit a specific context

Even if this book wasn't in his honour, it would be right to mention that education data had few advocates more enthusiastic than Tim Brighouse.

During his work in Birmingham in the 1990s, Tim encountered resistance when encouraging school leaders to learn from others. He would point to brilliant work in one school, only for a head teacher to say, 'That won't work here, we're different to them.'

Unconvinced, Tim was pleased to meet John Hill, a statistician who developed a model for grouping schools based on student demographics. Tim explained the power of this approach: 'What was different about what came to be called "family of schools" data sets, was that the schools could see each other's data in full detail so that they could visit and try to understand why some schools' practices differed so much' (Brighouse, 2013).

By making data transparent among similar schools, leaders could identify solutions tailored to their specific needs – and be less sniffy about the idea that it might work in their school too.

3. Facilitate more productive disagreements

In 2018, US President Barack Obama highlighted the importance of facts in fostering cooperation: 'Without facts, there is no basis for cooperation. If I say this is a podium and you say this is an elephant, it's going to be hard for us to cooperate.' This principle holds true in education too, where data can provide common ground for navigating complex debates.

Take teacher retention, for instance. Unions frequently sound the alarm about disgruntled teachers leaving the profession, but they do this every year. Others argue that it isn't a major concern as long as new recruits keep filling the gaps, which they always have. Who is right?

As I mentioned earlier, at Teacher Tapp, we have been surveying teachers for years about their plans to remain in the classroom. We ask the same questions, at the same time of year, to a similar group. In recent years, the percentage who say they intend to stay for at least three more years has fallen steadily from around 77% to just 59%. The data clearly show a troubling and new trend.

This isn't a matter of opinion: the numbers paint an objective picture of a growing decline in commitment to the job. To dismiss it by saying that new recruits will cover the gap, we would need evidence that more people are applying to be teachers. (They aren't.) The data is, therefore, an agreed-upon basis to show a problem and nudge everyone towards collaborating on solutions.

A conclusion

I will end by noting that quantitative evidence can be manipulated polit-ically, as the Department for Education's multiple warnings from the UK Statistics Authority remind us (Whittaker, 2022).

But, when combined with judgement and nuance, it empowers teachers, leaders, policymakers and the public to engage in more honest, constructive dialogue about the issues that matter most. And while it may not always point to a single 'right' answer, it can bridge ideological divides and foster collaborative problem-solving.

In a field as complex as education, that may be our best hope.

References

Brighouse, T. (2013). How Data Can Bring Schools Together. *The Guardian* (10 July). Available at: https://www.theguardian.com/teacher-network/teacher-blog/2013/jul/10/data-collaboration-school-families.

London School of Hygiene and Tropical Medicine (2019). John Snow Memorial Pump Marking Historic Cholera Outbreak Reinstalled in its Original Location (20 July). Available at: https://www.lshtm.ac.uk/newsevents/news/2019/john-snow-memorial-pump-marking-historic-cholera-outbreak-reinstalled-its.

Newsom, J. (chair) (1963). *Half Our Future: A Report of the Central Advisory Council for Education (England)* [Newsom Report]. London: Her Majesty's Stationery Office. Available at: https://www.education-uk.org/documents/newsom/newsom1963.html.

Obama, B. (2018). Transcript: Obama's Speech at the 2018 Nelson Mandela Annual Lecture. *NPR* (17 July). Available at: https://www.npr.org/2018/07/17/629862434/transcript-obamas-speech-at-the-2018-nelson-mandela-annual-lecture.

Teacher Tapp (2023). What Would Make You Stay in Teaching? (14 November). Available at: https://teachertapp.co.uk/articles/what-would-make-you-stay-in-teaching.

Whittaker, F. (2022). DfE to Correct Academy Claims After Stats Watchdog Slapdown. *Schools Week* (18 May). Available at: https://schoolsweek.co.uk/dfe-to-correct-academy-claims-after-stats-watchdog-slapdown.

Chapter 51

Leadership and life lessons from Tim Brighouse

Niall McWilliams

Niall was formally the head teacher of the Oxford Academy, a school well known to Tim. Niall first met Tim when he arrived in Oxford to teach in the early 1990s. He continuously sought his advice throughout his numerous headships and leadership roles, including the managing director role that Niall held at Oxford United.

In the spring of 1991, my life in education changed. I walked into a lecture without any expectations, and I walked out with a clear educational direction, my aspirations raised, determined to be a head teacher, for no other reason than I believed a head teacher could make the most significant positive impact on students. I still believe that.

I had just started at the Cherwell School, a large upper school in North Oxford, and was encouraged by my then head teacher, Martin Roberts, to attend a lecture given by Tim at the University of Oxford. Martin thought I might enjoy it, and it would probably be 'worthwhile' and 'enjoyable'. As it turned out, from my perspective, it was much more.

Although Tim had recently left his position as chief education officer in Oxfordshire to move to Keele he was returning to give a lecture to serving and trainee teachers. Even though I was early in my teaching career, I had already sat through many education talks from which I had instantly disengaged, so consequently I arrived without presumptions. Within minutes of Tim starting to speak, I was mesmerised and engaged. Mesmerised by Tim's sheer energy, including flailing arms, charisma, (clearly old) corduroy jacket and enthusiasm for life. Engaged by his humility, intelligence, passion for education and his intense interest in sport, including cricket and

Oxford United. This was pre-Ofsted, but Tim talked about the importance of supportive accountability and how 'poverty of aspiration' was a significant barrier to educational success.

From then on, I tracked Tim's career as he moved from Keele to Birmingham to London. I did not have time to catch up with him personally until I took on a new headship in West Oxfordshire where, unbeknown to me, Tim's grandson was a student.

It was my habit to be on duty in the morning to welcome the students. On this particular day, as the heavens opened, a car pulled up and the driver (Tim) rolled down the window and said to those of us on duty, 'You're doing very well.' I immediately felt energised. The fact that he had taken the time to compliment and thank us genuinely made a difference to our day and outlook. Tim then became a regular member of that team, standing with us, welcoming our students and talking to staff. He clearly loved being with people and being in and around schools.

I was able to call on Tim's advice and guidance for the next 16 years of my career as I moved to new challenges at the Oxford Academy, which Tim's children had attended years before. The school was back in challenging circumstances, despite the good work of committed staff, trustees and governors. At my request, Tim became a regular visitor to the school, often joining us on duty. He knew the area well: he was a governor at a primary on the same estate and he remained committed to local schools.

Tim knew that the pressure of Ofsted meant we had to improve rapidly and ensure the improvements were sustainable. We were able to call on his contacts and expertise from Birmingham, London and beyond to seek help and guidance from schools and school leaders who had been in similar situations. We learnt from them by continually looking outward. However, Tim was always keen that we continue to build on the good and often outstanding practice that already existed in the school.

I then made a remarkable career switch and became managing director at Oxford United, a football club close to Tim's heart. He was a longstanding season ticket-holder, sitting behind the technical areas enjoying the game and, perhaps, just as importantly, the real-life drama of the managers, coaches and fourth officials. I still sought his advice. Unsurprisingly, many of the principles that apply to successful schools also apply to successful football clubs. Tim was among the first people I talked to following our play-off final defeat at Wembley. I knew he would put the game into perspective; he didn't let me down, emphasising the positives and the ability to build on our success.

This book focuses on Tim's contribution to education and to him being the 'last of a kind'. I hope that isn't true, and that there are leaders out there who are prepared to find 'gaps in hedges' and go through them, who are prepared to make difficult decisions, to take communities with them and to positively influence future generations.

I am forever grateful that I spent so much time with Tim. I could write reams about his anecdotes, conversations, theories and musings. However, I thought it may be of interest to list the leadership tips that I took from Tim and use to this day:

● As a teacher 'you make the weather' – your influence makes the day good or challenging for students. As a school leader, or a leader in any organisation, this phrase is even more pertinent; the culture and cohesion you create determines whether that organisation thrives or not. Tim was an exceptional system leader, but he knew the importance of individual people within the system.

● Make the complex simple; never an easy concept but an important one. Clearly, Tim spent hours thinking about this. My belief remains that the most impactful improvement plans and processes are the simple ones.

● Partnership working is essential; and, within that, allow staff time to talk.

● Crisis management is the norm within educational leadership, so any leader needs to have unwarranted optimism to thrive.

● Listening is often more effective than talking.

● Look outwards, but never forget the good practice in your own organisation. Avoid initiative overload.

● Be high profile, build relationships and leave your ego at the door.

Much of this is outlined in what I believe is the best educational book ever written, *Essential Pieces: The Jigsaw of a Successful School* (2006), which was authored, of course, by Tim.

I think there will always be unfinished business in education – certainly for Tim. He would always be striving to improve on previous best. We must do the same.

References

Brighouse, T. (2006). *Essential Pieces: The Jigsaw of a Successful School.* Abingdon: RM.

Chapter 52

Professionalism and ethical leadership

Alison Peacock

Dame Alison Peacock is chief executive of the Chartered College of Teaching. Her career spans secondary, primary and early years education. She is a lifelong teacher committed to the inclusive values of 'learning without limits'. Alison is grateful that Sir Tim Brighouse was a great supporter of the Chartered College and thoroughly embraced the philosophy of reducing practices that label children.

The future of teaching must be underpinned by a collective understanding and endorsement of what it means to be viewed as a professional and to lead ethically.

Nature abhors a vacuum. In the absence of agreed pedagogical, curriculum design and assessment purpose in England, powerful political ideology thrives. There are many current issues to address. A review of curriculum and assessment is needed to ensure that all children are given the chance to follow a rich, meaningful path through school – a path that offers choice, celebrates a broad range of successes and extends beyond formal education into lifelong opportunity. With regard to pedagogy, there is a belief amongst some that centralised lesson planning is necessary in the name of reducing teacher workload. There is a world of difference, however, between the provision of a resourced scheme of work offering curriculum coherence and the blanket interpretation that all teachers must teach in the same way at the same time using identical resources. There is a danger that this latter approach erodes professional judgement, valuing compliance over charismatic, responsive teaching. As a profession, it is vital that we seek to balance these trends.

The Chartered College of Teaching is chairing a new Ethical Leadership Association that comprises representatives from teaching unions plus other membership bodies in England. The work of this group, with reference to the Committee on Standards in Public Life, will be to develop training related to the Framework for Ethical Leadership in Education (Association of School and College Leaders, 2019), to explore definitions of professionalism and to exemplify the Department for Education's (2011) Teachers' Standards (Part 2). This is not work that has been commissioned by the Department for Education; rather, it is work that the profession needs when making decisions that may be considered to have ethical impact. These dilemmas are faced by teachers and leaders in many areas of their work. The advent of a professional body, owned and governed by teacher members, offers, at last, the chance to provide guidance and advice to ministers, to ensure that 'evidence' combines with virtues and values.

The Chartered College of Teaching has its origins in the College of Preceptors, which was granted a Royal Charter in 1879. The latest iteration of the college, with supplemental charter, opened for membership in 2017. As a not-for-profit charitable professional body with ever increasing membership across schools and colleges, our core mission is encapsulated thus: *Empowering a knowledgeable and respected teaching profession through membership and accreditation.*

This is an essential aim if we are to maintain, sustain and grow a profession to which colleagues are proud to belong. Parents are often very keen to place trust in their local school, and it is the professionalism and compassion of colleagues who work within those schools that make all the difference. The micro-community embodied by each school is greatly enhanced when staffed with energetic, knowledgeable colleagues who are fuelled with intellectual curiosity and a passion to teach as effectively as possible. It is vital that we rediscover the joy of teaching as part of our national discourse, recognising the contribution that every school and college makes to children and their families.

As a professional membership body, the college has established rigorous accreditation standards against three core areas of defined professionalism: professional knowledge, professional practice and professional principles. Chartered study is not informed by models of compliance but by opportunities for qualified teachers to extend their repertoire of evidence-informed practice. Chartered teachers are required to maintain evidence of their exemplary practice throughout their career. This route is increasingly understood as being highly prestigious, and is aimed at developing highly influential thinkers within each school and college setting.

As a community, chartered teachers will be agents of change and less likely to accept ill-informed policy. Imagine the power and promise of enhanced collaboration through expert thinkers and trusted communities of schools and colleges. Colleagues inspired towards improvement, not through fear of pernicious accountability, but by a restless professional desire to support equitable improvement for all. If we were to harness the energy that currently goes into inspection preparation into a collective endeavour that aims for excellence in curriculum design, pedagogy and assessment practice, our profession could justifiably be proud of its transformation.

It is our contention that a member-led college could be the engine that enables this, providing a conduit for practice-informed theory. Increasingly, schools and colleges are appointing 'research champions' to work with their school to gain Institutional Member Status. Others are becoming part of a network of schools seeking Research Mark accreditation. Intellectual curiosity about not only 'what works' but also 'what might work' leads a drive towards engagement with sustained ethical study of classroom practice.

As a charity, the college is run by its members and is governed by a council elected from the membership. The college seeks to respect a plurality of voices, presenting articles, research summaries and opinion pieces that enable teachers as professionals to determine what they believe will work best for their children, their schools and their community. We are much more aligned as a profession than we are divided, and although professional debate will always rage, the truth is that as teachers we are united in wanting to find optimal ways of helping our students to succeed. The college is apolitical – rising above the political fray – whilst, nevertheless, brokering opportunities for consultation and informed debate. We are building a trusted group of professionals who are interested in the development of evidence-informed practice inspired by ethical leadership.

Teaching is a public service. If our professional body were to be designated a Royal College, this would be a source of great pride, giving recognition that the work of teachers as professionals is appreciated at the highest level. The collective sense of belonging and pride that a Royal College would contribute, both within and beyond the profession, has the potential to make a huge difference to the perception of what it means to become and remain a teacher.

As a professional body, the college will always advocate for teachers and leaders to engage in the highest quality professional learning. We are not a union, and although we work alongside our union colleagues, it is not our role to advocate for improved pay and conditions. We are confident, however, that the most effective education system will always require deep, sustained and generous investment if all our children are to thrive. The most important resource any child has access to is an empowered, knowledgeable and respected teacher.

As a Fellow of the Chartered College of Teaching, Sir Tim Brighouse was an avid supporter who understood why working in a collegiate and supportive way is foundational to teacher efficacy. What better tribute to his beliefs than building a universal and flourishing Royal College of Teaching that protects the profession from political ideology, ensuring that schools and colleges are staffed with trusted, inspired colleagues who are proud to teach.

References

Department for Education (2011). Teachers' Standards (updated 2021). Available at: https://www.gov.uk/government/publications/teachers-standards.

Association of School and College Leaders (2019). Framework for Ethical Leadership in Education. Available at: https://www.ascl.org.uk/ASCL/media/ASCL/Our%20view/Campaigns/Framework-for-Ethical-Leadership-in-Education.pdf.

Chapter 53

Education's AI transformation

Priya Lakhani

Priya Lakhani has deeply admired Tim's work for many years while building Century Tech. She was privileged to be on the National Teaching Awards board that honoured Tim with its inaugural Award for Lifetime Achievement, recognising his remarkable contribution to education.

Imagine a world where artificial intelligence (AI) doesn't just live in our phones or drive our cars but lives in the hallways of our schools, sits next to students at their desks and helps to mark their homework or blend their phonemes. It sounds like a scene from a science fiction novel, yet here we are, on the brink of a revolution that could change education as we know it.

Chatbots and machine learning algorithms have already begun to weave their magic across all sectors, from helping radiologists to detect tumours to revolutionising how businesses interact with customers. It is inevitable that their influence will extend into classrooms and lecture theatres, transforming the way knowledge is imparted and absorbed. But, like any tool, the impact of AI is contingent upon how we wield it, whether we take advantage of the opportunities it presents and how we safeguard against the risks.

The AI-powered personalisation of learning already exists in thousands of classrooms today. AI interactions augment traditional teaching methods and the classroom experience. Lessons and learning pathways are tailored not just to the class but to each individual student, considering their gaps in knowledge and skills, pace of learning and interests. A personalised learning experience has the power to make learning more engaging and more relevant in the moment to the learner.

This also helps to solve undoubtedly one of the biggest problems in education. Eighty per cent of teachers have contemplated leaving the profession, overwhelmed by their workload. On average, they clock in 50 hours a week, with a quarter of them pushing to 60 hours (Scott and Rogers, 2023). Despite these long hours, less than half of their time is dedicated to what they signed up for: teaching. The majority of their hours are buried under an avalanche of marking and lesson planning.

The AI driving the personalisation of learning for the student also, crucially, empowers our teachers. Classical AI platforms work by collecting and analysing vast amounts of data (billions of data points). The same technology offers the teacher instant insights to make timely, targeted interventions without the need to spend so much time marking. By automating administrative tasks and offering insights into student learning patterns, AI can free up teachers to spend more time on what they do best: teaching, inspiring, mentoring and connecting with their students on a personal level.

However, there is a pressing challenge ahead. In many parts of the world, access to quality education remains a significant challenge. We must ensure that these transformative tools – from personalised learning pathways and resources to 24/7 virtual tutors – are accessible to every child, preventing the emergence of an 'AI divide' in education. In doing so, AI can help us to democratise education, offering high-quality, personalised learning experiences to students regardless of their geographical or socio-economic status.

Preparation for life with AI also extends beyond the technical. What about silicon brains outsmarting human ones in an age of living with AI, or Elon Musk's claim that no human will need to work in future (Taylor, 2023)? Will teachers be relegated to the role of mere bystanders in their own classrooms? Education has always been about more than academic achievement. It is also about nurturing well-rounded individuals who are equipped to contribute meaningfully to society.

In an age where all of us are living with, working with or building AI, our bloated curriculum and assessment system, which is designed to result in a third of students failing, needs a rethink. An education system that prioritises memorisation strategies and rote learning is setting students up for future failure. Sadly, when it comes to superior memory capacity, humans cannot out-compete technology and AI. The modern workplace will prioritise increasing productivity and efficiencies through AI automation and augmentation, and demand human-centric cognitive skills and the cultivation of soft skills. As underscored by many reports (e.g. Iliadis, 2018; World Economic Forum, 2023), skills such as critical thinking, analytical reasoning and creative thinking, along with resilience, flexibility, agility and self-awareness, stand out as the most sought after. Our passionate educators need to be able to spend more time inspiring curiosity, encouraging deeper analysis and supporting ethical reasoning in an ever-changing world, fostering the social, emotional and ethical development of their students.

Our students are also growing up in a world where AI-driven algorithms cater to their preferences to keep them hooked and AI bots generate vast amounts of convincing information and media. While this abundance of knowledge undoubtedly empowers and enriches our lives in many ways, misinformation is rampant. There are now countless examples where we struggle to discern the truth amid the noise, which, if left unchecked and unprepared for, could result in deepening polarisation within our societies. The fourth industrial revolution curriculum must also ensure that students are armed with the ability to differentiate between fact and fiction, evaluate the credibility and reliability of information sources, and understand the implications of AI-driven technologies on trust.

Mick Waters (see Chapter 10) describes good schools as 'human places: exploiting every moment for learning, warm in every crevice and celebrating learning for every person'. AI may change the way we teach but not the reasons why we teach. The risk of dehumanising education cannot be ignored. As we integrate AI into our classrooms, we must ensure that it serves to augment rather than replace the irreplaceable human elements of education – the unique moments of connection, warmth, true empathy and understanding that only a teacher and a peer group can provide.

So, what is the game plan to achieve a future where personalised learning paths light the way for every student, where tech-savvy teachers are free to ignite sparks of curiosity and creativity, where every educational institution instils a culture of lifelong learning and the agility to embrace continuing technological advancement, and where education truly is the great equaliser? While there are understandable apprehensions about bias, privacy and over-reliance on AI, they should not lead us to boycott AI, any more than the advent of the calculator made us abandon teaching arithmetic.

Schools must become arenas of proactive change, preparing the ground for AI's integration into the educational fabric. AI integration will be disruptive, so schools must get out ahead of the curve by auditing current practices, identifying opportunities for AI augmentation and making a holistic transformation strategy. This journey requires leadership, vision and a community of educators and technologists marching in lockstep towards a shared goal. Yes, this means tech upgrades, but, crucially, a cultural shift towards embracing the new while developing on previous best.

References

Iliadis, N. (2018). *Learning to Learn: The Future-Proof Skill.* London: Big Innovation Centre, All-Party Parliamentary Group on AI and KPMG. Available at: https://assets.kpmg.com/content/dam/kpmg/uk/pdf/2018/10/learning-to-learn_report.pdf.

Scott, J. and Rogers, A. (2023). Teachers Working 60 Hour Weeks 'Being Driven Out of the Profession', Leaked Report Says. *Sky News* (31 March). Available at: https://news.sky.com/story/teachers-working-60-hour-weeks-being-driven-out-of-the-profession-leaked-report-says-12846562.

Taylor, C. (2023). Elon Musk Says AI Will Create a Future Where 'No Job is Needed': 'The AI Will Be Able To Do Everything'. *Fortune* (3 November). Available at: https://fortune.com/2023/11/03/elon-musk-ai-no-job-needed-work.

World Economic Forum (2023). *Future of Jobs Report 2023. Insight Report* (May). Geneva: World Economic Forum. Available at: https://www.weforum.org/publications/the-future-of-jobs-report-2023.

Inclusion, equity and diversity

Chapter 54

Taking an inclusive turn

Mel Ainscow

Mel Ainscow is emeritus professor, University of Manchester, professor of education, University of Glasgow and adjunct professor, Queensland University of Technology. He is internationally recognised as an authority on the promotion of inclusion and equity in education. Mel worked with Tim Brighouse on City Challenge in London and Greater Manchester.

Tim Brighouse was a source of inspiration to me over many years, as he was to many others. I frequently turned to him for advice, and his responses were always helpful, stimulating and challenging.

A concern that Tim and I shared is the need to make education systems inclusive. Whilst recent years have seen an increased interest in this idea, the field remains confused as to what it implies. Indeed, I recall hearing the Australian academic Roger Slee comment that it has travelled so much that it has become 'jet-lagged'.

An inclusive turn

In many countries, inclusive education is still thought of as an approach to serving children with disabilities within general education settings. Internationally, however, it is increasingly seen more broadly as a reform that supports and welcomes diversity amongst all learners (UNESCO, 2020). As such, it presumes that the aim is to eliminate exclusion that is a consequence of attitudes and responses to diversity in race, social class, ethnicity, religion, gender and capabilities.

Traditionally, the main response to difficulties experienced by learners has been through forms of special education. In recent years, this field has gone through a crisis of thinking about its guiding assumptions. As a result, the appropriateness of separate systems of education has been challenged, both from a human rights perspective and from the point of view of effectiveness.

More specifically, it is argued that the continued use of what is sometimes referred to as a 'medical model' of assessment – within which educational difficulties are explained in terms of a child's deficits – prevents progress in the field, not least because it distracts attention from questions about why schools fail to teach so many children successfully.

With this agenda as my overall focus, I have argued that what is needed is an 'inclusive turn' (Ainscow, 2024). This involves those within a par-ticular context working together to address barriers experienced by some learners. This is a radical approach to the way that we define and address difficulties in education. Furthermore, it is a change that is difficult to introduce, not least because the traditional perspectives and practices associated with special education continue to dominate thinking in the field, encouraged by what Sally Tomlinson (2012: 267) refers to as 'an expanded and expensive SEN industry'.

International developments

Over recent years, some countries have made great strides in terms of inclusive education. For example:

● For more than 30 years, New Brunswick in Canada has pioneered the concept of inclusive education through legislation, local authority policies and professional guidelines.

● The Italian government passed a law in 1977 that closed all special schools, units and other non-inclusive forms of provision. This legislation is still in force, and more recent amendments have further strengthened the inclusive nature of the education system.

● Having enacted legislation making disability discrimination within education unlawful, Portugal has gone much further in enacting an explicit legal framework for the inclusion of all students with and without disabilities in education.

- The success of Finland, a country that regularly outperforms most other countries in terms of educational outcomes, is partly explained by the progress of the lowest performing quintile of students who outperform those in other countries.

Meanwhile, a pattern that emerges from international research is the way in which education systems based on competition and choice – such as in England, Chile and Sweden – reduce connections between schools and their local communities. In these contexts, some families feel the need to choose schools away from their homes that seem more attractive. This is worrying in the light of research which indicates that to achieve greater inclusion, the work of schools with families and their local communities is vital (Kerr and Ainscow, 2022).

Collective effort

Developing inclusive schools requires a collective effort from teachers, families and the wider community. Therefore, a clear sense of what is intended is crucial. In particular, the term 'inclusion' must be defined in a way that will speak to everybody who needs to be involved. The following formulation provided by the United Nations Educational, Scientific and Cultural Organization (UNESCO, 2017: 12) is particularly helpful in that it avoids the use of jargon: 'Every learner matters and matters equally.'

Evidence from the Organisation for Economic Co-operation and Development (OECD, 2012) suggests that countries where teachers are supported, and where the profession is valued, are more effective for all students. This encourages teachers to see individual differences not as problems to be fixed but as opportunities for enriching their professional learning. Furthermore, this kind of approach is more likely to be successful in environments where there is a culture of collaboration that encourages collective problem-solving amongst staff.

Using evidence

It is also important to know who is included, who is segregated and who is excluded from schooling. Without such evidence there can be no accountability. But when data collection efforts are only focused on particular categories of students, as is currently the case in England, there is a risk of promoting negative views of those learners who share certain characteristics or come from similar backgrounds. This distracts attention from more fundamental questions, such as why are schools failing some learners, and what are the barriers experienced by these students?

Given the dangers associated with school isolation and competition, it is also clear that inclusion requires some form of local coordination. Unfortunately, in many parts of England no one organisation has the overall picture that would enable them to orchestrate more collaborative ways of working. This is why we need local area partnerships to monitor, support and challenge schools, including academies (see Ainscow et al., 2023).

A pathway to excellence

The ideas presented in this chapter echo suggestions made by Tim Brighouse (2023) for reducing exclusions. What connects these ideas is the importance of drawing together teachers, parents and the community around a common purpose.

Evidence from other parts of the world suggests that this approach has the potential to benefit all students. In this way, an emphasis on inclusion contributes to improvements in the overall quality of national educational provision.

References

Ainscow, M., Armstrong, P. W., Hughes, B. C. and Rayner, S. (2023). *Turning the Tide: A Study of Placed-Based Partnerships*. Manchester: The Staff College.

Ainscow, M. (2024). *Developing Inclusive Schools: Pathways to Success*. Abingdon and New York: Routledge.

Brighouse, T. (2023). Tim Brighouse's Nine Ways to Minimise Exclusions. *TES* (18 December). Available at: https://www.tes.com/magazine/teaching-learning/general/tim-brighouse-how-to-minimise-school-exclusions.

Kerr, K. and Ainscow, M. (2022). Promoting Equity in Market-Driven Education Systems: Lessons from England. *Education Science*, 12(7), 495. https://doi.org/10.3390/educsci12070495

Organisation for Economic Co-operation and Development (OECD) (2012). *Equity and Quality in Education: Supporting Disadvantaged Students and Schools.* Paris: OECD Publishing.

Tomlinson, S. (2012). The Irresistible Rise of the SEN Industry. *Oxford Review of Education*, 38(3), 267–268. DOI: 10.1080/03054985.2012.692055

United Nations Educational, Scientific and Cultural Organization (UNESCO) (2017). *A Guide for Ensuring Inclusion and Equity in Education.* Paris: UNESCO.

United Nations Educational, Scientific and Cultural Organization (UNESCO) (2020). *Towards Inclusion in Education: Status, Trends and Challenges.* Paris: UNESCO.

Chapter 55

Does labelling children reduce their life prospects?

Louise Blackburn

First and foremost, Louise Blackburn is an advocate for disadvantaged learners. Having worked in education for over 20 years, she now supports schools to deliver equitable approaches through Challenging Education, which works with leaders to tackle inequalities through Raising the Attainment of Disadvantaged Youngsters (RADY). It is this passion for equity that brought Louise into contact with Tim.

We can make life-changing differences to those who need it most, but it requires systemic changes. Why are our poorest learners continuing to underperform when compared to their peers? I describe below three things that Challenging Education believes are fundamental to the persistence of this gap. Each also contains our call to arms for all of us working in education.

Labels as the root of deficit thinking

At the Festival of Education in 2023, I was invited to sit alongside Sir Tim Brighouse as part of a panel participating in a provocation, 'Labelling pupils damages their life prospects'. Throughout the session, I listened to the evidence from the other panellists, which supported the idea that assigning labels to learners was at best problematic and at worst has a negative impact on prospects. My belief, and the one I shared at the event, is not that the label is damaging, but our (often unconscious) reaction to those labels kick-starts deficit thinking – the belief that we cannot change things for some learners. The label becomes the justification for a learner (or group of learners) not reaching their (lower) targets, or their parent not coming to an information event, or their home learning not being completed to the highest standard. Sometimes, a label triggers a sympathetic approach; we unconsciously expect less of some learners because we worry about adding to their difficulties by having high expectations, instead of giving them the extra support they need to reach the same standards as those not disadvantaged in the same way.

In our role as teachers, I believe it is essential that we know all we can about the learners in front of us. The more challenges a learner is facing, the more we need to know and understand to support them most effectively. This knowledge, which may well include labels, must inform our equitable approaches in the classroom.

Our first call to arms is for educators to make sure that labels are used in this way.

An unhealthy obsession with 'progress'

The extensive use of prior attainment data to measure progress has a profound impact, particularly on pupil premium (PP) learners. We believe this should not determine what learners will achieve, as their potential is in our hands. However, when fed into statistical estimation software, future achievements are predicted. The impact manifests as lower expectations for PP learners, hindering their ability to catch up with their non-disadvantaged peers, as seen in a substantial GCSE attainment gap.

I will explain further. In 2023, 51.6% of children eligible for free school meals achieved a 'good level of development' compared to 71.5% of their non-eligible peers.[1] If both groups made identical progress through their education, the potential attainment gap would remain a substantial 19.9 percentage points at GCSE. And GCSE grades are carried by our learners throughout their lives, impacting on the life choices they have available to them.

Consider a scenario where a hungry and distressed PP learner takes Key Stage 2 SATs, generating a statistical estimate of a grade 4 at GCSE.

---

1   See https://explore-education-statistics.service.gov.uk/find-statistics/early-years-foundation-stage-profile-results/2022-23.

This estimate becomes a target shared with teachers, parents and the learner, influencing their academic path. Hindered by hunger and poverty, the learner, confined to the school's middle set, cannot showcase their untapped potential. Making the same progress as their non-disadvantaged peers, they achieve a grade 4, aligning with statistical predictions and creating a self-fulfilling prophecy that is unlikely to reflect their true potential.

Progress data spanning eight years reveals that PP learners make less progress, repeatedly failing to meet lower average targets.[2] We are confident that lower expectations, both conscious and unconscious, along with the challenges of poverty, contribute to this trend.

Our second call to arms is for leaders to prioritise learners' true potential, considering untapped potential hidden by previous assessment results. Don't let prior attainment accurately predict future results by allowing it to dictate targets that are shared with all, including the pupil.

Evaluating the effectiveness of school improvement through the eyes of learners who need it least

As head of science, working with an incredible group of teachers and support staff under an inspirational head teacher, I was quite rightly held to account for the percentage of learners who achieved a grade C or above (showing my age) in various science qualifications. Many learners smashed those targets, and we were delighted. At no point did I have to think about the proportional representation of disadvantaged learners in that group who reached the C-or-above goal. And I didn't. I have no doubt that if I went back and reviewed that data now, our PP youngsters would have been severely underrepresented.

In another lifetime, visiting lessons with leaders, I am left wondering how they are evaluating the impact of the pedagogical approach they are reviewing on those learners who most need it to work for them. Are they

---

2   See https://explore-education-statistics.service.gov.uk/find-statistics/key-stage-4-performance.

consciously and deliberately focusing on those groups, or simply checking that a process is being carried out and noticing those already doing well benefiting further?

There is a group of learners in every school who rely 100% on the diet of teaching and learning experiences we give them. There are other learners who benefit from our purposeful curriculum and our effective diagnostic teaching alongside support outside school which enhances the impact of the work done in schools.

Our final call to arms is for leaders to make sure they evaluate the impact of strategies to improve their schools through the eyes of the poorest learners with the least support at home.

Our commitment: Raising the Attainment of Disadvantaged Youngsters

In 2012, Dave Hollomby used GCSE predictions to reveal that secondary schools aimed for an average attainment gap between PP and other learners. From this, Dave developed Raising the Attainment of Disadvantaged Youngsters (RADY), aimed at addressing this systemic error and helping schools to identify attainment gaps 'on entry', unlocking the potential of PP learners (Hollomby, 2013).

My work, and that of my fellow directors, Trevor Sutcliffe and Simon Blackburn, at Challenging Education is to help schools implement RADY and encourage them to address all the calls to arms outlined above – as Tim encouraged us to do.

References

Hollomby, D. (2013). *Raising the Attainment of Disadvantaged Youngsters: The RADY Project. Summary Report to the School Improvement Team Summer 2013.* Wallasey: Wirral Council.

Chapter 56

Confronting the roots of our education system

Rosemary Campbell-Stephens

Rosemary Campbell-Stephens is an international speaker, author and consultant on leadership and decolonising system change. She first met Tim Brighouse when he was Birmingham's chief education officer. Over the years, they have shared various platforms on numerous occasions. Most notably, their paths crossed during the London Challenge work from 2003 to 2011.

There is no way to sanitise or soften this, even as I sit in the shade of my verandah, marvelling at the breadfruit tree that my husband and I did not plant. The roots of the tree came from the parent tree next door in my sister's garden. Like all trees, it grows up simultaneously towards the sun and down deeper into the soil. I am reminded that understanding the roots of any ecosystem is important, not least to prevent preoccupation with the fruits without knowing from whence they came.

Crafting a short think-piece focused on recognising some of the many areas of commonality and concern that I shared with Sir Tim Brighouse, a man I admired and found inspirational, is the easy bit. Writing at that end of the spectrum predisposes one to focus on the many fruits, like our prolific breadfruit. On the other hand, the unfinished business is the uncomfortable end of the conversation, and that is most definitely directed to the roots of the British education system and what lies buried there, evolving.

Not to put too fine a point on it, there is a conspiracy of silence around race, with few notable exceptions, from even the most progressive White educationalists. I have found this both deeply frustrating and disappointing over the years. As a result, there is much unfinished business regarding race issues in schooling and educational policy.

The injustices visited on Black children over the years through education in Britain sit heavily within the Black collective memory, such as bussing, colour-bar policies in cities like Birmingham and the labelling in the 1960s of West Indian children as educationally subnormal. Teacher bias as seen through teacher assessment. Under-achievement baked in through standardised testing with eugenicist thinking about intelligence and false hierarchies based on a socially constructed notion of 'race'. Exclusion and the direct link to the school-to-prison pipeline. I could go on.

Race, and where it sits within the discourse of White scholars, practitioners and policymakers, is critical, given that the student demographic in most major cities is no longer ethnic minorities but young people of the Global Majority. Sadly, especially amongst the influential and admired, the silence on race was and remains deafening. Strategically, this not seeing or naming by the great and the good has enabled systemic racism to become normalised within educational practice. Like the infamous Japanese knotweed, almost impossible to get rid of.

To talk about race is difficult; to not talk about it is unethical, which must slowly but surely rot the soul. The call to action is an unequivocal call to White allies to see, talk and write about the elephant in the room: race in education. Start reparations by not just acknowledging and naming but opposing the kind of policies that structurally embed educational disadvantage based on race with the same rigour and focus that you bring to challenging gender or class-based inequity.

Start by deconstructing the foundational thinking about race that is baked into not only the system but also professional training. Adding that lens to your research and subsequent writing detracts nothing from your well-framed arguments on education and schooling; it adds much, however, by not being colour-blind, tone-deaf and way behind the curve in a racialised world.

The foundational thinking underpinning the British education system is rooted in eugenics and racism. It is way past its sell-by date when our schools have never been more ethnically, culturally or linguistically diverse in major cities such as London or Birmingham. The unfinished business is that we have never collectively, as a community of Black and

White and now junior elder educators, reckoned with the truth about how deeply embedded racism is in our education system. Nor have we used our agency collectively, with the proportionality required for the task at hand, to do something about it.

Whether examining curriculum, pedagogy, teacher training, school leadership, behaviour and discipline, or assessment; inspection, special needs, learning predispositions or neurodivergence; policy development, dogma, governance or practice, the now politicised and amplified false narrative of a neutral, post-racial and meritocratic education system remains. We all know that the education system may be many things, but neutral, post racial or meritocratic it is not.

Alongside the racism visited on Black children daily, resulting in the kind of morally bankrupt depravity of teachers taking a menstruating child from an exam to be intimately strip-searched by police in her school, there is the added indignity of Black educators' contribution to resisting racism and humanising education over decades, as academics, practitioners or activists, and sometimes all three, being completely erased from the discourse.

I remember reading the report on the London Challenge and wondering where the Black presence was. Because I was there, I recalled that we were right at the heart of the focus and the transformation. It is incredible how race can become conveniently invisible when the saviour narrative is the one on repeat.

Investing in diversity (IiD) was a leadership preparation programme addressing the under-representation of Black and Asian school leaders. Funded from 2003 to 2011, the programme was based within the Institute of Education, University College London. It enjoyed political support from Stephen Twigg, the schools minister, and more directly from Lord (Andrew) Adonis. As the programme creators, for eight years, we experienced the kind of autonomy and professional courtesy, if not acknowledgement, that Sir Tim Brighouse advocated for the profession.

Policymakers fail to mention the significant contribution that IiD made to changing not just the face but the heart of school leadership in London. Those rightfully applauding today's state comprehensives, like Brampton Manor, for the number of students sent to Oxbridge over the years, might be surprised to know of that school's roots and how many Black and other

Global Majority leaders and teachers at that school, and others like it, have been IiD alumni.

At a time when there is a global reckoning with race, we remain ill at ease in confronting collective legacies and entangled roots.

But confront those roots we must.

Chapter 57

Resisting a return to normal: capturing the COVID-19 edtech legacy

Kevan Collins

Tim's wisdom guided Kevan Collins' work as a school leader, local authority adviser and in his national work. He will always be grateful for the time Tim gave him and his unmatched ability to remind us that grace, humour and human connections are the lifeblood of our work.

The COVID-19 pandemic placed dramatic and unprecedented limitations on childhood. On average, pupils missed 115 days of school and were restricted from all out-of-home social activities. The pandemic revealed the best of our system: teachers turned on a sixpence to deliver online lessons, schools stayed open to support key workers and vulnerable children, and teachers went the extra mile to deliver learning resources to families. Parents played their part by leaning in to support their children's learning as never before, and our children revealed resilience and ingenuity as they adapted to new ways of learning.

For others, COVID-19 was a time of loss and isolation. Children facing education disadvantage were hit hardest, confronting the pandemic without access to education technology, parents were unable to work from home, and many households lacked the space and resources to learn and play. In 2022, 11-year-old pupils eligible for free school meals (FSM) were 8.7 months behind their peers in maths (up from 6.9 months before the pandemic) and at the end of Year 11, only 47% of pupils eligible for FSM achieved a standard pass (grade 9–4) in both English and maths GCSE compared to 75% of pupils not eligible.[1] COVID-19 wiped out a decade of work to narrow the gap.

Schools have strained every sinew to recover from the disruption, and many children have bounced back, but – and it is a big but – COVID-19 scarring is deep. School attendance, a pillar of the 'education contract', has plummeted. In February 2024, persistent absence rates were running at twice the pre-pandemic rates with 20% of pupils missing at least one day every fortnight.[2] More worrying, in a recent survey of more than one thousand parents, the Centre for Social Justice (2024) found that one in four parents (not adults) thought it was OK for children not to attend school every day.

Time lost from social activities, both in and out of school, has contributed to unprecedented numbers facing mental health issues. In a recent review, the Education Policy Institute reported a sharp rise in mental health concerns with an estimated 20% of 8–16-year-olds having a 'probable mental health disorder' in 2023 compared to 12% in 2017 (Joseph et al., 2023: 12).

The impact of the pandemic on childhood is broad, covering academic and non-academic domains. It continues to hit the most disadvantaged hardest, many of whom continue to live under its long shadow. Leaving aside the unforgivable failure to mount a national recovery strategy and reset the relationship between schools and families, there are still opportunities to capture lessons from COVID-19 to accelerate reform. Our response to the pandemic should be ambitious, reaching beyond recovery and harnessed as a platform to tackle the challenge of education disadvantage.

One example: the use of education technology.

We witnessed something of an education 'great leap forward' in the first days of the lockdown. Schools worked through a myriad of technical and safeguarding implications to deliver online learning. Without a huge

---

1   In January 2023, two million children were eligible for FSM (Francis-Devine et al., 2023).

2   See https://explore-education-statistics.service.gov.uk/find-statistics/pupil-absence-in-schools-in-england (Pupil absence in schools in England, academic year 2022/23).

national rollout plan driven by targets and the typical accountability architecture, schools took responsibility and rose to the challenge.

COVID-19 acted as an accelerator revealing the potential of education technology to enhance teaching and learning: the power of adaptive individualised learning to engage and challenge; real-time marking to guide and inform teacher interventions; and machine-led data management to provide insights and inform next steps. The benefits of education technology witnessed by so many during the pandemic opened the way for new opportunities to address the equity gap that shames our system: tutoring, previously the preserve of the more affluent, provides accessible diagnostic assessment; and personalised learning, to date an advantage of smaller classes, is available to all using digital technology.

Alongside the opportunities, we saw first hand how pupils without access to technology were excluded and how a shift to new ways of learning exacerbated education disadvantage. During the pandemic, the government flexed its muscles and, after a spluttering start, distributed over two million laptops. Negotiations with networks supported free access to key education sites. As with other COVID-19 examples, the power of the state was revealed. When the will and resources are aligned, we can deliver.

In the months since the end of the pandemic we have seen the technology take another step forward. Our special human power of language has been extended to machines that trawl unimaginable reservoirs of data to respond to our prompts and questions. Ofcom (2023) report that four in five (79%) of teenagers aged 13–17 now use artificial intelligence (AI) tools and services. As ever with technology, pupils led the way and jumped on the opportunity to ease their workload and improve their grades. Teachers have been quick to respond and are now using AI systems to reduce their huge workload. A recent survey indicated that one in three teachers in England now use large language models to support planning (Whittaker, 2023). Taken together, the shift to online learning during the pandemic and the potential of AI large language systems present an opportunity to power the next stage of education reform.

The education system's response to the pandemic revealed the latent capacity of our system to innovate and reform. The obligation to act, coupled with temporary freedom from the overbearing accountability framework that characterises our system, prompted a culture of responsibility, learning and informed disruption. We need to harness the same sense of endeavour, confidence and trust to ensure that teachers meet the advance of new technologies and own the risk and potential of education technology.

References

Whittaker, F. (2023). ChatGPT: One in Three Teachers Use AI to Help with School Work. *Schools Week* (14 September). Available at: https://schoolsweek.co.uk/chatgpt-one-in-three-teachers-use-ai-to-help-with-school-work.

Centre for Social Justice (2024). *The Missing Link: Restoring the Bond Between Schools and Families*. London: Centre for Social Justice. Available at: https://www.centreforsocialjustice.org.uk/wp-content/uploads/2024/01/CSJ-Persistent_and_Severe_Absence-1.pdf.

Francis-Devine, B., Malik, X. and Danechi, S. (2023). *Food Poverty: Households, Food Banks and Free School Meals*. House of Commons Library Research Briefing (24 August). Available at https://researchbriefings.files.parliament.uk/documents/CBP-9209/CBP-9209.pdf.

Joseph, A., Jennings, W-C. and Marchant, I. (2023). *Children and Young People's Mental Health Services: Targets, Progress and Barriers to Improvement*. London: Education Policy Institute. Available at: https://epi.org.uk/publications-and-research/children-and-young-peoples-mental-health-services.

Ofcom (2023). *Online Nation Report* (28 November). Available at: https://www.ofcom.org.uk/__data/assets/pdf_file/0029/272288/online-nation-2023-report.pdf.

Chapter 58

Changing the world one day at a time

Ellie Costello

Ellie Costello is executive director at Square Peg and a long-time fangirl of Sir Tim. Square Peg is a community interest company working to ensure that any young people who are marginalised or unable to attend, access or remain in education are at the heart of policy, development and improvement, giving us a brighter future for all.

I was fortunate enough to meet the late, great Sir Tim Brighouse in person in the summer before he died at the 2023 Festival of Education.

He had invited me to join a panel he was hosting – a series of provocations on education, schools and schooling. I was in awe of being asked and in awe of meeting Tim. I had wanted to meet him forever! As a relative newbie to the education landscape, I was familiar with Tim's writing and his work in Birmingham and London. He had written an endorsement of our book, *Square Pegs: Compassion, Inclusion and Fitting In – A Guide for Schools* (Morgan and Costello, 2023) published earlier that year.

Square Pegs, conceived in lockdown as a resource for tired and stretched school leaders, addled policy writers, those in governance at all levels, practitioners, teachers and parent carers, was the book we wished we'd had access to when our children faced barriers to school attendance. It was the book we wished the common assessment framework or early help team had read. It was a book written to inspire, empower and enable change in the education landscape.

Tim had graciously said that a copy should be sent to every school in England, much as Michael Gove had sent a copy of the King James Bible.

We couldn't quite believe he had said it, but we hugged ourselves with glee that he had! To receive Tim's endorsement meant the world to us. A titan of influence and a beacon of hope, innovation and inspiration, Tim understood deeply the importance of community and the inclusion of everyone in the conversation about, around, for and with families and their children attending school.

He opened our panel at the Festival of Education with a wonderful poem narrated by a young pupil describing how their identity, self-belief and agency was forged within a school system that didn't believe in them. It set the scene beautifully.

Tim observed that parents were often left outside the school gates, prevented from being part of the shared endeavour of raising and educating children within schools. He said that one of the first things that must happen urgently is for schools to welcome parents in, to create a genuinely inclusive and collaborative community. I was nodding like the Churchill dog as this is at the heart of Square Peg's solutions-focused work.

With school attendance high on everyone's agenda, following a virus that had ravaged the globe and disrupted systems, keeping children (and families) wedded to schools has become a government priority.

The founder of Square Peg, Fran Morgan, and I both had our own school non-attenders and stumbled into the 'not fitting school' landscape accidentally (no one plans it or wants it, believe me), with our journeys commencing more than 15 and 10 years ago respectively – long before COVID-19 had evolved.

Our children, like the 1.7 million persistent absentees now, were the victims of stretched budgets, inflexible practice, off-rolling, unsupported and unrecognised mental ill health, and a system where if you weren't going to boost exam results, you were quickly labelled as a problem. Defiant, disruptive, challenging, wilful, an anomaly, a peculiarity, a burden, a nuisance: core messages no child or family should acquire.

We also experienced some of the best practice and found multidisciplinary professional allies who could help us to stabilise, recover and start to heal. But, as is so common, it was often very late in the day, by which time wounds ran deep and disabling clinical anxiety an ever-present bête noire.

Fran and I had a clear purpose. It was time to do things differently and, armed with strategic local area working via our parent-carer forums, to effect change. Square Peg was born.

Sir Tim absolutely recognised the necessity of doing things differently. He was the ultimate pioneer of finding another way. With a quiet dignity, tenacity and determination, he truly delivered transformational change across the education landscape. Thank heavens for Tim; he got it, and delivered with bells on.

Once our panel had finished, I spent several minutes with him as the venue emptied, thanking him for inviting me whilst plucking up the courage to ask him to sign my copy of our book. He took it and wrote, 'Just keep changing the world Ellie' and handed it back with a twinkly eye. I gasped when I read his inscription. 'Really?' I said. 'Yes,' he replied, nodding firmly. 'Let's talk more after the summer,' and affirming, 'We *will* talk more, Ellie – let's make sure we do.'

I left the cool chapel at Wellington College and hit the bright sunshine outside floating on air, boosted, validated and encouraged in ways few words can adequately describe. I regret enormously not being able to follow up with Tim, but I have no doubt that he would approve of Square Peg's continued work, vision and aspirations for a dynamic, agile, welcoming and inclusive education system.

We advocate for holding on to trying another way, for authentically inclusive, relationship-focused practice. We believe in the innate goodness in every child, and in each of us who show up every day to guide, teach, care for and nurture every child and young person. We are committed to life-wide learning that is open to all, where curiosity, creativity and courage are cherished in everyone. We believe in the importance of inclusive, accessible community schools where every child thrives and looks forward to school every day. We know it is possible – we have seen it in action!

The way forward in addressing concerns about attendance lies in creating a system where all are valued and join together to ensure every child and young person develops to believe in themselves and find their unique talents, purpose and place, with a lifelong curiosity and appetite for learning and continuous personal growth. I think that is what Tim worked for.

Thank you, Sir Tim Brighouse – your legacy will shine in us all.

References

Morgan, F. and Costello, E. (2023). *Square Pegs: Compassion, Inclusion and Fitting In – A Guide for Schools*. Carmarthen: Independent Thinking Press.

Chapter 59

It takes a city to raise a child: how multiculturalism survived 14 years of Tory education policy in Birmingham's schools

Colin Diamond

Colin Diamond first met Tim in 2000 when visiting Birmingham. He recalls his abundant energy and chaotic office! Fast forward to 2015, and Colin took over as director of education in Birmingham, where everyone talked admiringly of the 'Tim years' and his legacy, and Colin felt that he was walking on the shoulders of a giant.

Birmingham is a super-diverse city. Its citizens come from over two hundred countries. It is the youngest city in Europe with almost 40% of the population made up of under 25-year-olds. The 2021 census revealed that over 51% of its residents are from ethnic minorities with the largest groups from South Asia.[1]

Nothing stands still here. From the agricultural workers uprooted by the Industrial Revolution to the Irish starved by the Brits into seeking lives abroad, via the Windrush generation and the establishment of the largest Mirpuri community outside Pakistan, new residents continue to arrive from Afghanistan, Syria and Ukraine.

Tim Brighouse, appointed as chief education officer in 1993, recognised the importance of a curriculum that reflected the diversity of cultures in

---

1   See https://www.ons.gov.uk/census.

the city and the need to counter racism. Uniquely in that era, he ensured that data on the performance of pupils was on the table for analysis and action in schools. Targets were set for the improvement of underachieving groups, and the recruitment and training of teachers from minority ethnic groups was prioritised. Some of the most successful and influential leaders in the city's education system today were enabled to become teachers via Tim's initiative, having been previously rejected by local colleges and universities.

By the time Tim left Birmingham in 2002, primary and secondary schools had transformed their results, and the local authority had earned an international reputation for urban education. Its school leaders were empowered and optimistic.

What remains of his legacy, and where has it left multicultural education and anti-racism?

English education policy turned its back on urban education research and multiculturalism from 2010. The incoming government favoured a school improvement model driven by teachers' expertise based on a 'knowledge rich', one-size-fits-all, academic curriculum. Prime Minister David Cameron equated multiculturalism with separate and segregated communities (Helm et al., 2011). In 2014, then Secretary of State for Education Michael Gove announced that all schools must promote 'Fundemental British Values' (Travis, 2014). It was an opportunistic political slogan, devoid of any nuance around assimilation versus integration and driven by a version of cultural capital that reified Shakespeare and relegated Zephaniah as an irrelevance in our schools. Both West Midlands authors, of course.

Multiculturalism is no silver bullet, and improving urban schools requires a sophisticated blend of ingredients. There has been progress but unevenly so. We have more school leaders from the Global Majority and some ethnic groups have made significant leaps.

I spent four years researching Birmingham's education history in the run-up to the Trojan Horse affair which erupted in 2014: how had this happened, what lay beneath the hysterical headlines about an Islamist takeover of certain schools and how did Birmingham's education system recover? (Diamond, 2022).

When we examine school performance between 2004 and 2014, we discover, unsurprisingly, that the biggest determinant of progress was socio-economic status, with those from cash-poor backgrounds starting behind in Key Stage 1 and influencing progress through to Key Stage 5, regardless of ethnicity. However, when we dig further, we find big differences in starting points and progress between ethnic groups. White pupils do best overall. British Pakistani heritage pupils start behind and make some limited progress, whereas Indian heritage pupils start high and end up higher. Bangladeshi pupils start low and finish high with spectacular progress. Worryingly, Black pupils (African and Caribbean heritage) made least progress overall. Birmingham's progress data matches the national picture, and the same direction of travel has continued since 2014 according to the city's data. Overall, attainment in all key stages mirrors national data and usually lags a few points behind (Perry, 2022).

If we accept that multiculturalism and anti-racism are key ingredients in authentic, sustainable school improvement, what can we learn from schools where all pupils succeed? Herminder Channa led Ark Boulton, a historically underperforming secondary school much damaged by poor governance, from its nadir in 2015 to becoming one of the most improved schools in the city by 2019. She believes that 'it takes a whole community to bring up a child', mobilised this approach by engaging with parents and fused it with powerful school improvement techniques (Channa, 2022). Azita Zohhadi led Nelson Mandela Primary School from 2009 until 2020, winning recognition for high levels of progress, attainment and inclusion. In common with over 250 schools in the city, she adopted the UNICEF Rights Respecting Schools Award as a tool to enable all pupils to talk confidently about their rights and responsibilities (Zohhadi, 2022).

The 'Sankofa' is a proverb used by the Akan people of Ghana and means, 'It's not wrong to go back for that which you have forgotten' (Birmingham Race Impact Group, 2024: 2). It is apposite here as the progress led by Tim, driving forward multiculturalism, has been discounted by successive governments since 2010. A generation of teachers has been weaned on a narrow version of what constitutes success in schools. Civic leadership of education has been dismantled in the name of 'freedom' – a classic ingredient of the neoliberal policy playbook.

Brummies have long memories, and rarely does a week go by without Tim's name coming up in the conversation. The love and affection remain undimmed. His multicultural legacy lives on in the DNA of Birmingham's most successful schools, to the chagrin of those who sought to homogenise this super-diverse city and turn them into Union Jack-waving clones.

References

Birmingham Race Impact Group (2024). *Global Position Paper: Education.* Available at: https://www.wearebrig.co.uk/position-papers.

Channa, H. (2022). It Takes a Whole Community to Bring up a Child. From Golden Hillock to Ark Boulton: A Case Study in Transformative Leadership. In C. Diamond (ed.), *The Birmingham Book: Lessons in Urban Education Leadership and Policy from the Trojan Horse Affair.* Carmarthen: Crown House Publishing, pp. 213–226.

Diamond, C. (ed.) (2022). *The Birmingham Book: Lessons in Urban Education Leadership and Policy from the Trojan Horse Affair.* Carmarthen: Crown House Publishing.

Helm, T., Taylor, M. and Davis, R. (2011). David Cameron Sparks Fury from Critics Who Say Attack on Multiculturalism Has Boosted English Defence League. *The Guardian* (5 February). Available at: https://www.theguardian.com/politics/2011/feb/05/david-cameron-speech-criticised-edl.

Perry, T. (2022). The Educational Achievement of Birmingham's Children, 2002–2018. In C. Diamond (ed.), *The Birmingham Book: Lessons in Urban Education Leadership and Policy from the Trojan Horse Affair.* Carmarthen: Crown House Publishing, pp. 73–98.

Travis, A. (2014). Gove's Sticking Plaster of 'British Values' in Schools Comes Unstuck. *The Guardian* (10 June). Available at: https://www.theguardian.com/politics/2014/jun/10/michael-gove-british-values-schools.

Zohhadi, A. (2022). The Pedagogy of Equality: The Role of the UNICEF Rights Respecting Schools Award in Making Schools Safer and More Inclusive. In C. Diamond (ed.), *The Birmingham Book: Lessons in Urban Education Leadership and Policy from the Trojan Horse Affair.* Carmarthen: Crown House Publishing, pp. 129–164.

Chapter 60

Shaping educational policy to support families and communities living with disadvantage

Javed Khan

Javed Khan is a former CEO of Barnardo's and a director of education. He first met Tim as a teacher in Birmingham, and was appointed to Tim's team in 2000 as assistant director where he saw Tim's magical impact at close quarters – and credits his success since then to what he learned.

Tim Brighouse always found common ground because of his belief that a good education provides a beacon of hope for all children, and that this was especially true for the most disadvantaged – those whose life chances are constrained from very early on in their lives. It is no longer a case of Dickensian Britain with children sleeping on streets, in gutters and in alleyways. Today's challenges are just less visible. In post-COVID-19 Britain, we have over four million children living in poverty; one in twenty are being sexually abused; three children in every classroom have a diagnosable mental health condition; we are seeing a rise in serious youth violence; young people are being criminally exploited and groomed via their smartphones; and the list goes on. The very nature of vulnerability is changing.

The glaring truth persists that, despite great efforts over many decades, it is usually the most disadvantaged children who have the worst education and health outcomes. And then in later life socio-economic disparities, systemic inequalities and resource deficiencies cast long shadows over the educational, health and employment landscape, particularly for families and communities grappling with multiple disadvantages.

We have known for a long time that at the heart of educational disparity lies the unequal distribution of resources, perpetuating a legacy of disadvantage that moves seamlessly from generation to generation. While equitable funding serves as the cornerstone, a paradigm shift is needed to transcend traditional funding formulas. We need better recognition that greater sustained investment in education now is an 'invest to save' choice, which can make a critical difference to families and communities living within this cycle of poverty and inequality. In addition, we should facilitate interdependence between educational institutions, businesses and philanthropic organisations to harness additional funding and resources for schools in underserved areas.

Intrinsic to tackling disadvantage must be an unwavering commitment to inclusion. This is not merely in physical presence but also in the embrace of diversity and the celebration of individuality and community. Tim's pioneering work in inclusive education should serve as an inspirational North Star, advocating for transformative pedagogical paradigms. And we must insist on culturally intelligent pedagogy, recognising and honouring the cultural diversity of students and the lived experience they carry, integrating culturally responsive teaching practices that validate students' identities, experiences and perspectives, and fostering a sense of belonging and empowerment within their haven of learning.

The role of family engagement also has to be key to educational success. To help tackle intergenerational disadvantage, our schools should be enveloped in family learning, cultivating vibrant lifelong learning communities that extend beyond the school walls, empowering families as active partners in their children's education through reciprocal learning experiences, parent education plans and community-based initiatives.

But our family engagement approaches must also be culturally intelligent, building in cultural diversity and embracing the unique strengths and perspectives of families from diverse backgrounds, fostering trust, mutual respect and meaningful collaboration. This has got to be much more than the well-trodden 'saris, samosas and steel bands' approach! The school gate should be experienced as a signal of welcome, not a passport control infused with security measures that signal fear of the very communities that schools are there to serve. We have enough good examples to know that this is possible, and that herein lies great rewards and respect.

In the face of adversity, hope and resilience will be key, guiding students through the tumultuous waters of life. So, we also need an integrated and holistic health and well-being curriculum that prioritises mental health, social-emotional learning and mindfulness practices, nurturing students' resilience, empathy and self-awareness.

Let us also think about how to ignite the often latent leadership spark within our young people to help them shape their communities and build their social capital, from which we will all learn and benefit. Their civic engagement and advocacy will amplify their voice and lived experience.

Amid the myriad challenges at the centre of disadvantage, perhaps none is as insidious as tackling the 'poverty of hope' faced by many young people and their families – a pervasive sense of despair and resignation that undermines their aspirations and dreams. To combat this silent adversary, at the risk of stating the obvious, we need to do much more to recognise and celebrate the unique strengths, talents and potential of every student. We need to foster a culture of optimism, resilience and self-belief that does not accept that their futures will be limited by their past.

If we are to fully understand and address the underlying root causes of hopelessness and despair, we will need to engage communities in true collaboration. And we will need a systemic commitment to connecting students with positive role models and mentors from their communities who can provide guidance, support and inspiration, instilling a sense of hope and possibility for the future.

Young people stuck in a cycle of despair also need experiential learning opportunities, with hands-on experiences, internships and apprenticeships that expose them to diverse career pathways and opportunities, broadening their horizons and igniting their passion for learning and personal growth. Experiential learning is so important in locating the young person at the centre – the starting point as a co-creator and as somebody we work with and not just somebody we work on.

In charting a new course for education policy in the UK, we need to embrace a journey that will require continuous innovation, creativity, compassion and cultural intelligence. By embracing financial equity, catalysing inclusive excellence, nurturing holistic interdependent action, cultivating resilient ecosystems and combatting the poverty of hope, we may just have a chance for a more equitable, inclusive, cohesive and empowering education system. Anything less won't break the cycles of deprivation that some of our children and families find themselves in. Together, let us dare to dream, innovate and pioneer a brighter future for all children, as Tim would have implored us to do, igniting the flames of hope and possibility in the hearts of generations to come.

Chapter 61

The fucking legend

Chris Kilkenny

Chris Kilkenny is a campaigner and activist striving to end the impact of poverty, when he is not busy sorting out his own life. He is currently working to get into university to become a teacher and make a difference for children from difficult circumstances, like his own. Tim Brighouse encouraged his ambitions.

David Cameron, one of the co-editors of this book, insisted that I use this title for my contribution, because that is what I always called Sir Tim Brighouse, and it still seems like a pretty good summing up of what Tim was to me.

I met him at an Essex secondary head teachers' conference in November 2016. The conference was called 'Mapping the Territory', and the idea was to look at education from all possible viewpoints. The 'legend' was the voice of those who had led major reforms and who had radically improved systems. I was the voice of experience, and it wasn't a great experience.

Here is the short version from a chapter that I wrote for *The Working Class* (Kilkenny, 2018):

> My mum was a heroin addict for most of my life. That made things hard for me and my brothers and sister. When I was a child there were times when I would collect my younger siblings from school and take them home. It wasn't that I was worried about them walking home on their own. It was because on many of those days the door would be locked and there would be nobody in. I was the oldest, even if I was still at primary school, and it was up to me to lead our tiny tribe around to the drug den or wherever we might find my mum. It wasn't even her that we really needed to find. She would be out of

it anyway, sometimes unconscious. She couldn't help us. It's just that she had the keys.

I would take the keys and lead the tribe back to the flat. I couldn't do anything for my mum. I couldn't even do much for my brothers and sister, but I did serve them black-slab pizza. These were the days before the *Bake Off* and I was short on knowledge or advice about cooking. Mary Berry wasn't a huge presence in the area where I lived. I did my best and we survived, even if we didn't exactly thrive.

I could say a lot more about that period of my life. I remember a lot of it very clearly. Mostly, though, I just remember being hungry and humiliated.

Education didn't work for me. I know that I am bright enough. I am pretty good with words. I have spoken in front of five hundred teachers at the Northern Rocks conference. I have worked with head teachers and pupils. You don't get to do that if you are an idiot. I think that I just had too much on my mind when I was at school, especially at secondary school. I worried about my brothers and sister who were in care by that time. I worried about my mum, and about what I might have to deal with when I got home. I worried about being embarrassed, humiliated, bullied. I wanted attention, but I didn't really know how to get it. I would be the class clown, because that seemed to get a laugh, but it didn't feel like they were laughing with me.

From my teachers, I got rows and punishments, but at least it was something. Looking back now, with the experience I have as a pupil support worker and from working in pupil referral units, I know I wasn't bad enough. If my behaviour had been worse, I might have got more special attention. Instead, I just spent a lot of time outside classes and staring at walls. After a while, things fell apart and I lost any stability at all. I never sat any certificate exams. I left school with no qualifications.

Although I have gained a lot of confidence since then, my experiences have left a lot of scars. Events like a head teachers' conference are still terrifying; it is hard to feel that you fit or deserve to be there. Given that the speakers at that Essex secondary heads' conference in 2016, apart from Tim, included other contributors to this book – Fiona Millar, Melissa Benn and Ben Davis – my feeling of inadequacy was even stronger. Everyone involved helped me, but it was Tim who became the legend. He spent more time listening to me than he did talking to me. He made me feel interesting and worthwhile When he did speak, he spoke to me in exactly the same way as he spoke to everyone else. He never patronised me or talked down to me. By the time we sat down for a very posh conference dinner, it felt like we were friends. He was a great laugh and had a great laugh. All of this made me completely relaxed and made me feel differently about the whole event. I actually enjoyed it.

And it didn't stop there. Tim continued to ask for me, continued to take an interest in me and always sent his regards whenever he met anyone who knew me. He had to be a legend to find the time for that, given all that he did and all the people to whom he was connected.

For a lot of people in education, I am only ever the person they talk about. With Tim, I was the person he talked and listened to. He listened, and I believe he genuinely cared about me. That makes him a fucking legend in my book.

References

Kilkenny, Chris (2018). Down But Not Out. In I. Gilbert (ed.), *The Working Class: Poverty, Education and Alternative Voices*. Carmarthen: Independent Thinking Press, pp. 103–106.

Chapter 62

Better serving our underserved learners

Rachel Macfarlane

Rachel Macfarlane writes and leads training on various aspects of educational equity. As a programme leader for the London Leadership Strategy, Rachel heard Tim speak on many occasions. He kindly addressed leaders at various conferences that she organised from 2005 to 2023. On each occasion, he sprinkled gold dust and lifted and challenged colleagues.

Tim Brighouse understood more than anyone the importance of all learners feeling a sense of safety and belonging at school. He spoke movingly about how unhappy he was at the grammar school he was sent to aged 11 and, contrastingly, how he felt instantly included when he changed schools following a family move. He described the process as moving from monochrome to experiencing education in colour.

Whenever Tim spoke to audiences of teachers and leaders, he peppered his talks with examples of relationship-building – simple ways to get to know pupils more deeply and to demonstrate interest in and care for them. He would describe this as 'the Kes effect', in reference to the way that Billy's teacher, in Barry Hines's *A Kestrel for a Knave*, invites Billy to talk about his kestrel and the boy comes alive in class for the first time.

Tim understood deeply the link between belonging, status and self-efficacy. He noticed the underserved learners who can so easily get overlooked and marginalised – the economically disadvantaged, young carers, looked-after children, refugees, those lacking parental support, those with special educational needs and disabilities, protected characteristics or a disjointed education. Tim spoke of the need to 'fill their pockets with confidence'.

When he came to talk to the staff of my new 4–18 school a few weeks after we had opened, he rightly took me to task for the bare 'hospital corridor' walls. We set to, erecting displays to ensure that all our learners saw themselves, their cultures, their religions and their lives represented on the walls.

When he addressed my team of advisers at HFL Education, he challenged us to co-create a lexicon of inclusive language that we all use when in schools, settings and trusts. We have spent the last two years doing just that. The process has deepened our understanding of inclusion.

Societal inequities have, arguably, never impacted on educational experience more than they do at the current time. We see the impact through the contrasting progress, participation, attendance and suspension rates of the underserved and their more advantaged peers and the stubborn attainment gaps at all key stages.

How do we effect change?

First, we need our new government to engage more urgently than past governments have around provision for the underserved. For that to happen, the power, voice and resource of the minister championing the needs of the underserved must be magnified. Decisions about the allocation of funding and reforms to laws, systems and structures must be approached through the lens of better serving the currently underserved.

In the Department for Education, responsibility for children in care, children in need, child protection, disadvantaged and vulnerable children, behaviour, attendance and exclusion, young people's mental health, online safety and bullying, and children's social care all rest with the parliamentary under-secretary of state for children, families and wellbeing.

Yet, the position of parliamentary under-secretary is the most junior of all the ministerial posts, sitting under the ministers of state, who themselves sit under the secretary of state.

What message does this convey?

Furthermore, since 2019, there have been no fewer than nine incumbents. With an average tenure of under six months, what depth of understanding, pertinence of judgement and impact of action can a junior minister who advocates for underserved learners be expected to have? The new government would do well to prioritise greater stability.

Second, in addition to more impactful support from the government to enable school leaders to prioritise action to tackle disadvantage, we must address the current pressures that disincentivise education leaders from putting the underserved first.

The high-accountability performance culture that exists in the UK education system results in too many schools chasing short-term strategies – often involving arid and didactic teaching and learning techniques – to maximise exam results. This is at the expense of ensuring a well-rounded curriculum, multimodal assessment opportunities, collaborative learning and great personal, social and emotional support for pupils.

The result is a school experience that is neither engaging nor inclusive, in which it is hard to foster high levels of safety, belonging, status and self-efficacy for the underserved. Many are voting with their feet and not even attending.

Tim signed up to Rethinking Assessment's campaign for the adoption of a learner profile in schools, a personal online portfolio for every pupil, including academic qualifications alongside a record of other achievements. I am convinced that, were the government to introduce such a profile for all learners, the less well served could be supported by their teachers to showcase a much wider range of evidence of their strengths. They could be coached to reflect metacognitively on themselves and develop their learning strength. The profile would assist them in transitioning into well-suited, high-quality employment or higher education, thereby leaving school with a greater sense of achievement and self-worth.

Finally, reform of our school inspection system must address the frequent failure of inspectors to look through a lens of social equity when making judgements about schools. Too frequently, schools are graded outstanding despite having huge disadvantage gaps, significantly negative outcomes for pupil premium eligible pupils, zero tolerance behaviour policies, fixed mindset grouping arrangements, and non-inclusive admissions, off-rolling and exams entry practices. And data shows an over-representation of outstanding schools in affluent areas serving catchments with very few underserved learners.

As Sir Martyn Oliver, His Majesty's Chief Inspector, has acknowledged, 'we don't want disadvantage or vulnerability to be a barrier. Because if you get it right for the most disadvantaged, you get it right for everyone' (Ofsted and Oliver, 2024).

Whether inspections continue in a similar format, or whether an alternative model of accountability and judgement of school effectiveness – such as a report card or balance score card – is introduced, inspectors must be required to look for evidence that curriculum design, pedagogical approaches and classroom activities are fostering opportunities for underserved learners to exercise agency and result in them making great progress and attaining in line with their more advantaged peers. No school should be awarded a top grade or descriptor without being a beacon of inclusive practice and serving underserved learners exceptionally well.

References

Ofsted and Oliver, M. (2024). Sir Martyn Oliver's Speech at the 2024 ASCL Annual Conference (8 March). Available at: https://www.gov.uk/government/speeches/sir-martyn-olivers-speech-at-the-2024-ascl-annual-conference.

Chapter 63
Be more Tim

David Cameron

David Cameron has had a long and varied career in education. He met Tim at a conference years ago. Tim said he would tell people to book him instead of Tim. He did. They became colleagues and friends. David sees that as one of the greatest honours of his life and hopes this book repays that to some small extent.

I think we have set ourselves a real challenge in this book.

On one hand we wanted it to be a tribute to someone who was admired, respected and loved by every contributor. We have certainly succeeded in that. The chapters show Sir Tim Brighouse as inspiring, charismatic, eccentric, frighteningly wise and intimidatingly competent. We have exhortations to 'clone Tim Brighouse' if one wishes to address virtually any educational problem and we have run the risk of elevating him to sainthood, if not deity.

I make no apology for any of that. He deserves that sort of regard.

We also wanted the book to be a call to action. It is called *Unfinished Business* because we still have much to do to realise Tim's ambitions. Mick Waters has made that very clear in his chapter, 'From Opinions to Action: Improving on Previous Best' (Chapter 10), where he sets out these ambitions. They are at the heart of *About Our Schools* (Brighouse and Waters, 2022), the final book that Tim was involved in writing.

Clearly, we are not going to finish the business by trying to *be Tim*. We have made too strong a case for him being unique, but we might do it by being *more Tim*. That, for me, means looking at the core elements in the way he worked and how he conducted himself. Fortunately, that is not a difficult task and, even more fortunately, those qualities are not beyond any of us.

Tim understood that improvement for children and young people in schools happens as a result of practice. He often quoted Haim Ginott's comments about his role as a teacher:

> I have come to a frightening conclusion. I am the decisive element in the classroom. It is my personal approach that creates the climate. It is my daily mood that makes the weather. As a teacher I possess tremendous power to make a child's life miserable or joyous. I can be a tool of torture or an instrument of inspiration. I can humiliate or humor, hurt or heal. In all situations it is my response that decides whether a crisis will be escalated or de-escalated, and a child humanized or de-humanized. (Ginott, 1975: 13)

He knew the importance of the educator's contribution from research, experience and insight. I remember him being challenged about what 'the answers' were in education at a conference in Scotland. While other expert speakers equivocated, Tim told them that the answer was already in that school and eulogised the practice of a teacher he had spent time with that morning. That was what made a difference for the children – care, humanity and reflective, thoughtful practice.

Tim sought power to enable and liberate, never to centralise and control. He saw his role as being clear about the wider moral purpose of education. He always saw education as being central, not only to individual lives but to society more generally. We needed to support attainment, but we also needed to help children become good people.

In my work with schools, I often say that the purpose of education is to hold up a mirror to learners in which they see a better reflection of themselves, and then work with them to make that reflection a reality. I don't think I stole the words from Tim, but I certainly took the spirit.

Tim combined terrific self-belief and certainty with openness. He was a compass and never a satnav; he pointed a direction but allowed you to find a route. Because of this he could work with people who did not share all of his views and build wide and strong alliances.

That sat well with his understanding that collaboration was key to improvement, but he was always careful to avoid hierarchies in this. He encouraged schools to work with others that were similar and to seek what he called 'aspirational comparisons' – the quest for marginal and achievable goals rather than the quest for perfection.

He recognised the importance of culture, of focusing on how we behave and how we make each other feel. Tim modelled that too. He was unrelentingly courteous, curious and interested. We praise him as speaker, but he was a genius at listening and, having listened, he responded with the power of praise, respect and recognition. All of that brought loyalty and, in his terms, 'sustained discretionary effort'.

It may have been those working in schools who made the weather, but he built the shelter-belts. He did his best to stop the incoming hurricanes of misguided policies and ideologically inspired demands.

For me, Tim was the classic example of 'either and' rather than 'either or'. He was the romantic who used the data, the statistician who could instil passion, the researcher who encouraged dreams. He was the person who was always busy, and yet always had time for others. Tim got results and made lasting, significant and substantial change.

He showed us how to be more Tim. He showed us the qualities that make a difference and, in doing so, set a path to make sure the business can be finished.

References

Brighouse, T. and Waters, M. (2022). *About Our Schools: Improving on Previous Best*. Carmarthen: Crown House Publishing.

Ginott, H. G. (1975). *Teacher and Child: A Book for Parents and Teachers*. New York: Avon.

About Our Schools

Improving on Previous Best

Tim Brighouse and Mick Waters

Foreword by Danny Dorling.

ISBN: 9781785835865

About Our Schools examines in detail the turbulent years of education policy and practice from the late 1970s to the present day – and sets out what policy-makers and education leaders can do to enable our schools to improve on their previous best.

Through revealing and forthright interviews with 14 secretaries of state – from Kenneth Baker to Michael Gove and Gavin Williamson, together with many other leading figures in education – Tim Brighouse and Mick Waters provide fascinating insights into the various evolutions and revolutions that have taken place in English state education since 1976.

In so doing they highlight key areas for improvement and assess where we should go from here to enable teachers and schools to improve the learning and broaden the horizons of each and every one of their pupils – whatever their talents, challenges, advantages or problems.

Split into four parts, the book shares a range of perspectives and informed viewpoints on education, covering areas such as curriculum, pedagogy and assessment; school improvement and leadership; admissions, attendance, exclusions and behaviour; special educational needs and disabilities; and governance and finance of schooling.

Suitable for teachers, head teachers, school governors and policy-makers, as well as parents and anyone interested in the politics of schooling.

Twenty things that teachers do

1. The morning: offer a welcome to every child.
2. Notice – name and identify thoughts.
3. Listen – to ask questions about thoughts.
4. Create a past – to reminisce about.
5. Laugh – share a joke.
6. Remember – a birthday or event.
7. Admire – out loud to others.
8. Praise in writing.
9. Respect – family, history, culture.
10. Share – football teams, pop stars, sweets.
11. Steal crisps.
12. Promote – tell good stories to others/staff/kids/families.
13. Acknowledge something they are better at than you.
14. Recognise – around the school, beyond the school, cheerfully.
15. 'I saw this and thought of you.' Give them a cutting from a newspaper or magazine, about their team, etc.
16. Collect.
17. Contribute – to the X factor.
18. Mark – privately, journals of progress, intimate conversations.
19. Find – the invisible child.
20. Confess – to private interest.

Scan this code to download a poster for your school staffroom